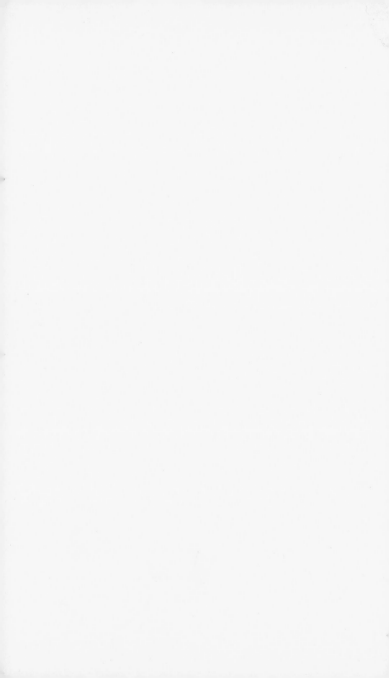

Every time I think I have a handle on Japan, it's as if another layer of an onion gets peeled back, and I end up saying "I don't understand the country at all."

An American researcher writing after his second year at a Japanese scientific center.

About the Author

Alison Lanier is the author of many intercultural works including: *Update Japan* (Intercultural Press) and *Japan Today* (Yohan Publications, Inc. Tokyo). In addition to several other books, she has also authored many articles and continues to write and edit "The International Assignment." Ms. Lanier has taught in the Navy, at the Foreign Service Institute, the American Management Association, the World Trade Institute and at the New School for Social Research. She is a graduate of Bryn Mawr College and a full Commander in the U.S. Navy (Ret.). She has been selected for the World's Who's Who of Women as a result of her pioneering and continuing work in intercultural relations.

Table of Contents

PART IV: PATTERNS OF COMMUNI-
          CATION

WITH HEARTFELT THANKS:

Many people have helped me with this book—in many ways. I am deeply indebted to them all: those who gave me introductions to knowledgeable people; those who sent me relevant clippings and references; the ones who were sustainedly interested and encouraging throughout; those who commented on various of the chapters for me, sharing their experience and their knowledge. I am, above all, indebted to the one at home who was unfailingly understanding and supportive—no matter what.

Three Unwitting Influences

I would like to pay special tribute to three writers whom I have never met: *John C. Condon,* and *Edward T.* and *Mildred Reed Hall*. They have unwittingly been "mentors" to me for many years. Their multiple excellent books **(See Recommended Reading, Page 290)** have long illuminated the whole field of intercultural relations for many of us. Dr. Hall's early book, *Silent Language,* was, in fact, a major influence leading to my original entry into the international field many years ago. I suspect that may have been true for other people as well.

These "mentors" are woven into this book far beyond the footnoted quotes. Although I have tried to give credit as it is due, their words and thoughts have long become interwoven into my own work and surely are to be found throughout this book. I owe them a deep and lasting debt of gratitude. I recommend their books wholeheartedly to anyone who may be looking for help in understanding any people (not necessarily Japanese) who come from different pasts, and, therefore, live by different guidelines in today's world.

Knowledgeable Friends

Others who have been particularly generous in their supportive assistance include *Virginia McKay*, a good and

steady friend and author of *Moving Abroad: A Guide to International Living,* published by VLM Enterprises, P.O. Box 7236, Wilmington, DE 19803. I highly recommend her book to anyone who is moving about the world or is planning to do so—and *Roberta Seret,* another good friend, President of American Welcome Services in New York, and author of the excellent—and recently revised— book, *Welcome to New York.* She has briefed a great many Japanese who have come to the United States and has also given pre-departure briefings to many Americans who were headed for assignments in other parts of the world— including many to Japan. She has shared her knowledge generously, as have: *Noel Kreiker,* President of International Orientation Resources, in Northbrook, Illinois and her colleague, *Jane Tyner; Carol Sage,* Training and De- velopment Consultant and free lance writer, who gave me much time and many useful introductions; *Stacey Klein Simon,* Director of Metro International in New York, who lived in Japan for several years. She was one of my earli- est "encouragers" about this book and has shared her experience generously.

Others who gave helpful leads, comments, and advice include: *Elizabeth Andoh,* Executive Director of the asso- ciated Japan American Societies of the U.S. Inc.: *Kristin K. Connell,* who was in Japan for IBM for eleven years; *Thomas Elbe,* of Nikko Hotels International; *Negar Rafikian,* of IBJ Schroder Bank and Trust Company; *Diane G. Rothman,* of the New Otani Hotels; *John J. Scafiddi,* Bank of California International; *Heinz O. Schmid,* of Mitsubishi International Corporation.

And not least: my warmest thanks and appreciation go to a skilled and enormously helpful editorial assistant, *Linda Robbins,* who together with *Cheryl Cavanaugh,* both helped me to put this book into proper final shape for the publisher.

PART I

THE
BACKGROUND OF
DIFFERENCE

Tokyo Metropolitan Government office

(photo by Kenji Arai)

Section 1: Who the Book is For

The book is for:

I. Non-Japanese people—of any country—who, though outside Japan find themselves:

a) Working for Japanese bosses;
b) Negotiating with Japanese people;
c) Working beside Japanese colleagues;
d) Or simply encountering increasing numbers of Japanese men and women, either at work or socially.

It is also for:

II. Japanese people who are interested in seeing their own culture through other eyes.

Some 550,000 Americans visit Japan each year, according to a study done by the London *Economist* ; 2.1 million Japanese go to the USA each year; of these 20,000 are studying in American universities.[1]

Countless millions more Japanese are to be found in Brazil, in France, in Britain, in Italy, in Canada, Australia, throughout Southeast Asia—wherever planes can carry them and doors are open.

But outside Japan, the Japanese are different. Over the years, many books have been written to help those actually going *to* Japan to adjust to the very different ways of working, thinking, and living that one finds in that country.

However, when Japanese people come to work in other countries, they do not operate in quite the same ways that they do on their own home ground. They are then dealing in new and unfamiliar terms themselves.

1 *The Economist Business Traveller's Guides: Japan Prentice Hall, New York, 1987.*

They are speaking in unfamiliar languages, surrounded by people who operate on wavelengths different from those they have previously known. We need to be aware of what they—and we—are both likely to find most perplexing about the other, as we go about our various businesses and live our daily lives.

Clearly the Japanese are an increasing presence throughout the world. We and they both need to work consciously and hard at the task of making our relationships harmonious and fruitful, rather than bewildering, harsh, or negative—as they sometimes are.

This book is a small effort in that direction.

Section 2:
What the Book is About: Our Basically Different Approaches

In his well-known book *Beyond Culture*, Dr. Edward Hall writes: "Cultures can be thought of as 'screens' between man and the outside world. In its many forms," he says, "culture designates what we pay attention to and what we ignore. Without it we would all go into 'overload'," he suggests.[2] Elsewhere he says, "Culture can be likened to an enormous, subtle, extraordinarily complex computer. It programs the actions and responses of every person, and these programs must be mastered by anyone wishing to make the program work."[3]

2 *Reprinted by permission of Bantam Doubleday Dell Publishing Group. Edward T. Hall, Beyond Culture (Garden City, NY: Anchor Press/Doubleday,1987), p. 74.*

3 *Reprinted by permission of Bantam Doubleday Dell Publishing Group. Edward T. and Mildred Reed Hall, Hidden Differences: Doing Business with the Japanese (Garden City, NY: Anchor Press/Doubleday, 1987), p. 4.*

We and the Japanese Think Differently

"It is impossible to interface an American appliance with a European outlet without an adaptor and a transformer," Dr. Hall points out. "Not only are the voltages different, but the contacts on one are round and on the other thin and flat." He suggests that there is a parallel with the interface between Western and Japanese cultures.[4]

The Japanese find Western man's logical "one-two-three" approaches to be blunt and abrupt. They themselves are far more apt to suggest—to look for nuances and subtle shadings. A Japanese advertisement will not tell you all the fine points of, let us say, a watch. It is more likely to say something like "It floats upon time like a leaf." You are supposed to read into that, by the "feeling" created, that it is delicately designed, runs silently, and is no trouble at all!

Images play a tremendous part in the way the Japanese think, as well as in how they express themselves. Americans— and other Westerners too-assume that "we are all alike under the skin." Nothing could be farther from the truth. No one who operated on that assumption will ever be able to "feel" or truly understand any culture—including subcultures in their own countries. In Japanese eyes more can be accomplished by what is not quite said—or what is said obliquely—or hinted at—than is accomplished by "coming right out with it," and "calling a spade a spade." Neither approach is ultimately right or wrong. Each is, however, quite different from the other. Both East and West stem from basically different heritages of thought.

Western thought stems from schooling and training that is basically Aristotelian. We think, to a considerable degree, in scientific and analytical terms. This means that we take things apart mentally. We think in percentages and figures, in fragmented items of fact. We love statistics. Just listen to our weather forecasts or to baseball reporters! We

4 *Ibid., p. 33.*

arrange and rearrange facts and figures as we seek to put them into coherent wholes.

People from other cultures—notably the Japanese—are more likely to think in complete images: whole panoramas, rather than the fragmented segments that we often combine to form concepts (*i.e.*, If A and B are true, then C must be true). One can liken the process to a ray of light. Some people see this as a single, white ray. Others of us unconsciously and automatically put it through our mental prisms, breaking up the spectrum into its component colors. Both groups are, in fact, seeing the same ray of light, but through such different eyes (*i.e.*, different cultural approaches) that it shows up entirely differently.

This difference of approach is apparent throughout all phases of our contacts together. For example, Japan sees its technical culture and technology as one integrated system and in their eyes it is technology, rather than science, that is the driving force. With many Westerners, the pursuit of science is the driving force; the technology comes second. According to one observer: "Japan keeps looking ahead to the next phases of research and technology, to new markets and new correlations between the technologist and industrialists—as if these were all one piece of cloth." Westerners have different roles for scientists, for marketing people, for industrialists. Each segment develops on its own in separated departments, coordinated only loosely with the other parts.

Wil Lepkowski points out that not only are scientific and technological policies melded at early stages in Japanese operations, but they are also coordinated closely with policy statements from both government and industry. "They seek to do it in great big chunks of perception," he writes. He quotes Justin Bloom, former U.S. Science Attache in Tokyo, as saying: "The place is in a ferment...new programs, new organizations in science and technology are sprouting all over, and they are being done more by

enthusiasm and determination than by simply throwing money at them. There is greater openness to the participation of foreign researchers."[5]

If one looks at all this in terms of relationships between people, one can see where differences can be very great. In the United States, for example, interpersonal relations are not usually the first priority. The business at hand matters more than the personalities involved. But, as we will see later in this book, interrelationships between people are of *major* importance to the Japanese. If necessary they can easily take precedence over the business in hand. It is not at all unusual for a deal to be broken off simply and entirely because the "harmonies" were not good.

In working with people of another culture, one has to be consciously aware of what each person is—and is not— taken into account. Clearly none of us can take *everything* into account. That would lead to the "overload" to which Dr. Hall referred. We must all be selective. However, the point is: we tend to "select" differently, depending on our training and our past heritage.

Tolerance for Difference

Consciously or unconsciously, many of us are judgmental and quite intolerant of difference. If something is different we often read it as being "inferior." We say, "the British are cold, the Greeks are noisy, the Chinese are inscrutable...." We consider indirect, poetic approaches to be "inferior" to direct, scientific ones ... so it goes. We tend to judge, based on our own accustomed train of thought. "Non-verbal systems," writes Dr. Hall, "are closely tied to ethnicity.

5 Wil Lepkowski, "Japan's Science and Technology Aim Toward Globalization," *abstracted with permission from Chemical & Engineering News, 8 May 1989, 67 (19), pp. 7-14. ©1989 American Chemical Society.*

This creates problems," he says, "for those who are intolerant of difference."[6] A real understanding of other peoples' behavior, a search for the meaning behind their actions and their words is fundamental to smooth relations with them.

Our Own Self-Image

However, understanding can take place only if people have a desire to learn from one another, and the willingness to work at it. Otherwise our own self-image—together with an instinctive, defensive justification of that self-image—gets in the way.

If people keep us waiting for long periods in an office anteroom, for example, we Westerners are likely to start pacing up and down after a while, getting more and more irritated. Time to us is valuable. "Don't they realize that my time is short? I don't have all day to wait," we say to ourselves. We do not stop to think that a quite different sense of priorities is possible in another culture. The man who is keeping us waiting may feel it is more important not to be discourteous to the previous guest in his office than it is to maintain an arbitrary time frame. The fact that his second guest has just come in from New York or Sao Paulo or Frankfort has no bearing on the matter.

Similarly, in many parts of the world dinner guests will arrive at 8:30 or 9:00 p.m. regardless of the hour that you gave on the invitation. They are not meaning to be rude. They are simply operating on the time frame that is familiar to them in their own country.

Space is another area where cultures collide. We are likely to think people are "fresh" or "intrusive" or "rude" if they stand too close to us and put faces right close to ours. On the other hand, if they stand too far away, we "read" them as being "offish" or cold and unfriendly. We are used to our space, not to their patterns.

6 *Edward T. Hall, Beyond Culture, p. 71.*

Instinctively and unconsciously most of us judge one another in a hundred little ways by our *own* cultural signposts—not theirs. Until we realize that there are other ways of doing almost anything, that we are NOT all alike under the skin, we remain narrow and provincial, whether we realize it or not. In terms of doing business, we "stand in our own light."

Section 3:   The Asian World and the West: Brass Tacks and Bamboo

Moving between Asia and the Western world requires many adjustments. The hardest of these are neither visible nor tangible, being of the mind and spirit. We look at life from different windows so no wonder our views are different. Our priorities are often far apart. We work differently; we eat differently; we think differently.

Asians have learned *endurance* from centuries of hardship. They have learned that strength comes from "yielding before the wind like bamboo." Westerners tend to be more like the British oak—strong but unyielding—at the risk of being flattened by the same wind which passes harmlessly over the more flexible bamboo.

But yielding is not the Western way. Western emphasis is placed less on enduring than on conquering—whether it be frontiers, rival powers, medical scourges, or space.

The West harnesses water; it tames the wilderness; it conquers space. It sharply divides good and evil, and is quite sure that the latter can be destroyed by a sufficient amount of righteousness. One sees this eternal combat between good and evil portrayed in our myths and stories from the earliest days, such as David and Goliath, or Saint George and the Dragon or, more recently, Superman.

Life in the East is, generally speaking, a balance or a

compromise, rather than a head-on conflict. Things can be both good *and* bad at the same time; right *and* wrong, black *and* white. We in the West operate like a metronome: good OR bad; right OR wrong; black OR white. It is hard for us to accept two conflicting ideas at the same time. Easterners can, and often do.

Since much Western philosophy stems from Socrates and Aristotle, we as a people have been taught since childhood to be "rational." We take everything apart mentally, analyzing: why? how? when? Westerners go in a straight line from A to B. For Asians, however, point A is more likely to be on a circle, inextricably linked with point B on the same circle.

The Western desire for speedy action—especially in the U.S.—is often hard for Asians to understand. They dislike being rushed. They tend to mistrust those who press them for quick decisions. They want time to establish trust, to develop rapport with the new person. Westerners, on the other hand, want to "get down to business."

Americans in particular tend to move fast and to make quick decisions. They do not like long deliberations. They make up their minds quickly about whom they feel they can trust. They often communicate by short memos, check lists, or other impersonal media. They use fax machines and conference phone calls to the maximum possible extent in order to "save" time. The human element becomes steadily less and less visible in the marketplace.

Contrasted with this emphasis on speed, is the Asian concept of flexibility. Asia's symbol of strength is water, which conforms to what it touches. It drifts around obstacles and trickles into crannies without stress, yet it can cut canyons out of rock. It is strong, but its strength can be very quiet.

Western philosophical views of such qualities as honesty, equality, justice and morals have been inherited from the Greeks and Romans. It is not surprising that they are

fundamentally different in many respects from the heritage of the East—just as many Eastern values are unfamiliar in the West.

As we scrutinize and debate our ideas, our values, and even our ethics, we need to be slow to judge, quick to explore, and alert to new ideas from unfamiliar sources. When East and West sit down together, each side has much to learn from the other.

Section 4: The Power of Japan

Power

The power of money is the power of today's world.

It is interesting that all ten of the largest banks throughout the entire world (in terms of deposits), are now Japanese banks. Leading financial firms on Wall Street, in London, in Germany and elsewhere are finding it increasingly expedient to take on Japanese partners so they can more easily obtain capital for their own needs. The Japanese own significant minority interests in such large and respected Wall Street brokerage firms as Shearson-Lehman-Hutton, Paine Webber, and Goldman Sachs. As this continues, and as Japan invests more and more—not only in banks and security markets across the world, but also in real estate, businesses and industries—it becomes imperative to increase our understanding of one another.

Clearly—as is only human-Japanese interests are always going to be their own No. 1 priority. With money comes power—wherever it may be located, and in whoever's hands it may be. This being the case, non-Japanese people throughout the world need to become more deeply aware of what lies behind this new dynamo in the economic world. We all need to understand—at least to some degree—how Japanese people think and work; what their

expectations and priorities are; how we can work harmoniously with them now that they are in our streets, banks, technological enterprises and manufacturing plants, for that is where they are now operating, and where they will continue to operate for the visible future. They will be working, selling, organizing, manufacturing, and living wherever resources, markets, and work forces are to be found, *i.e.*, on your street and mine, in your club, your office, your plant, and mine; in your country and mine.

There is too little space in Japan; they are too far from raw materials and from global markets for them to use their own islands as their industrial base. As a result, they and we will be working side by side, more and more closely, in all corners of the earth, for as long as we can foresee. We need to understand them—and they us.

Section 5: Japan and the West: Four Fundamental Differences

In order to understand the Japanese, Westerners have to start with bedrock awareness of four major points that affect all Japanese from birth to death:

I. *They Have No Space*

A Japanese journalist once wrote:

"The silent, stifling pressure of expanding millions in a small space makes production a matter of life and death."

The Japanese have grown up crammed into one of the most densely populated countries in the world. Their population, sixth largest in the world and growing at about one million a year, is roughly half that of the U.S.A. However, they are jammed into a land space about the size of California—or Finland. Furthermore, only roughly 10% of that small space can be lived in. The rest is mountainous, rocky, and rugged—unsuitable either for farming or for

cities. One can begin to get a sense of the intensity of their population pressure when you realize that not only are these numbers of people crowded in so small a space, but in addition nearly a quarter of the total number—over 30 million—live within the Greater Tokyo area! Tokyo currently vies with Shanghai as the biggest city in the world in terms of population; in some parts their population density is THREE TIMES that of New York.

This means that all Japanese people have grown up since babyhood pressed and jostled in the streets, in their schools, jammed into subways, stalled in traffic jams, and lined up perpetually for service in stores, the post office, the bank. They are always waiting to get in—or out—of wherever they want to go. This means that they have HAD to be extremely competitive. They start with special tutoring and special classes even to get into kindergarten, then to move to the "right" school, the "right" university, the "right" job, and the "right" company.

Such lifelong pressure affects many subtle things that are found in the national character, and that affects how they do business—and expect others to do business-wherever they are:

1) Their "vertical" society of hierarchy, which includes their sense of deference to age and rank;
2) Their emphasis on respect, on not hurting feelings, on *Wa* or harmony in relationships;
3) Their concern as to how they are "seen" by others (Face);
4) The fact that they are indirect rather than direct in speech—they try to soften all edges;
5) Their stress on working, playing, and living in groups; following formal, well-recognized rules of behavior and courtesy;
6) Their careful reciprocity in such matters as the giving of gifts and the doing of favors.

Constant lifelong crowding requires of the Japanese people:

a) Self-discipline
b) Individual restraint
c) Group cooperation

All these things affect their perception not only of themselves, but also of us—the people with whom they deal. We may—or may not—consider discipline and restraint to be important matters. They do.

Japan has HAD to be formal, stylized, rigid in its priorities and manners or—with that many people in that small a space—they would have lived in chaos through the years. Life would have been unlivable if there had not been well-developed codes of behavior, rigidly-adhered-to rules, clear-cut sequences, well-recognized ranks, and a universally recognized value system.

II. *They are a Remarkably Homogeneous People*

Another factor that makes the Japanese noticeably different from most other nations, comes from the fact that they are an island nation which, for centuries, was tightly controlled and kept almost completely isolated from the rest of the world. If a foreigner set foot in Japan he was executed. As a result they are still one of the most homogeneous people on earth. 99.4% of them are of ethnically Japanese stock (0.5% Korean).[7]

The time of their isolation is well over. Since World War II they have put their indefatigable energies into learning a great deal about the rest of the world. Not only do children learn about it— in depth—in school, but books, publications and TV are full of it. Anyone going to Tokyo is struck with the range of restaurants, movies, concerts, books, from *everywhere*. You can have a Finnish Sauna *à la Japonaise*; you can bowl in an alley that might have been

---

7 *Figures from the World Almanac and Book of Facts. Newspaper Enterprise Ass'n., 1987.*

transported from Cedar Rapids, Iowa; you can read best seller books from most countries of the world. In October 1988, the 70,000th overseas trainee was welcomed to Japan. One agency alone (The Japan International Cooperation Agency [JICA]), accepts some 5,000 overseas trainees every year—from about 100 countries. They come for courses ranging from rice cultivation to nuclear power. That is just one further indication of the enormous shift in attitude that there has been in Japan since the days of tight island isolation.

It is we Westerners who are now isolated, at least in terms of our knowledge about Japan. How many of us have read a Japanese novel, even in translation? Or know the names of Japan's four major islands? Or can name—let alone place—its four largest cities? Or know more than a word or two of Japanese—if we know even that?

III. *They are Dependent on Outsiders*

Japanese feel vulnerable, however, even now while they are prospering. This is because they have no raw materials. They are, therefore, dependent on "outsiders" to a strong degree. They look to them for fuel, building materials, metals, and many other essentials. Their entry into World War II was primarily because of their compelling drive not only for space but also for raw materials. This sense of vulnerability is one of the fundamental reasons why they are—and always have been—extremely competitive people. They MUST be competitive in order to survive. It is born and bred into them. In today's world, although their material needs, their financial power and their global role have all changed, the pressure of dependence on the outside world for vital materials still remains a driving force. It is a strong element in their national character.

IV. *Flattened by World War II: They have Risen Again*

Prior to World War II, most of the world considered that Japan made shoddy, cheap goods. One bought their prod-

ucts at Woolworth's—little paper umbrellas, paper toys, cheap combs, cheap but gaudy slippers....Then came the war. Their cities were in ruins. In 1945 they had no materials with which to rebuild. Their country seemed to be totally destroyed, both literally and metaphorically.

However, in the incredibly short span of less than fifty years—nothing in the life of a nation—Japan has risen from virtually total devastation to become the second major industrial economy in the world, if not No. 1. Today Japan is unquestionably an economic dynamo among the nations of the world. No longer are they a country of feudal sweatshops. They are a great World Economic Power. Wages doubled in the 1950's and tripled in the 1960's.[8] Large scale, highly automated facilities now rival—often excel—those to be found anywhere else in the world. These allow for high-value, high-speed production. Capital and high technology have been substituted for labor. Surely no people anywhere have changed their country so much—so rapidly.

Japan started to expand into international markets as early as the 1970's—a mere twenty-five years after the end of World War II! At that time, not able yet to compete where western countries were well established, they searched out niches in the market, developing specialties where other countries had not yet established themselves. They started early to develop markets in certain not-yet advanced parts of the world—such as Brazil. They concentrated on the quality and ingenuity of their products, making new—or better—goods that would not only compete, but could quickly excel over products made elsewhere.

They concentrated also on goods that did well in mass markets, such as cars, consumer electronics, and the like.

8 *The Economist Business Traveller's Guides: Japan.* Prentice Hall, New York, 1987, p. 18.

As they succeeded in these lines, they moved on into computers, semiconductors, and increasingly into advanced electronic fields.

During the nineteen seventies and eighties they have avidly pursued technology, seeking their sources in both Europe and the USA. Their governmental direction at home has been increasingly flexible, allowing for rapid growth and change. They continue to concentrate hard on research and development so as to keep moving steadily ahead.

As Japan advances in terms of economic power, and as it moves increasingly throughout the world, it has come to realize that it must increase its ability to innovate, as well as to imitate. It is, therefore, encouraging more individualism in its own people. Heretofore, through previous centuries, they have always been taught the imperative necessity for obedience and subservience. A move towards greater individualism and therefore greater creativity, is a very real part of the rapidly changing scene in today's Japan.

PART II

JAPAN'S FAST-CHANGING WORLD ROLE

Skyscrapers in Shinjuku, Tokyo

(photo by Kenji Arai)

Section 1:
Power Changes and Globalization

Who is "up" and who is "down" in the world is a matter of perpetual change.

China, the Incas and Aztecs, the Romans and Greeks, the Ottoman Empire, the British Empire, the USA and the Soviet Union have all been part of the world's rising and falling "Super Power" pattern through the ages.

Japan—A Super Power?

All over the world the question is being asked: Is Japan about to become a Super Power?

Japan is not ready to be one—yet. They are going through the long, slow, very Japanese process of determining their own national consensus—seeking a consensus that their entire society can support. This will take time. They are not yet sure "who they want to be." They have long been accustomed to allowing other nations to take the lead on global economic matters. But as their economic strength grows, they are searching for a new identity.

With their new Emperor, new currents seem to be moving. But they are not sure what these will be. Ian Buruma, writing in *The New York Times Magazine* speaks of the current movement in Japan to bring state and religion closer together than they have been at any time since World War II. One evidence of this that he cites was the mix of Shinto rituals into Emperor Hirohito's state funeral. Shintoism may not seem relevant any longer in a period of "high-tech" Japan. Says Mr. Buruma: "Japan may be enjoying an unprecedented economic success but, partly as a result, is deeply uncertain about its relations with the outside world and about where the nation is heading. The

attempt to revive native values in Japan, as in other countries, is usually a sign of crisis."

He goes on to say: "The threat of Japanese militarism so often raised by Japan's neighbors, as well as by leftist critics at home, appears remote. But a revival of racial and imperial myths—really the same thing in Japan—could have serious consequences nonetheless. It could help close Japanese society at a time when it must open up, for the sake of domestic democracy and international relations. To look for signs of resurgent militarism in Japan is to misunderstand the issue. The problem is rather the ever closer links between state and religion that General McArthur's occupation authorities thought they had severed by making a state religion unconstitutional."[1]

Clearly the Japanese have not liked being considered America's postwar ward. There is now a new feeling in the air which brings forth an often arrogant "Japan Is Number ONE" attitude. However, this often conflicts with another strong element in the Japanese soul: they feel more secure when someone else leads and Japan follows. They are groping to find their own world role.

In the 1945 Constitution [Article 9] Japan "renounced" being a major military force. Neither its Asian neighbors nor the rest of the world are anxious to see it assume a military posture ever again. Mr. Buruma may be right that they are not going to become militaristic again. However, one should not overlook the extent of their current military strength. By agreement they spend little more than 1% of their GNP on defense. What many people do not realize is that with their fast-growing GNP, this now amounts to $30 billion a year, according to Mike Mansfield, former (1977-1989) United States Ambassador to Japan. An article in *Newsweek*[2] stated that Japan is currently ranked no less

1 *Ian Bruma, The New York Times Magazine, 28 May 1989, p. 28.*

2 *"Hour of Power," Newsweek, 27 February 1989.*

than third in world military power, behind only USA and USSR. Former Ambassador Mansfield says that Japan's defense spending ranks with that of Britain, France, or West Germany.

Editorial writer Kiyofuku Chuma says in an article in the liberal newspaper, *Asahi Shimbun* of Tokyo: "Japan's defense budget has increased at least 5% a year in real terms since 1981. Japan's GNP exceeds $2 trillion and is growing. I am not alone in wondering how big our military establishment will become if the arms budget continues to grow at the present rate. Being the free world's No. 2 economy is responsibility enough. Do we really want to add the dubious distinction of being a military colossus?"[3]

An Economic Super Power

Without a national consensus and without at any rate brandishing its Big Stick, Japan may, in fact, become the first nation in history to become a Super Power in purely economic terms. It has the highest per capita gross national product in the world according to law professor, Masataka Kosaka, at Kyoto University. "In view of this," he says "Japan needs more than ever to act in a responsible manner." It is fast becoming the world's banker and economic leader; probably—as things are going—it can be considered the world's most technologically advanced nation.

The USA, and soon the European Community, will almost surely remain its two greatest markets for some time to come. However, with major help from Japan, Third World countries are likely to develop their economies too, to the point that they will also become markets for ever more Japanese goods—goods which are already being produced in countries scattered all over the world.

Mr. Yoshi Ysurumi, President of the Pacific Rim Basin Foundation says: "In terms of per capita income and annual

3 *Quoted in World Press Review, April 1989.*

consumption levels, Japan, with her population of 22 million has long surpassed the levels of her European counterparts; it is now passing the U.S. standard. Today, Japan's average manufacturing worker earns $18.00 an hour, while his/her American counterpart makes $14.00 an hour. While the social and economic gap between rich and poor widens in the United States. Japan's similar gap is shrinking. National medical insurance frees all Japanese from the fear of sudden poverty due to serious illness. Japan is considered to be almost crime- and drug-free by American standards.[4]

Biggest Creditor Nation

As both the United States trade deficit and Japan's trade surplus have grown, Japan has already become the world's biggest creditor nation. It is deeply involved in stocks, bonds, and real estate in country after country. It is also deeply involved in the massive U.S. deficit. Japan's Central Bank is holding some $98 billion of U.S. Treasury bonds; private interests in Japan are said to hold an estimated half that much in addition.

In 1987 Japan's GNP saw an incremental gain of $420 billion—compared with $250 billion in the USA. "An even larger gain is likely to be recorded in 1989," according to Ms. Keiko Atsumi, Publisher and Editor of *Nippon Finance*. However, Ms. Atsumi points out that this has not yet been translated into a greatly improved quality of life in Japan. "This," she says, "is far inferior to that of other industrialized nations."

She points out that their housing and social infrastructure are, as she says, "insufficient." "Young Japanese workers have given up any hope of ever owning a house," she says. "If they were to buy one in Tokyo it would require

4 *Nippon Supplement, The New York Times, 26 March 1989.*

them to spend 20-30 years of their annual earnings; in distant suburbs it would take 10-15 years' salary. So they spend on expensive goods rather than saving for an impossible house."[5]

She also points out that they go on working 300 hours longer each year than their Western counterparts and says they are "dragged down by a vague anxiety about what their old age will be like."

Isamu Miyazaki, Chairman of Daiwa Securities Research Institute Mayekawa Commission, says: "Japan's foremost international responsibility is to ensure the smooth recycling of money. As our surplus is a destabilizing factor in the world, we have no friends abroad. The world's political climate is improving with the U.S.-Soviet rapprochement, with *Perestroika* in the Soviet Union, and with regional conflicts on their way to being solved in many areas of the world. All these events are making it easier for Japan to fulfill its responsibilities. But can we?"[6]

Within various elements of Japan there is fear that perhaps they cannot. Some of the Japanese fear that their growth has been too rapid; that the money being spent so lavishly across the world is not "real" money.

"Once we were famous for our tremendous national savings," said one, "but we are not saving any more. We are spending; more of our people are learning about buying on credit cards. We are paying three to four times the market value for housing, for food, for all manner of things. There is no base in Japan for this fantastic growth."

Many worry deeply—and perhaps primarily—about changes in values among the younger generation.

"They no longer have a work ethic," they say. "They care too much about status symbols; they buy only the best and most expensive. They want what they want immediately, without working for it."

5 *Ibid.*
6 *Japan Press quoted in World Press Review, April 1989.*

Women's fast-growing independence is another concern. Japanese worry over what this will do to their family stability—the age-old strength of Japan.

"We also watch the Koreans and Taiwanese. They concern us too," said one. "They are making very solid progress in competition with us."

Dr. Kosaka believes that frictions between Japan and the West need attention not only in economic terms but also in social ones. He says: "Japanese society is being called on to create new lifestyles, industry and values. People's desires are transcending material wants and focusing more on broader personal fulfillment. A steady change towards a new sense of values and new lifestyles has begun."

Clearly Japan is to be reckoned with in a new way, not only at home but throughout the world. This could hardly be otherwise with a nation that has become the world's largest creditor nation, and the country with the largest trade surplus. Those who think of it merely as a "Third World" developing country, or a "nation of little yellow men whom we remember as our enemy," are in for a rude shock.

He Who Pays the Piper Calls the Tune

Because of its own huge budget and trade deficits, the USA no longer has money to spare. The question therefore arises: "How long will Tokyo continue to put up the money but let Washington call the tune?"

There is little doubt that things are changing rapidly in this regard. The Japanese are already starting to demand "more voice" in world decisions, especially those regarding the use of their own aid money. They have already won No. 2 status for themselves at the World Bank. Pressures are rising in the Japanese Diet (Parliament) to achieve a similar new status at the IMF (International Monetary

Fund) as well. Currently, despite its massive contributions, Japan ranks only fifth in voting rights in that body, after the USA, Britain, France, and West Germany.

Makoto Utsumi, Director of the Finance Ministry's International Finance Bureau, made the situation plain: "This is becoming a serious political issue," he said. "In March [1989] we were urged by many members of the Diet to make our share of IMF reflect economic realities."

Even if the United States were to agree to a greater Japanese role at the IMF, how would the leading European contributors feel at being what they might consider "demoted"? It remains to be seen.

Foreign Aid: A Major World Donor

More than two years ago the Japanese announced that they would recycle $30 billion from their trade surpluses to international lending agencies. In 1988 in addition to that, they announced a 5-year, $50 billion aid fund for poor countries. Their own "economic miracle" and the sharp rise of the yen against the dollar, have transformed Japan into the world's largest bilateral provider of aid in 25 countries, including such crucial ones among their neighbors as Indonesia, China, Thailand, India, and the Philippines.[7]

The Japanese are spreading their largesse across the world. They have become a large donor in a number of African countries and, as noted elsewhere, are active regarding the rescheduling of debt in Mexico, Brazil, and other South American countries. They have 1,200 volunteers working in 29 countries around the world, through an organization modeled on the Peace Corps (Japan Overseas Cooperation Volunteers). They also contribute to a num-

7 *Steven R . Weisman, "Foreign Aid Isn't Easy for Japan,"
   The New York Times, 20 August 1989, sec. 4.*

ber of the United Nations Funds, including the Peace-Keeping Fund, and they sent men to aid the peace-keeping forces in Namibia. They are now helping to get that country on its feet financially.

Much U.S. aid is given more for political than humanitarian reasons. Much less is being given than used to be the case, and of that the bulk now goes to Israel, Egypt, Pakistan, and Turkey.[8]

In 1988, the last year for which figures were available, Japan and the USA were almost neck and neck in the amount of foreign aid distributed—despite the great contrast in the size of the two countries and their per capita numbers (i.e. Japan $9.1 billion; USA $9.8 billion).[9] According to Urban C. Lehner, writing in *The Wall Street Journal*, "Over the five years ending in 1992, Japan will have doled out some $50 billion to developing lands, twice what it spent in the previous five years."[10] It perhaps should not be too surprising that officials in Tokyo are starting to demand global influence commensurate with their economic power and contributions.

In Thailand, the third largest recipient of Japanese aid after Indonesia and China, the Japanese are omnipresent. Two-thirds of all foreign aid reaching Thailand is from Japan. "The Japanese are changing the skyline of Bangkok, bringing primitive villages into the 20th century," and also "setting some teeth on edge," according to Mary Williams Marsh, writing in *The Wall Street Journal*.[11]

Not only are the Japanese providing aid in a broad range of countries, they are also investing in them heavily. Japan

8   *Ibid.*

9   *Ibid.*

10 *Urban C. Lehner, "Throwing Money—Japan Still Is Not Sure What Purpose It Serves," The Wall Street Journal, 3 July 1989.*

11 *Mary Williams Marsh, "Japanese Largesse Annoys Some Thais," The Wall Street Journal, 6 April 1989.*

is Thailand's leading investor, as well as donor, for example, providing 31% of their total. For years the Thais have feared—and for a long time resisted—the Japanese economic takeover. However, thanks to Japanese money, they have themselves reached the point of exporting goods to their impoverished neighbors. Japan, in turn, is now selling Thailand high-tech wares.

"We are becoming a newly industrialized country," says Mr. Thirayuth, who was actually one of the key leaders of *anti*-Japanese protests in Bangkok in the 1970's. "As we start to make foreign investments ourselves we think there could be room in Asia for both Thais and Japanese ... together we can exploit."

Industrialized Countries are Restless

This picture of growing power concerns many people in industrialized countries. Are the Japanese using aid in order to buy increasing political and commercial advantages throughout the Third World? Is that their long-term plan? The United States, which continues to provide Japan with military protection, is particularly concerned about this.

Republican Senator Frank Markowski of Alaska says: "I don't want to see us as the world's cop while Japan moves into the role of world benefactor."[12] The United States has already played the role of "cop," or policeman once—to Japan's great benefit—when it patrolled the oil lines in the Persian Gulf, protecting oil vital to Japan's supply.

Critics of rapidly spreading Japanese aid programs complain that some of it is "tied" to the purchase of Japanese goods and services. People claim that by means

12 *Senator Frank Markowski, "The Cop and the Bene-factor," Newsweek, 6 February 1989.*

of giving—or withholding—its aid, Japan is making in-roads into new markets and "shutting others out." Mr. Fujikawa, of the Finance Ministry, refutes this, saying, as quoted in "Japan Takes a Leading Role in the Third World Debt Crisis" by S. R. Weisman [*N.Y. Times* 4/17/89.]: "Our loans are all completely untied and unconditional." Even if the loans are not "unconditional," however, it would be nothing new. In fact it is commonly true of aid programs from many countries. A great number of programs extended over the past decades have had various strings attached. According to a 1987 OECD report, 66.8% of United States overseas development assistance was "entirely or partially tied" to the purchase of American goods and services. At that time this was true of only 35.1% of Japanese aid.

There is no doubt that Japan indeed seeks the extension of power that comes with the dispersal of large amounts of money—just as other nations have always done when they were in the same kind of position. Philippine Congressman Herminio Aquino says: "It would be a rarity for Japanese aid project contracts not to go to Japanese companies." There is widespread apprehension about this, but it is not a new phenomenon, nor is it confined only to Japanese donors.

Globalization

The trend towards "globalization" is something we all have to get used to. Americans have been prime movers in development for decades, operating a vast network of international subsidiaries all over the world since soon after World War II. Many people think it is rather odd for Americans to object now to foreign acquisitions and investments coming into the United States. We have been buying and operating plants in their countries for years! They point out, furthermore, that a lot of the wealth

actually comes back to the USA in the form of dividends to American shareholders. The same is now true, of course, for shareholders in the firms of other countries as well. According to the Securities Industry Association, 93.8% of all United States corporate stock is still [1989] held by Americans. However, this is changing as the amount of foreign ownership of U.S. stocks and bonds is gradually rising. Who can predict what will happen in that regard in the years immediately ahead?

In the past few years the American pace has quickened. More and more high-paying jobs, including those for engineers and other professionals, are going out of the USA. According to the National Science Foundation, spending and research by U.S. manufacturers is rising more quickly overseas than at home—to the great concern of many U.S. laboratories and universities which have previously been doing much of this corporate research. **(See Part III-Section 3: "Research and Development," page 117)**

Another aspect of globalization is the extent to which far-flung companies increasingly supply their foreign markets from their own overseas operations rather than exporting from their own home bases. This does not help any country's trade deficit, nor its employment rate, but it makes profitable good sense to the companies involved. They are developing customers all over the world at a rapid rate. Multinational companies find it extremely lucrative to produce where the marketing action is, rather than half a world away. So they are adjusting their plants to their markets. Louis Uchitelle, writing in *The New York Times* reports, for example, that sales on many American products are growing more rapidly in Europe and Asia than they are in the USA these days.[13]

American companies are obviously still spending far

13   *Louis Uchitelle, "U.S. Business Loosen Links to Mother Country," The New York Times, 21 May 1989.*

more on plants and equipment at home than abroad—to the tune of $488 billion domestically in 1988, for example, as compared with $42 billion overseas. However, the writing is on the wall. It has been clear for people to read since the mid-80's.

In his article, Louis Uchitelle reports that the "biggies," such as Ford, IBM, Motorola, and others, now collect 30% or more of their revenues and big proportions of their profits from products *outside* the USA. "According to the National Bureau of Economic Research," he says, "nearly 17% of total corporate assets are now overseas, up from 14.4% as recently as 1984." It may surprise people to learn that that is more than three times the percentage of Japan's overseas holdings. We need to remember this as we chafe at "foreigners" setting up businesses in our home countries. It is interesting to note, moreover, that the percentages of overseas holdings are rising not only in Japan and in the United States, but in all developed countries. It is the trend of the times. It is what is meant by the word "globalizing."

Horst Urban, Chairman of Continental A.G., the West German tire company, is clear about this for his own country. "We cannot do business the way we used to," he says. "We used not to look beyond Germany, but the globalization of our industry has meant that we must expand…into other parts of the world. There is no choice."

During the 1980's, more and more United States investment overseas has been in the form of joint ventures. The Conference Board, a U.S. business organization, did a survey which showed that in 1988, 40% of all U.S. overseas investment was in joint ventures. This, of course, spreads technology rapidly across national borders.

"Global firms are buying up what were previously regional or national firms in various parts of the world," says Robert Reich, professor of political economy and

management at Harvard's Kennedy School of Government, "or they are joint-venturing with one another, or they are sub-contracting work around the globe. In twenty years—even sooner perhaps—a majority of Americans will be working directly or indirectly, for global entities which have no particular nationality. More and more it will be the marketplace rather than individual governments that will dictate the trend towards globalization," he concluded.

The whole globalization process has been called a *decoupling* of the corporate world. Corporations across the world are steadily moving more and more out of the national into the international arena.

It should be understood that "globalizing" is not the same as "internationalizing." The latter basically means moving companies and plants across borders. "Globalizing," however, means "the blending of society, finance and technology with the rest of the world; it means participating in addressing the Third World nations' needs so they become part of the world market; it means establishing plants all over the world and staffing them with foreigners; building a single web of communications and technology across the globe. It means a broad exchange of scientists, academicians, and others, who can work together in joint multinational, cooperative research and development projects."[14]

Those who see globalization as the future trend of the world look for industrial nations to move rapidly in this direction. Computerization of information, the development of coordinated data bases, and now the "fax" machine, have revolutionized the ways of doing business, opening enormous global possibilities for all to see.

14 *Wil Lepkowski, "Japan's Science and Technology Aim Toward Globalization," abstracted with permission from Chemical & Engineering News, 8 May 1989, 67(19), pp. 7-14. ©1989 American Chemical Society.*

The Japanese "invasion" of the USA—and the world—should be seen not in isolation but merely as one significant part of the entire, rapid, world-changing process that is going on before our very eyes.

Section 2:
Japan and the Rest of the World

"Spearheading Japan's world thrust," writes Wil Lepkowski, "is innovation, propelled by high technology and basic science, sped on by the persuasive power of lots and lots of capital."[15]

Relationships are undergoing rapid and fundamental restructuring and change between Japan and the USA...Japan and Europe...Japan and the Soviet Union...Japan and the rest of Southeast Asia...Japan and the Third World.

Japan and the USA

Many in the USA see the picture only with resentment. They see Japan as "buying up America," " beating us at our own game," "pushing in everywhere."

Most who say these things, have no idea about the way we Americans are similarly investing in other countries; nor the extent to which "globalization" has become part of the world scene, in just a few short years. A few figures may help:

15 *Wil Lepkowski, "Japan's Science and Technology Aim Toward Globalization," abstracted with permission from Chemical & Engineering News, 8 May 1989, 67(19), pp. 7-14. ©1989 American Chemical Society.*

In 1987, U.S. investment abroad was $309 billion; investment in the USA from all countries—Japan, Britain, Netherlands, and everywhere—was $262 billion.

Foreigners currently own less than 1% of American farmland and—not counting a few highly concentrated areas like Los Angeles and New York—the figure is roughly the same for all U.S. real estate, according to Robert J. Samuelson, writing in *The New Republic* (June 12, 1989).[16]

"In the popular mind," says Mr. Samuelson, "foreign ownership connotes foreign influence, as if American interests and values are always replaced and destroyed when a property passes into foreign hands. Sometimes this happens, but typically the truth is less dramatic. Foreign owners and investors are often indistinguishable from Americans. What can foreign landlords do with American buildings? Take them home? Increase the rents? If rents rise too high, tenants will move elsewhere. Similar practical considerations apply to U.S. ownership of companies and factories ..."

Nonetheless, Americans do worry over the dominance of trade between Japan and the USA.

Carla Hills, U.S. Trade Representative and Robert Mosbach, Secretary of Commerce under President Bush, have been firm with Japan (and with other nations as well) insisting that they *must* buy more products from the United States, or risk retaliation.

The "free trade" group in the Administration, on the other hand, argue that too much retaliation against U.S. trading partners (of any country), could erode the foundations of economic order, and eventually ignite a trade war. The whole question is in ferment in Washington.

The Japanese feel that the USA has some responsibilities on its side too.

16 *Robert J. Samuelson, "America for Sale?" The New Republic, 12 June 1989.*

Ko Nakauchi, President of Daiei, Inc.—Japan's largest supermarket chain operator—says: "American manufacturers of industrial products are lacking in export-mindedness. To my sorrow they do not think about selling their goods to foreign countries since their domestic market is so huge. I want U.S. manufacturers to study more about the Japanese market and make products that are tailored to the needs of each market. McDonald's, IBM, Nescafe and some others are making efforts, but most firms are not. Although the Japanese side has problems, U.S. manufacturers also have to become more export-minded."[17]

In a *New York Times* column, A. M. Rosenthal puts the whole thing in a nutshell. He explains our trade differences very clearly: "They (the Japanese) are selling much more to Americans than they buy. That is simply because they have more of what we want, and we have more of what they don't want. This is called marketing."[18]

Clearly the U.S. does have to tackle its huge trade deficit. Clearly also it has another vitally important goal: that of expanding its own exports.

"Every one billion dollars in exports means 25,000 more jobs for Americans," says John Dillin, writing in *The Christian Science Monitor*. "Half the earnings of America's twenty-three largest banks come from overseas, and exports now account for 9% of the nation's output."[19] Many agree that U.S. exports should—and could—be much higher.

The U.S. must take a firm line globally, but it often risks

---

17 *Keiko Kambara (writing from Tokyo), "Retailer says: Government Out," The Christian Science Monitor, 16 June 1989.*

18 *A.M. Rosenthal, "The Whine Industry," The New York Times, 31 March 1989.*

19 *John Dillin, "Education's New International Wave," The Christian Science Monitor, 1 March 1989.*

getting the reputation of being a big bully, "bashing" other nations to get its own way. Does one hear the U.S. talking about reducing its own trade barriers? Frequently, it is asking for unilateral concessions. WIRES Ltd., a business and public affairs consulting firm for companies both in the USA and abroad, says:

"The process (of retaliation) threatens to generate enormous resentment abroad."[20]

Many other countries worry about Japan's growth in their parts of the world as well. There is growing fear. People look at the burgeoning extent of Japanese investment in real estate, stocks, and bonds in various countries. They worry over that. They see the whole "invasion" process mushrooming. Every time a major Japanese company sets up shop anywhere in the world, a raft of major suppliers always follows, each setting up its *own* plant or service in the locality. Obviously this adds to the Japanese impact on whatever area has been chosen.

Feeling in the USA is rising—both pro and con—as to the Japanese presence:

Con: 30,000 Americans are members of a grassroots lobbying group called "Citizens Against Foreign Control of America." These people are calling for curbs and stricter disclosure laws. Labor unions across the country are also apprehensive, fearing that the new foreign owners will be increasingly anti-union, and that therefore, they will lose out; heads of many companies feel threatened by takeovers; other people simply do not like "foreigners"—from any nation—coming in droves into their country.

Pro: On the other hand, many people actively welcome the Japanese and encourage them to come. These include state and local officials who rejoice to see local industries revitalized; investment coming into their areas; employ-

20 *"U.S. Trade Dilemma: Get Tough But Not Nasty," The Christian Science Monitor, 3 May 1989.*

ment and prosperity booming; idle property again becoming productive. Many people feel that a great number of small and middle-sized companies across the nation had been stagnating. Mergers were affecting them. Unemployment was a growing concern. These people now see foreign ownership bringing new life and vitality to what were fast-fading industries.

There is no question, however, that frictions are growing. Many people in the USA see the Japanese as a major economic threat in the future. They also resent the fact that the U.S. is still paying for Japanese defense; they complain about restricted Japanese markets.

Less than six months into its first year, the Bush Administration declared Japan to be "an unfair trading partner," thereby taking the cover of smiles, bows, and polite talk off the reality of growing tensions in the US-Japanese relationship.

The Japanese say that the American government has not been lily-white either in its trade relations. It, too, has a number of blocks and restraints of trade. Many in Congress consider Japan to be an untrustworthy commercial ally and have said so. The Japanese bitterly resent the accusations made about them. They feel they have been publicly disgraced in the eyes of the world, and they resent it. They particularly resent threats of unilateral trade sanctions on the part of the USA. Many Japanese consider the U.S. is using "bullying" tactics. They feel that the U.S. is becoming more and more anti-Japanese; they resent the statements that they are "questionable" as an ally.

Says Mr. Jay Epstein, in his article "The Japanese Are Different": "…The U.S. has already forced Japan to raise the value of the yen (which by making Japanese labor comparatively more expensive, further accelerated the conversion of Japan to a robot empire); ... It can now threaten to withdraw its air bases from Japanese territory (though those bases are as much needed to keep Soviet

naval and submarine power in check as to defend Japan)."
"If carried out," points out Mr. Epstein, "this threat would
drive Japan to create its own high-tech, and probably
highly roboticized military equipment. Furthermore,
these pilotless planes, ships and tanks might also
become exports ... Finally, the U.S. can threaten to em-
bargo Japanese goods. But since Japan provides a large
part of the electronic innards for American products,
this would retard American technology and the
American standard of living...So," he asks, "how far can
the U.S. go in pressuring the Japanese government to
change its policies without having the pressures boomer-
ang?"[21]

Actually, despite frictions, there still seems little desire
on the part of the Japanese to distance themselves far from
the United States. They believe that the U.S. will remain a
leader in the western world and that both countries need
each other. According to *The Economist*: "The U.S. is
Japan's main trading partner; Japan is America's No. 2
partner, after Canada. Japanese-American trade reached
$112 billion last year (1988); Japanese firms are the fourth
biggest direct investors in the U.S., with holdings of $40
billion, while American companies are the biggest in Japan
(about $17 billion)."[22]

For the U.S., with its low savings rate and huge trade
deficits, Japanese capital is vital. Without it the country
could not sustain the dollar and America's investments.

For Japan, the vast market of the U.S. is equally critical.
Japan absolutely MUST export both its goods and its
surplus capital in order to survive. Their islands are small;
they have many mouths to feed; they have no raw materi-

21 *Edward Jay Epstein, "The Japanese Are Different," Lear's
Magazine, July/August 1989.*
22 *"The Tie that Binds-Money" as quoted World Press Review, April 1989, p.13.*

als. Trade must not falter. There must be steady markets for their goods.

Whatever the legal battles over trade laws may be, Japan's money represents a huge vote of confidence in the U.S. economy. Clearly new jobs, new plants, new technologies have stemmed from their vast infusion of money into the USA. Even though the amount of that investment stirs controversy, it unquestionably also benefits the country.

"The issue should not even be debated," according to Edward Lincoln of the Brookings Institute. "Their trade balance is going to be reduced more by direct investment abroad than it is by changing their domestic market, anyway." [*Newsweek,* 23 February 1987.]

U.S. companies are clearly going to face increasingly intense competition right in their own backyards. But, says *Newsweek:* "For many American businessmen it is time to put up or shut up. Now some of the American companies that have been accusing Japan of pricing below cost and dumping their products illegally in the U.S. market, have more than the 'level playing field' they have been asking for. Now they have the home court advantage as well."

Edward Lincoln says Japan's investment in the U.S. "is a challenge to us. If we can't meet it well, we deserve to work for the Japanese."

In his article "America for Sale?", Mr. Robert Samuelson says: "Technology is mobile because once something is sold around the world, customers learn how it works. Companies routinely move production among plants in different countries. The emergence of global markets mainly reflects improvements in transportation and communications that have made it less expensive to produce and sell around the world."

He goes on: "The American challenge is to come to grips with these changes...not to deny them...We can't meet global competition by staying isolated from it...

Retreating from worldwide competition is a formula for economic mediocrity...Economic markets now transcend political borders. We cannot undo that, unsettling as it may be."[23]

What the U.S. Should Be Doing

A.M. Rosenthal, *The New York Times'* columnist, who formerly lived in Japan for some time, says: "Makoto Kuroda, a very blunt top Japanese economic coordinator suggested to me that we take some steps pretty quickly. That is, put more money into long range investments and research, and show the guts to stay in the battle long enough to win..."

He also proposed that we "invest in an education system that, like Japan's, expects a little more from high school graduates than the ability to count on their fingers."

Mr. Rosenthal goes on to say: "So far, the United States has neither a coherent strategy for dealing with Japan nor a set of educational and business priorities that would get us back into real competition. Maybe someday we will stop whining long enough to turn and look in the mirror."[24]

The Japanese own, part- own, or are otherwise affiliated with over 8,000 companies in Canada and the USA, according to a report given by JETRO [4/89]. About 600 factories and hundreds more banks, trade and service offices in the U.S. are Japanese-owned. More and more major corporations such as Firestone, Union Bank, Reichhold Chemicals, and Fotomat—to name a few— have been bought by Japanese owners. However, the important fact should not be forgotten by the people of the USA that an estimated 90% of the workers in all these

23 *R. J. Samuelson, "America For Sale?" The New Republic, 12 June 1989.*

24 *Rosenthal, "The Whine Industry." NY Times, 31 March 1989.*

various plants are American. They are not Japanese. 300,000 Americans are working for Japanese "bosses."

Japan's MITI (Ministry of Internal Trade and Industry), predicts that Japanese investment will spawn an *additional* 840,000 American jobs in the next decade. Some people think that even this figure may be conservative. The same kind of employment growth is going on in other countries as well. "Globalization" is working rapidly.

Small Town America

Not only major cities but also the heartland of America— Kentucky, Tennessee, Ohio, and other neighboring states— are getting to know the Japanese well. They have moved in great numbers to rural states and small towns as well as to cities and suburban areas all over the country. Tennessee has a particularly high concentration of Japanese invest- ment with more than 36 plants, employing over 8,000 people, and an investment in that one state alone of over $1.2 billion.[25]

Fort Lee, New Jersey is another example. It is so full of Japanese people and shops that one wonders if it is really America. Los Angeles is the same. According to Daniel B. Wood, writing in *The Christian Science Monitor*, "There are roughly 150,000 Japanese-Americans in Los Angeles County, the largest concentration in the U.S. Of these some 15,000 are Japanese businessmen on 3-5 year stints with local subsidiaries of Japanese companies." Japanese can go days there without having to speak English. There is an eight block "Little Tokyo" section crammed with Japanese shops, nightclubs, bars, and supermarkets. One shopping center in Gardena, California (owned by a Japanese), has forty businesses in it, all catering to Japanese tastes from

25 *Business Week, 14 July 1986.*

raw fish to golf clubs.[26] In Battle Creek, Michigan, there are already eleven Japanese industrial plants, with more about to join them.

In addition, hundreds of thousands of Japanese tourists flock to such cities as New York and San Francisco each year; 60,000 live within the New York metropolitan area and roughly 50,000 Americans work for Japanese companies in that same area. New York's 550 Japanese companies make up the largest single group of foreign businesses in that city.

There is no question that the Japanese presence in the United States is far-reaching and, to many people, formidable.

Martin and Susan Tolchin say that Japanese real estate acquisitions in Hawaii have "driven prices so high that some housing is moving beyond the reach of U.S. citizens."[27] This is reported to be happening in other areas as well.

Because they are by nature reticent, and because they find great differences in cultural habits and the ways of daily life, Japanese often have a hard time in feeling comfortable outside Japan, however well they may be doing in terms of business. Often they stay off by themselves in their own clubs and groups.

Others, however, struggle with the language and the customs, and work hard to become part of the scene. Some join business clubs; many play golf at local country clubs, or join local baseball teams. The children frequently try to fit in by joining the Scouts or the Little League, or other youth groups. Japanese restaurants with their *sushi* and

26 *Daniel B.Wood, "U.S., Japan Swap Conversation. Putting a Human Face on Trade." The Christian Science Monitor, 6 June 1989.*

27 *Martin and Susan Tolchin, "Buying Into America: How Foreign Money Is Changing the Face of Our Nation," Business Week, 7 March 1989, p. 14.*

sake are becoming known in towns all over the world that never heard of such foods before.

In many areas of the U.S., Midwest where life and employment possibilities were getting alarmingly slow, Japanese investment, with its many jobs, has been welcome. However, fear comes with it. As the numbers, the money, and Japanese power increase, people ask themselves "What will their political leverage become?" In a *Business Week* survey, 63% of those responding said they thought Japan's investment will result in "too much influence over U.S. Government policies."

The Japanese are astute people. They know how to butter their bread. They are already seeking representation from U.S. senators and representatives to an increasing degree, with the purpose of weakening voting strength for protectionism. If Congress stopped the flow of plants, equipment or spare parts from Japan, it would very quickly cost increasing numbers of U.S. jobs in their states and constituencies. This might easily cause a voter backlash. More and more Congressmen realize that they have to consider that fact.

The Japanese are working hard to project a desirable image. Yoshitaka Sajiwa, Vice President of Mitsui Co. (USA), which has many operations going throughout the heartland, speaks plainly on the subject: "If the Japanese show they can contribute to the better life of the community," he says, "this will affect the politicians' view in Washington."

The Japanese see themselves as "providers" not as a threat. However, they do not find it easy to get everyone in other countries to perceive them in that light. December 7 is still remembered as "the day of infamy." Across the world, the generation that fought World War II knew, observed—and some of them felt—Japanese atrocities. These men and women are still active throughout the business world. They find it hard to let bygones be by-

gones—hard to forget what is seared into their souls. However, younger generations are now filling the ranks of business more and more. These are young men and women without those memories. For them the point is: there are jobs. Particularly in rural areas, where various kinds of farming and tobacco are in trouble, foreign investment is the chief hope of keeping towns from sliding into total decay. Because this is so, some states and local governments are willing to offer Japanese compelling incentives, such as major tax breaks and other attentions.

In some areas these incentives are working well. Japanese are moving with growing impact into U.S. farmland, ranches, and food-processing plants.

Iowa, for example, has encouraged the flow by loosening its state's anti-foreign ownership law; there is also considerable Japanese activity in rural California. Several other states, however, have reacted in the opposite way, with a backlash of resentment. There is considerable hostility in Montana, for example, which is considering a law to ban foreign ownership of agricultural land. Of all fifty states, Nebraska is the one in which the Japanese have met their stiffest resistance.[28]

Hostile attitudes arise from several causes:
1. Anger on the part of local people at being outbid for good properties by outsiders;
2. Residual post World War II dislike of the Japanese;
3. Racism and the dislike of any foreigners;
4. America's sense of itself. "I just don't believe we should be selling our land to foreigners," said a cattle rancher from Nebraska. "This is America."

Despite tensions of this sort, the Japanese are happy to find hardworking, non-unionized labor and easy access to major markets. When this is coupled with a ready market,

28 *William Celis III, "Japanese Investment in U.S. Farm Belt Boosts Its Economy But Sparks Backlash," The Wall Street Journal, 19 May 1989.*

plus tax and other incentives, they keep coming! However, everyone is aware that problems lie not too far below the surface.

As large Japanese companies, such as Toyota, develop their own multi-leveled tiers of support systems, financial resources, distributors and parts suppliers, they try to ease the situation by setting them up in locations ranging as far as 100 miles from their base plant, often even in other states, in order not to overload any one locality. This is only partly successful, however, in keeping hostility down. Although they may refrain from overloading one region with Japanese faces and families, nevertheless, local bankers, auto parts manufacturers, restaurant owners and other small business people still realize quite clearly that business which might come to them is, in fact, going to an increasing degree, to incoming Japanese banks, parts suppliers, and restaurants. This does not sit well with them. Honda and Nissan have done better than some companies, but many Japanese firms need to move with more understanding and sensitivity than they are doing now, if they expect to set up their customary highly-integrated manufacturing system without creating the impression—now firmly believed in many areas—that local firms are gradually being locked out. And there are many similar problems—as deep or deeper than these—in local communities.

As the Japanese move more and more into small towns all over the world, some collision of cultures and styles is inevitable. *Both* sides will have to take great pains to adapt well and thoughtfully if an integrated partnership is going to work.

Japan and Europe

The Japanese are speeding their expansion in Europe rapidly with an eye to the new phases of the European

Community. In the five years from 1984 to 1989, Japanese companies have established strong European footholds—companies such as Sony, Fuji, Nissan, Bridgestone, Toyota, and Fujitsu. In the cases of Nissan and Toyota, initial investment was over a billion dollars in value; each of the others have also invested many millions. Nissan expects to be producing 200,000 cars a year in Europe by 1992, out of the North Sea port of Sunderland.

The total number of Japanese companies in Europe is close to 500 (as of autumn 1989). That is more than double the number that were there in 1983, and the rate of growth is escalating rapidly. The greatest number are in Britain, France, West Germany, and Spain. The Japanese are especially interested in Spain, because they look on it as a particularly dynamic economy. They see Spain as being a place "ripe" for Japanese investment, providing low-cost space, low-cost (but trainable) labor, and a great desire to grow economically.

Increasingly, Japanese corporations are jumping on the takeover-and-"buy-into" bandwagon throughout Europe, rather than maintaining the slower route they had been following, i.e., building their own factories and establishing a European foothold that way. Although in 1988 they ranked second in buying up businesses in the USA they are relatively new to that process in Europe. However, knowledgeable people predict that the value of Japanese deals in Europe will double to $ 2.6 billion in 1990 and reach $5 billion by 1992.[29]

Britain is especially favored by Japan for both large and small firms, because of its fast-growing economy; its strong network of roads, ports, and telecommunications; its well-trained and reasonably docile workers; and the financial services that are readily available to them since so

29 *Mark Dixon, editor, 1992 M&A Monthly (London), quoted in The Wall Street Journal, 21 July 1989.*

many major Japanese banks have already been established in Britain. The Japanese also like Britain's free market economy better than the mixed economies of many European countries. Among the European Community only the United Kingdom has no quantitative restrictions against Japan (only a voluntary quota of 11% on cars, as of 1989). In addition, Britain has been giving substantial development grants and favors to Japanese firms that establish plants there. The Japanese also like being able to speak English, which most of them have studied throughout their school years, and they like the great number of golf courses! Furthermore, the Japanese feel more welcome in Britain than they do in other countries. The British feel hospitable to Japanese investment which has brought thousands of jobs and a technological lift to British industries, especially in the North where Britain has badly needed a lift for many years. To date the Japanese have invested over $17 billion in Britain (1989).[30]

Two-thirds of the hundred or more Japanese companies now established in Britain have arrived there in the five years from 1984 to 1989. Other European countries are not too happy with Britain's disproportionate and growing share of the Japanese investment. Some of them are talking about putting European Community restrictions and subsidies on foreign investors.

Among examples of the new move towards buying into European companies is that of Honda which, in mid-1989, bought 20% of Britain's Rover Group, PLC. This made it the first Japanese car maker to own part of any European auto producer. Together with that news came the announcement that Honda was planning to follow the lead of Toyota and Nissan and build its first major European car

---

30 *Julian Baum, "The Changing Strategy for Europe in 1992: Think British," The Christian Science Monitor, 19 May 1989.*

factory—this one to be located also in England—at Swindon.

France is starting to get into the act too. Mr. Roger Fauroux, Minister of Industry for France, recently said: "It is essential that we attract Japanese investors to France rather than have them go to neighboring European countries." This is a new note for France. Until recently it has dragged its feet on—or totally blocked—a number of Japanese prospects. French—and also Italian-industrialists are still leery. They demand quotas and protection for European markets and jobs, especially in areas such as semiconductor research, where they greatly fear Japanese domination.

"We welcome Japanese investment in industries like photo equipment that have already died in Europe because of the Japanese," said Mme Edith Cresson, France's Minister for European Affairs. "We are less enthusiastic about Japanese investment in industries where the Europeans are still doing well."[31]

Many across Europe see the photo equipment industry as a clear example of what can happen. They fear that Japan will come to dominate and eliminate whole sectors of the economy in a similar way, just as they have done in some sectors of the U.S. economy (the making of television sets, for example, with only one U.S. company remaining in that field). That fear lies behind the pressure on the part of many industrialists in the European Community to erect trade barriers. These industrialists have two goals of their own:
1. To allow labor-intensive industries (such as cars, or consumer electronics) to grow more competitive in Europe;
2. To protect the industries of tomorrow—such as semiconductors.

31 *"Europe Agonizing Over Japan," The New York Times, 30 April 1989.*

Actually there is considerable hostility to the Japanese in parts of Europe. The European Commission in Brussels, the executive arm of the 12-nation Community, has pressured Japan regarding anti-dumping measures for several ranges of items which they believe do not contain a sufficient content of components made in Europe. They are also demanding that countries trading extensively in Europe establish research and development units there. Europeans worry too about the impact of Japanese manufacturing on their own local operations and their standards of manufacturing. A British businessman likens them to "Trojan Horses." He fears that "unless we apply our own tough standards," the Japanese will get a foothold in Europe, then undermine the Community's competitiveness.

Individual countries vary greatly in their sense of hostility to the Japanese. The French and the Swiss, for example, feel quite hostile. The French, who consider their culture to be superior to all others, simply resent Japanese "coming over."

"We would rather stay hungry than rent to them," said one Frenchman. Actually the French are not famous for welcoming any foreign presence. "We will not eat our pride nor sell ourselves," they say. Nonetheless, the Japanese are there. They have been investing steadily in land and buildings, especially office buildings, in and around Paris, according to Healey and Baker, Inc., a real estate firm. Japanese investments total roughly $1.04 billion to date, second only to the British who have invested approximately $1.65 billion in France.

The Swiss are also not exactly welcoming to outsiders (except to skiers and tourists). They expelled many Arabs not too long ago. But they say of the Japanese: "They are using their minds—then their money. The Arabs used their money but not their minds. The Arabs were too conspicuous, so we threw them out." In contrast the Japanese slip in quietly and inconspicuously.

As they need to build new plants in Europe, it is likely that the Japanese will continue to do so as often as possible in areas of high unemployment, such as Wales, Ireland, or Spain, where they are eagerly welcomed for their impact on troubled economies, and where labor costs are low. Even there they keep a low profile. So far they have made strong bases in the Netherlands and Italy, as well as Britain.

Europeans worry especially about the automotive industry. They are afraid that the advent of Japanese auto factories will only intensify the major problems of overcapacity which already exist in Europe.

Raymond Levy, Chairman of Renault, looks with deep concern at the $1.2 billion investment Toyota has made in Britain. "We, too, could build a modern plant and build 200,000 cars a year with 3,000 employees," he said. "But if we did that we would have to close one of our plants that employs 10,000 people."[32] This same concern exists among many other manufacturers across Europe.

On the other hand, others, who strongly favor Japanese investment in Europe, say: "It is better to have foreign-owned companies which provide employment for our people, than it is to import goods. Japanese goods made in Europe not only increase employment; they also help to reduce the $22.8 billion trade deficit that the European Community has with Japan."[33]

The Rest of Europe

As the Japanese worry over new European protectionism and look for available and potentially profitable European targets, they are eyeing prospects in all the European countries.

In late March of 1989, for example, the Suntory Wine

32 *Ibid.*
33 *Ibid.*

and Spirits Group became the first Japanese owner of a French cognac house; Kao Corporation, a strong world competitor in the soaps and toiletries field, spent $139.5 million to buy a 75% share of a leading German toiletries manufacturer, "with the rights to acquire the rest later." That same firm, Kao Corporation, had recently bought the Cincinnati-based Jergens, Co., well-known hand lotion.[34] Globalization in action!

Mr. Fukazawa is an officer of the Long Term Credit Bank—one of the ten or eleven Japanese banks and security houses that have established themselves in London in order to help Japanese clients find European candidates for "buy-outs" or "take-overs" or "buy-into's." "So far these have mostly been small, friendly targets, or minority stakes," Mr. Fukazawa says. "However, this will not be the case for long. The Japanese are learning their way into the field with remarkable speed, far more speed than is customary for the cautious Japanese."

At first they kept missing out on deals because of their slowness in making decisions. It was reported, for example, that one Japanese company was trying to buy a machine tool manufacturing firm in Dusseldorf. Eight such German firms showed interest. However, seven withdrew from negotiations after the trading house dithered for five months. The targets got tired of the delays. "Waiting does not work here," said one dryly.

Mr. Fukazawa says: "The Japanese are moving carefully, conscious of prevalent local opposition. There is an anti-Japanese psychological barrier from the European side."[35]

However, the Japanese are learning quickly to combine Japanese caution with the European need for quick deci-

34 Joann S. Lublin, *"Japanese Increasingly View Take-Overs as A Faster, Cheaper Way to Enter Europe,"* The Wall Street Journal, 21 July 1989.
35 *Ibid.*

sions. They are beginning to score increasing numbers of victories and are "becoming bolder and more aggressive," observers report. A number of merger brokers in the field say that because the Japanese are speeding up their decision-making processes they are becoming very competitive. Says one such firm in Brussels (which includes Sony Corporation as one of its clients): "In one or two years, the Japanese are going to be a force to be reckoned with throughout the whole European M&A [Merger and Acquisition] market."

Japan and the Soviet Union

Gorbachev is currently courting Japan. Up to recently the relationship between Japan and the USSR has been a cold and distant one—in part, at least, because of the disputed ownership of four islands in the Kurile chain. These the Soviets have occupied since 1945. The Japanese consider them to be part of *their* chain of islands, and have steadily claimed them as their own. In the past year or two, Mr. Gorbachev has been targeting Japan with his "charm offensive."

Japan has the somewhat tricky task of relaxing the various tensions which exist between their country and the Soviet Union, while at the same time remaining a strong and effective military deterrent in northeast Asia *against* the Soviet Union. "Despite a general easing of tension in East-West relations, the USSR is actually stepping up the qualitative improvement of its naval and air forces in that part of Asia," says Seizaburo Sato, a professor at Tokyo University, writing in the *Japan Times*.[36]

Given this situation, the West is forced to recognize and acknowledge the value of Japan's defensive contributions

36 *Seizaburo Sato, "The Time to Accept New Responsibility: What Japan Should Do Next," World Press Review, April 1989.*

in this area. Japanese military power in that critical area, in fact, plays a significant part in the whole context of security for all western nations.

"If Moscow truly wants to reduce tensions," says one Japanese diplomat, "it must revise its previous policy of continually strengthening its military presence in that area (900,000 troops, a third of its nuclear arsenal, 840 ships, and 140 submarines). There is considerable concern in some quarters that the repositioning of Soviet troops withdrawn from Afghanistan may lead to further strengthening of Russia's Pacific Front."[37]

Writing in France's *Le Monde* (January 1989), Philippe Pons quotes Makoto Momoi, former director of Japan's Institute for Defense, as saying: "The Soviet threat in the Pacific is essentially naval, and no reductions in this sphere are anticipated. In fact," he continued, "the Soviets are trying to *strengthen* their bases. It is possible that they will use Kompong Som, the Cambodian port from which Japan's attack on Singapore and Malaysia was launched in 1941."[38]

However things develop in these days of *rapprochement* between the Soviets and the rest of the world, it must be recognized that relations between the USSR and Japan are vitally important to the West as well—though many of us give that little thought. We need to be alert as these relationships develop further one way or the other.

As yet Japan is not cottoning up to *Gorbymania*. Japan is still America's closest friend in Asia, still has tightly woven connections in trade and finance, and close agreements regarding the nuclear umbrella. Russia still remains the greatest threat to Japan's security. For now Japan has too much to lose to be tempted away from the West easily.

But in the not-too-distant future, one may see changes.

37 *Philippe Pons, "The Japanese and the Soviets" Le Monde, see World Press Review, April 1989.*
38 *Ibid.*

America's military "embrace" has already started to irritate South Korea and the Philippines. Japan may begin to chafe as well, and seek a freer hand. If the Soviet Union becomes less of a threat, because of its military cuts and new economic involvements at home and abroad, and if Japan's economic self-confidence continues to grow at its present pace, Japanese leaders may start to look increasingly towards Russia and Eastern Europe—not just America and Western Europe—both for its continued growth, and for further outlets for its expanding energy. If it starts to go in that direction, major new world balances could be in the making.

Japan and Southeast Asia

Japan worries about increasing U.S. pressure and threats of protectionism and is apprehensive also, as to what the European Community plans to do in regard to world trade.

Partly as a result of this deep-seated anxiety, Japan is actively exploring new avenues of economic cooperation throughout the Asia-Pacific area. Asian trading nations believe that joint cooperation would give them needed collective bargaining strength. With this new strength they would be better able to counter the worry that they all feel regarding the growing pressures of protectionism in the western world. "Since they (meaning southeast Asian countries) are all trading nations based on a multilateral system, they fear unilateralism," said an official of MITI. "What they mean by this is that they fear punitive retaliation for trade imbalances."

Japan is, therefore, working closely with Australia, whose Prime Minister, Bob Hawkes, proposed early in 1989 that Australia, New Zealand, Japan, Korea, Hong Kong, China, and the six Southeast Asian nations of ASEAN try to coordinate their government policies on trade and regional development projects. Japan is suppor-

tive of this idea, although it believes it necessary to include both the USA and Canada as well. The Australians hope that a permanent secretariat will be formed for this group. Planning meetings are already underway.

Because the Asian countries all worry increasingly about western "protectionism" they understandably want to keep the world trade system open. They have discussed this whole matter with the world trade body, GATT (General Agreement on Tariffs and Trade). They are exploring ways in which they can act together in loose alliance, finding it useful to work together more and more, in order to explore carefully—and then (if all goes well), to pursue avenues of closer economic cooperation throughout the vast and populous Asian-Pacific region.[39]

The Japanese are doing this carefully with one eye on the South Koreans and the Taiwanese, both of whom they see as powerful competitors. They are particularly wary of the South Koreans whose business acumen and solid, careful preparation they respect, despite long-term antagonisms between the two countries. "We Japanese go into our dealings a bit half-cocked sometimes," a Japanese admitted. "We want to get into deals quickly. The Koreans are more thorough and more patient."

The Japanese would not win popularity contests anywhere in Southeast Asia, despite the fact that the aid and trade they provide throughout the non-communist parts of the area is tremendous. Japan buys nearly a quarter of all six ASEAN nations' exports; it provides about a third of their non-military aid, and it owns up to half the foreign investment in all of them, except Brunei (tiny and oil-rich) and the Philippines.

A poll that the Japanese government itself took in 1987 found that 37% of the people who responded throughout

39 *David Sneider, "Trade Clouds Gather Over Japan," The Christian Science Monitor, 6 April 1989.*

the area, consider Japan to be a military threat. Many worry that the United States will someday decide that the Japanese should have a greater part of the military burden of the region, in which case they fear that they would see Japan re-arm in earnest. The whole area suffered greatly under the Japanese in World War II. They are now "gun shy" in the face of what they consider to be a rebirth of Japanese arrogance. They complain that the Japanese exploit local labor forces in their countries, manipulate and control markets and prices, and, in general, give them "the sticky end of the gum brush." They still—or again—look on Japan as "an imperialist threat."[40]

Japan and China

Before the Chinese upheaval in 1989, Japan was developing substantial economic ties. Japanese investment was the third largest foreign investment in that vast country—a total of $2.2 billion since 1979, according to Jeremy Mark, writing in *The Wall Street Journal*.[41] Most of that was invested in just the last three years he reported (1986-1989). Bilateral trade between China and Japan was $19.33 billion in 1988; Japan was China's second largest trading partner after Hong Kong. Before the uprising, Japan had about 300 offices and 1,000 businessmen in Beijing—the largest foreign business community in that city.[42]

The most severe impact of the Tiananmen crackdown is likely to fall in the area of investment. Japan had long been wary of Beijing's "about faces" in policy. It was slower than many countries to commit substantial investments in

40 *Steven Erlanger, "In Southeast Asia Japan Dominates…,"*
    The New York Times, 2 July 1989.

41 *Jeremy Mark, "Japanese Are Less Eager Than It Seems to*
    Resume Business as Usual in Beijing," The Wall Street
    Journal, 9 August 1989.

42 *Ibid.*

China. Although some companies—such as Hitachi Ltd.—resumed talks with China within a couple of months after the turmoil, Japan's worst worries about China's stability have been realized; it is unlikely that they will be anything but cautious and conservative in their approach for a considerable time to come.

Japan and the Third World

Japan's enormous trade surplus has enabled it to make its financial impact felt all across the world—and very rapidly. It is starting to take a leading role in dealing with the crushing $41.3 TRILLION debt which is strangling many of the world's poor nations, especially in Latin America. Estimates are that loans to Latin American nations total $135.8 billion. Of these, U.S. banks hold $39.7 billion; Japanese banks hold $40.9 billion.[43] People worry over whether the Japanese—who have never been known for their altruism—are really seeking to assist the Third World in getting on its own feet, or whether the focus is simply what the Third World can do for Japan. There is considerable skepticism. Many people, in many nations, feel that the loans may be aimed purely at financing Japanese exports (or commercial lending).

The impetus can also come from the other way around, however, as well. Mexico, for example, is struggling with its economy and is eager to make itself less overwhelmingly dependent on the USA. It is turning strongly to the Orient as an alternative source for credit and investment, as well as trade. President Salinas of Mexico (whom some call "Salinas-san") finds Japan an eager and responsive partner. The Japanese look to increase their access to

43 Steven R. Weisman, "Japan Takes a Leading Role in the Third World Debt Crisis," The New York Times, 17 April 1989.

markets in the USA. They also have a sharp eye out all over the world for sources of cheap and plentiful labor. They are flocking to Mexico, particularly to areas along the U.S. border where they are creating what some call the "border boom." "More than 25 Japanese firms have been established in the Tijuana area alone (up from 5 in 1985) and more than 50 are scattered along the 2,000 mile border," according to Brook Larmer, writing from Tijuana for *The Christian Science Monitor:* Most of these are assembly plants. Mr. Larmer goes on to say, "Japan has become Mexico's fourth largest trading partner, second largest creditor [its banks are owed $15 billion of Mexico's $100 billion debt] and fourth largest foreign investor [its $1.3 billion equals about 10 percent of U.S. investment in Mexico]".[44]

The Japanese say they are not comfortable with a "leadership" role and are not seeking it. They point out, however, that greater Japanese involvement in Latin America and other areas of major debt would, in fact, help debtor nations to get on their feet. This would enable them to increase their imports which would in turn help the industrialized countries to reduce their burgeoning trade deficits. Like western nations, Japan itself has become a creditor in Latin America in the past ten years. It has a legitimate interest in the fiscal health of debtor nations.

"The Japanese used to view the Latin American debt as a fire on the other side of the river," said one Japanese official. "Recently that has changed."

Whether they seek a leadership role or not, the Japanese are moving towards one. In 1988 they announced that they were going to "recycle" $30 billion from their trade surpluses to various international lending agencies for use primarily in the Third World. The following year they

44 *Brook Larmer, "Mexico Looks to Asia for Economic Boost," The Christian Science Monitor, 8 August 1989.*

announced their own five-year $50 billion aid program for poor countries.[45]

"We realize that there are some suspicious eyes, so we have to be careful," said Mikio Wakatsuki, Director of Policy Planning for the Bank of Japan. "But there is a national consensus in Japan now that we should be doing things suitable to our national strength. This is the reality."[46]

Section 3: What May Lie Ahead?

Power is Frightening

Clearly it remains extremely hard for many people to accept the growing power of Japan. Not only do World War II veterans and their families all over the world have vivid memories; so do former workers in auto, electronic, and other plants who have lost longtime, high-paying jobs, because of Japanese competition. Furthermore, many people across the world who now work under Japanese managers are uncomfortable with their somewhat rigid, paternalistic style. And, as the Japanese grow more aggressive economically, people are reminded increasingly of the hated militaristic side that was evident during World War II. This still hurts the Japanese image badly throughout the world. Nevertheless, the combination of their economic drive, their hard work, and their financial astuteness makes them formidable competitors, whether popular or not.

45 Steven R. Weismann, "Japan Takes a Leading Role in the Third World Debt Crisis."
46 Jeremy Mark, "Japanese Are Less Eager Than It Seems to Resume Business as Usual in Beijing."

One of the deepest concerns that people feel—perhaps THE deepest—is that they dislike feeling that they are working to fill Japan's coffers. There are profound worries about the uneasily changing balances caused by their immense wealth and growing world power.

R. Taggart Murphy, Managing Director of Japan Private Placement, at Chase Manhattan Asia Ltd., in Tokyo, had an article in the February 1989 issue of the *Harvard Business Review*. In it he warns that even a small number of Japanese money managers could destabilize the United States and world markets in a matter of hours. Both he and Nicholas F. Brady, now U.S. Secretary of the Treasury, believe that it was fund managers in Tokyo who set off the stock market crash in October 1987, acting on the basis of a mistranslated press report.

"If at some future time," Mr. Murphy suggests, "Japanese money managers decide to pull funds out of banks in any part of the world, or if they decide to *dump* securities in any country, they could wield awesome power over the financial fate of the world. Heavy Japanese trade surpluses can—and do—generate heavy dependence on Japanese capital. The hope is that the Japanese will open their markets more widely to foreign goods; that they will make the yen available as a world currency; that they will take on more of the responsibilities of a world financial leader."

"If other countries do *not* have the chance to earn its (Japan's) currency," he continues, "that currency will continually appreciate and the whole global balance of payments will be thrown out of kilter."

Partnerships

Obviously the gigantic shifts in financial relationships taking place globally in such a short span of time, are profoundly significant. They deeply affect international psychology. They are changing the world's attitudes towards

Japan, and even more so, Japan's attitudes towards the rest of the world.

The hope is that there will be steadily increasing international partnerships—especially in high-tech research and development. Increasing numbers of these are already underway. A variety of U.S.-Japanese consortiums, for example, are working even now on such projects as a super high-speed aircraft, capable of flying between New York and Tokyo in 3-5 hours; rapid (300 m.p.h.) surface transportation; high definition television; fiber optic cables that can carry tens of thousands of phone calls simultaneously between one continent or country and another...

In February 1989, the European Community and Japan signed an agreement related to cooperation on fusion power research. This was the first formal agreement between the two parties in the scientific field "reflecting the important role of the European Community in science and technology, and Japan's emphasis on research with long-term goals," according to a Reuters report.[47]

Under this agreement, Japan will be working with all countries in the Community that are carrying on controlled nuclear fusion research. It will work also with Sweden and Switzerland, who are closely associated with the fusion power program, even though they are not part of the European Economic Community. Japan, the USA, and the Soviet Union all have comparable fusion research programs as well. "Cooperation among them is possible because their strategies are broadly similar," says Reuters. The goal, of course, is to develop a new, safe, and environmentally advantageous source of energy which would run on almost inexhaustible and widely available raw materials. What a difference that would make in every corner of this spinning globe!

47 *Europe, April 1989, p. 43.*

Shared Global Problems

The fear of Japanese domination is likely to recede as people realize increasingly the extent to which the Japanese are providing beneficial investment and jobs (as well, of course, as competition and challenge), in a broad range of countries; and also as we turn increasingly to partnerships with one another, in order to deal with massive and frightening global problems that affect us all.

Obviously the world needs to encourage and accept scientific skills from any nation that can contribute, since we all face the same crucial environmental issues. A number of these issues are potentially nothing less than catastrophic to our universe: absorption of the world's ozone; the increasing penetration of ultraviolet rays; the spread of acid rain; decreasing water supplies; the destruction of the world's forests and the pollution of its waters, including even the oceans...not to mention cancer, AIDS, and other major problems that we share throughout the world.

Economic rather than Territorial Friction

Nonetheless, apprehensions remain. The man who has the money calls the tune. There is no doubt that Japan will continue to grow increasingly powerful. If and when they reach a consensus as to their own role in the world, the Japanese could move quickly. Who knows in what direction?

Twice before in the course of history, Japan has unpredictably, abruptly and radically changed the entire direction of its own national course. Once was in 1868 when—under Emperor Meiji—they changed decisively—and with remarkable speed—from being a feudal, agricultural society to becoming an industrial nation. Then again, in 1945, they dramatically changed course, when, at the end of World War II Emperor Hirohito stepped down from his

"divine" role. Almost overnight the country became a relatively smoothly-running democracy.

What lies ahead for the world appears to be intense *economic* competition rather than the primarily territorial competition of past centuries. Already new world impacts are changing social orders. They are affecting whole populations and "globalizing" us all, not only in economic terms but also in the shrinkage of the world. We now move about it with incredible speed; we can communicate almost instantaneously virtually anywhere; our companies are merging with one another across national boundaries; we are in the throes of developing larger political units, to varying degrees, on a cooperative, regional basis—as in the European Community, the Pacific Rim, and the Caribbean Basin.

"By the beginning of the 21st century (only a few years off), the economic terrain will be one of large trading blocs, instead of individual countries trying to maximize their growth through trade," said Governor L. Baliles of Virginia, Chairman of the National Governor's Association (NGA) in their recently issued report surveying the efforts of the U.S. fifty states to improve international studies.

Additional factors that are bound to affect nations' relationships with each other during the coming years include fast-changing patterns in the world's system of interlocking financial and loan agreements, and extensive new trading patterns. There will be increasingly effective economic competition from additional sources also, such as the four Asian "dragons," the European Community, and other blocs of nations.

Whether either side likes it or not (and despite their fundamental differences), Japan and the USA have much to make them *inter*dependent. Competitive though they are, there are economic imperatives that are so strong that—at least for some years—these will almost surely take precedence over the various discords, emotional reac-

tions, and rivalries of the two countries. But one can expect that roles will change on both sides as time goes on.

It is not expected that Japan will "go military" again— though it is not impossible. Their current direction *could* veer in those—or other—unexpected ways:

1. Will they, in fact, sometime look upon themselves as a military power again?
2. Do they like the "feel" of democracy, or will they abandon it for some other approach?
3. What will their new, younger generation—the *Shinjinrui* —see as Japan's place in the world? What will their demands be in the international arena?

All this—and much more—remains to be seen. All we know for now is that Japanese energy is already transforming the power structures of much of the world. Money is power—and they have it.

PART III

"READING"
THE JAPANESE

Kinkakuji Temple (Golden Pavilion) in Kyoto
(photo by Kenji Arai)

Section 1:
Basic Beliefs and Attitudes

Who are the "Elite" in Japan?

All countries have their own levels of "elite." However, the criteria on which elitism (or class) is decided vary considerably from country to country. In *France*, for example, it is based basically on brains. Graduates of leading intellectual centers have high status in France, regardless of their family strain or heritage. In *England* the elite are those "to the Manor born." This naturally includes "The Royals" and all connected with them, but it also includes titled nobility, high church officials, top military officers, and others with titles of one kind or another who are honored and respected as being a bit "above" everyone else, even if they now live in modest circumstances. They still bear their titles—and with them their prestige.

In the *USA* money will do it. If you live on Park Avenue, or own a palatial house in the "proper" suburbs—if you have a yacht, or a stretch Cadillac with tinted glass—you will generally be able to step into the so-called "exclusive" clubs or boxes at the opera, with no questions asked. No one cares what your origin may have been. You can have made your "pile" on Wall Street; by selling cosmetics; by making movies in Hollywood; or by entertaining in night clubs. Your parents can have been virtually illiterate, or drunks, or no-goods; you can have had very little education yourself. But if you have the wherewithal to buy the "right" things and be seen in the "right" places, you can raise yourself to the point of being considered by many as one of America's "social luminaries," or part of the "jet-set."

In Japan

Japan's social interaction works differently. They have a highly complex hierarchical and ranking system tied in closely with their educational system—starting in kindergarten. "Upper" to the Japanese generally means "older, wiser, more revered." It rarely means class or birth. "Status" is related to occupation and position in your group, rather than to heritage. Wealth is now beginning to be a factor in social position.

However, they do not have "socially exclusive" circles the way the Europeans, South or North Americans do. A published "Social Register" listing the "socially elite" would be unthinkable there. For them, education is the basic passport to success if it is education in the "right" school, *i.e.,* a status school. In most countries ability and determination are the vital ingredients for success, not the name of the school you attended. In Japan, however, it is far harder to rise to the top—whatever one's ability and determination—without proper credentials. This starts with attendance at the "right" school, and thus subsequent entry into the "right" university.

Examinations at every level are, therefore, all-important to them. Much is learned by rote, to be given back on examination papers. Individual thinking, reasoning, initiative, and creativity count far less in their school system than a knowledge of *facts*. Students move ahead a) if they conform well to the group, and b) if they can display a great and accurate knowledge of the required facts.

Once in the proper channel, you rise with your age group primarily on the basis of time, rather than through social or blood lines or money, or individual ability. As we will see, this is changing rapidly, but it has long been the pattern in Japan.

Giri

Japanese lives are interwoven with *giri*, meaning the whole pervasive idea of "obligation" and duty, both to those above one in rank, and to those below as well. Obligations often last all of a life time, to a degree seldom seen in the West. *Giri* is a strongly motivating force to many Japanese people. It is a strong strand in the social and self-control fabrics that are both schooled into them from babyhood—so much so that they have become key parts of the Japanese character.

A Group Society

The Japanese interact primarily in groups, not as individuals. They have groups which operate within a wide variety of frameworks and contexts, but social "acceptability" is not often one of the deciding factors. People belong to university groups, business groups, shop and company groups, legal or medical groups, or military groups. Farmers, fishermen, and others interact through cooperatives. In addition—and cutting across social lines in a quite different way—are a broad range of recreational and sports groups, and a variety of clubs. In the past decades money has become a factor in forming new types of exclusive clubs and groups for the wealthy. Within this varied network of groupings, people find their own levels, based to a large extent on age, occupation, or interest. **(See page 101, Section 2 for more on Japanese "Groupness.")**

Religion

The Japanese are not much interested in religion. Their interests tend to be more worldly. There is no state religion, no religious teaching in the schools, little or no connection between religion and national functions. As a result, Japa-

nese people are tolerant about other people's religions. In fact, they are themselves quite often partly Shinto, partly Buddhist, and maybe partly Christian as well. They may be christened with a Shinto ceremony and buried with a Buddhist ceremony. It all blends easily together for them. It seems quite normal to them to turn to one religion to express life's joys and to another for solace over sorrows. In their view "harmony in life is many-sided." Things do not have to be segmented, separated, clearly defined, with sharp distinctive boundaries. Matters of the spirit—and indeed most of life—can flow quite flexibly for them.

Shinto is the old, natural, indigenous religion, based on the concept that all natural objects (rocks, trees, rivers, *etc.*), have their own gods. Japan is covered with small shrines erected to these various local gods. People go to them not only to mark births, deaths, or major world events, but also to ask for such personal favors as help in passing exams, avoiding accidents, having a son, and the like. You often see small shrines in people's homes—even sometimes in their offices, with flowers or food offered there to the gods.

Buddhism which came to Japan via China and Korea, is a major factor in their arts, literature, morals, and ways of thought, even when not practiced as a religion.

Those who want to understand Japanese people really well are advised to learn a bit about it. Buddhism has no God. Buddha himself was a teacher. The Buddhist goal is to achieve tolerance and equality; to rid oneself of hate and jealousy; to "tap" the infinite love that exists. Believers try to reach out to *The Truth*—they look for self-enlightenment. Zen Buddhists, especially, believe you attain an enlightened mental state through long, frequent meditation. Buddhists strive to keep increasing their own sense of serenity. This is very important to them. You see the influence of Buddhism in many aspects of Japanese life: the quietness of the tea ceremony; the "spareness" of

flower arrangements (*ikebana*); the simplicity of most houses, the "temporariness" of life. Major or cherished works of art, for example, may be displayed for only one day out of each year, with the idea that this very "temporariness" makes them more appreciated and honored.

Superstition

Those working with Japanese people will often find them to be quite superstitious. Many turn readily to astrologers or fortune tellers if they have decisions to make. You will find this to be true even with efficient, Western-oriented businessmen. Many things for them are "lucky" or "unlucky." The start of a new venture or major undertaking may be affected by what are—or are not—considered to be "propitious" circumstances or dates. This is not done "for fun," or "tongue in cheek." It is taken very seriously by many Japanese, even those who are well-educated, mature, and in positions of high authority.

Wa or "Harmony"

One of the subtle but crucially important Japanese attitudes relates to what is called *Wa*. This can be defined as "Harmony." In daily life it means maintaining a comfortable atmosphere of acceptance and respect at all times, with all people. *Wa* avoids abruptness; it includes a highly developed sensitivity to peoples' feelings. Their antennae are always out, feeling the air for tension or harmony. The Japanese are tuned to a high degree to other peoples' moods, needs, desires, antagonisms, hesitations...Disharmonies and any kind of confrontation are avoided whenever possible. Such frictions are really painful to Japanese people. They run contrary to their deep sense of what is right. The Japanese absolutely HATE a row, or scene, or confrontation. They will rarely argue if

they can possibly avoid it, and they are masters at avoiding conflicts of all sorts. It would be startling, for example, to see a Japanese tennis player argue with the umpire no matter how great the aggravation.

Wa is often reflected in cautious, indirect—sometimes somewhat hesitating—speech. This gives the speaker time to sense the other person's mood before coming up with something that might not be "harmonious." They will rarely disagree with someone in public. Even if they do not agree with what is being said, they often appear to go along with it, especially if the speaker is clearly feeling strongly about it. This can be confusing— often annoying— to Westerners. But to the Japanese, harmony is more important than accuracy *at that moment*. They will come back to the subject later with the facts, if necessary. But first they will focus on preserving the harmonies. In other words, we of different cultures must always understand that they will give leeway in speech, and at least the appearance of agreement, for the sake of smooth relationships and "harmony." Those who have been "out in the Western world" for some time naturally get used to Western ways to varying degrees. However, the basic Japanese instinct is to keep things smooth and unruffled to the fullest possible extent.

Go-Betweens

Most Westerners are not used to the system of "Go-Betweens," *i.e.*, middlemen who go back and forth between two parties, helping them come to agreements, or settle disputes, or feel out future possibilities (even including marriage possibilities!).

In a country that abhors friction and debates, "Go-Betweens" are useful because they can stay neutral. They can let each side know the possibilities and pitfalls; they can make sure that both sides are serious; they can feel out

how much leeway there is on either side; and can keep each side informed as to the other one's hopes, intentions, fears, or roadblocks. If the news is bad, they can smooth it over and put it into a gentle light; if there is disagreement they can interpret one side's view to the other, without heat. In Japan intermediaries frequently are the ones who discuss money matters in detail, thus sparing the protagonists from what is usually the thorniest part of any agreement.

Most Westerners are not comfortable with "Go-Betweens." We prefer to speak for ourselves. In addition, we want to "get on with it." We are anxious not to "waste time." Going through an intermediary seems to us a "roundabout" method. We are apt to trust our own ability better than someone else's. However, when dealing with Japanese people, the direct approach is often not the quickest. John C. Condon suggests: "In Japan the shortest distance between two points may be a curved line."[1]

Who Makes a Good Leader in Japanese Eyes?

The Japanese often choose their leaders with personal qualities in mind rather than particular skills, experience, or knowledge. Young people are observed as they come up through the ranks. Those selected for promotion are not necessarily the brightest and quickest. They are likely to be the best listeners, the best harmonizers, the ones who work loyally, steadily, and quietly. Even at top levels, promotions are frequently given for loyalty and seniority, rather than for actual achievement.

In many countries—the USA, for example, or Australia, or Britain, or throughout South America—a leader is a person who draws others to him, who has an air of power

1 *Used with permission John C. Condon, With Respect to the Japanese (Yarmouth, ME: Intellectual Press, Inc. 1984) p. 15.*

about him, is charismatic and strong, and preferably likeable. He (or she) is expected to be able to analyze a situation, make decisions, delegate responsibilities, and "follow through" on projects or activities, keeping track of their developments, offering guidance as needed, drawing all the different parts and phases of the undertaking together. In short, he (or she) "keeps the reins" in his (or her) hands.

This is not the kind of leader that the Japanese are used to or respond to well. What has happened to consensus? Where are the *ringi* ideas, seeping upwards through the ranks? Where are the delicacies of innuendo and suggestion? What happens to the harmonies if final decisions are clear cut and come from the top down? *Nemawashi* is lost, *i.e.*, persuasion, adequate time for evaluation along the way by people of lower ranks.

Japan is Woven Like a Cloth

To understand Japan—and the Japanese—one must liken the country to a tapestry. No one thread stands out; the whole is superior to its parts. We, in large scale America, are used to looking for heroes or villains; we search for the individual who "stands out" in any plant or office, in sports, or in the government. Japan—like equally tiny Switzerland—functions more smoothly as a melded, interwoven whole. The Japanese mistrust towering individuals. That makes a subtle difference in every aspect of life.

It is an area in which new currents are stirring, however. Most of the increasing number of Japanese who have studied and lived and worked abroad have enjoyed the feeling of "being somebody." They like the feel of choice, of initiative, of having a voice, rather than being a mere cog in a wheel. Once freedom and initiative and creativity have been experienced, that memory never fades. Silent confor-

mity then comes hard—if it comes at all. Japanese who have experienced the heady taste of individuality are taking a new look at patient subservience—and a new look at themselves.

Consistency

Another common Western priority is that of "being consistent." We expect people to be "true to their word." We consider this to be vital in human relations (except in situations with which we ourselves are familiar, such as being polite, exaggerating for effect, or using other shadings that, because we use them too, we recognize them).

Being consistent, however, frequently conflicts with the Japanese priority of "flexibility." It must be understood that flexibility is just as important to them as *consistency* is to us. The difference is that with them, the situation matters. They adjust to the personalities involved, the need for "harmonies." We, on the other hand, are apt to have a standard (or norm) that holds true regardless of the situation. Basically, we link our behavior to that standard— with some variations—regardless of the specific circumstances. What seems to them to be "sensitively flexible" is often read by people from another background as "wavering," or frequently even "evasive."

To the Japanese it is not. They know how to interpret the nuances in their culture just as we do in ours. The problem is that we each have trouble with the other one's subtleties.

One needs to try consciously and hard simply to suspend judgement until one understands any other culture. In doing business with the Japanese, Westerners need to remember that however "Westernized" the Japanese appear, they always remain deeply and fundamentally Japanese. Their outlook on the world is always uniquely Japanese. That fundamental assumption is basic to understanding these global, effective, but very different people.

What if...?

The deep sense of caution found in most Japanese people frequently affects how they react to a new suggestion. Their immediate—almost instinctive—tendency is to avoid committing themselves. Japanese people need to be sure they will not fail. Failure to them carries great loss of face. It becomes a matter of shame. Most Westerners are likely to feel "Let's try it; if it doesn't work we will try something else. Let's at least explore it." But the Japanese are rarely exploratory. "Better safe than sorry," is their more usual motto. We seldom mind making mistakes. If we turn out to be wrong we are apt to say, "Oh, really? Well, I'm sorry about that. I thought it was the other way. My error." We go merrily on our way, unabashed at having made a mistake. A Japanese, however, will be very chagrined if he is round to be in error. He is therefore, generally hesitant to speculate on uncertainties—whether these be in or out of business. As a result, when Westerners start asking about "percentage of chances," or cost estimate on things that are not yet more than hypothetical dreams, it is often hard for Japanese people to follow the concept. Most of them simply have not been trained to think that way. In the West, children are taught from a young age to explore, to think "what if ... ?", to experiment. Their toys and training from early childhood include taking things apart and putting them back together again, wondering what *might* be possible, what *might* happen next if...The Japanese are not. But they are raising a new generation who are.

Formality

Stacey Simon, Director of Metro International in New York, who lived and worked in Japan for some years, points to what she found to be an interesting phenomenon regarding the Japanese sense of formality: "They are quite formal with one another in the mornings," she says. "You

might say most offices are a little stiff with formality. However, if things go along well as the day progresses, they grow increasingly informal. The language the Japanese use with one another grows less formal; there is more teasing and laughter...a kind of family feeling takes over. But the surprising thing is," she continued, "that the next morning they will start with the same formality again."

Ethics, Morals and Points of View

One of the intriguing things about this world is the range of human reactions that seem "ethical" or "moral" or "right" in one culture but which are given an entirely different interpretation by another. A clear example of this is found among Eskimos, certain desert tribes, and some South Sea Island people who consider that it is hospitable—and a special honor to a guest—to lend them their wives overnight. To them this is perfectly "moral." Since morals relate to the everyday sense of right and wrong by which each nation lives, they vary widely from country to country. The same is true of manners, treatment of women, and much else. Again, one needs to avoid being judgmental.

In the USA, for example, honesty in speech is considered to be a high priority, no matter what the consequences. But what Americans consider (with pride) to be "honest forthrightness," other people frequently see as "bluntness," "lack of discretion," "lack of sensitivity," or sometimes "blatant interference."

Says Edward T. Hall, particularly highly esteemed qualities in Japanese eyes are: 1) being dependable; 2) taking responsibility when things go wrong; 3) keeping one's word. "Having a strong reputation for these qualities," he says, "is like having money in the bank. Each person is expected to accept full responsibility for his/her

own job." He says: "The Japanese dislike excuses." They expect commitment; they expect a person to do whatever he has agreed to do—and they will do the same.[2]

When Problems Occur

No matter what happens, no matter whose fault it may have been, in Japan *the person in charge always takes the blame*. It is like the captain of a ship who is expected to take the blame, even if he was not on the bridge at the time of a disaster.

If you are working with Japanese people, it is well to understand this. If you are in charge, you must be ready not only to take the blame yourself, but also to downplay blame in others.[3] The important thing will be to straighten out the "harmonies" again, to get everyone back on an even keel as quickly as possible. Blame is considered negative and is rarely helpful. They are not accustomed to self-analysis based on our Western suppositions.

Wherever Japanese people may be, they retain a deep sense of the formal hierarchy through which they see social relationships. It is part of their warp and woof. In addition, one must not forget their complex and deeply ingrained sense of individual obligations (*Giri*). Understandably they will follow these and various other instincts which have been bred in them from birth. We Westerners must allow for their accustomed "style" of behavior, just as the Japanese must allow for our breezy informality and our desire for speed.

2 *Reprinted by permission of Bantam Doubleday Dell Publishing Group. Edward T. and Mildred Reed Hall, Hidden Differences. Doing Business With the Japanese (Garden City, NY: Anchor Press/Doubleday. 1987) p. 70.*
3 *Ibid., p. 113.*

Different Concepts of Time

A United Nations Committee was discussing the pros and cons of no less enormous a project than diverting the entire course of the Platte River in South America. The impact would be felt over half the continent; the lives, the jobs, the homes of millions of people could or would be affected by the project, if it were approved.

Every time the American delegate spoke it was in terms of short approaches. He kept emphasizing the costs. Many of the rest of the group were eloquent as to the long-term benefits, the sweeping economic changes that would accrue, the broad vision that the project opened up for the whole area over the coming decades.

The meeting continued for some hours. Finally the American announced that his country would be willing to consider the project but only in terms of the next two years.

The Chairman, an Argentinean, exploded. He banged his fist down on the table and said, "That is just like you Americans. Here we are discussing a 20-year plan, a 10-year budget, and 5-year personnel. At best you can think only in terms of a 2-year plan, a 1-year budget, and 1-year personnel."

Although Americans think of themselves as "future-oriented," Japanese see them as lacking in foresight and long-range planning; shackled by their own politics, their short-term budgets, and their short-term personnel.

The Japanese deeply revere the past. Nevertheless, they are thinking now in terms of rapid world-changing innovation. They are forging ahead with new technologies. Theirs is a long-term view of the future. Not only the USA but many other Western countries, however, are still thinking of the future in 2-5 year terms, with one eye on their own parliaments, political parties and budgets. We are hobbled by the facts and figures of here and now.

Nonetheless—perhaps for the very reason that we *are*

working in a foreshortened time frame—we of the West often press hard for completion once a project has begun and the clock starts running. We act like Harvey, the Rabbit. When someone casually said to him "You must come up and see me sometime," his immediate answer was "When?" If the Japanese say they will "study a proposal" we will almost surely say "When? When will you get back to us? In two weeks? A month?" The Japanese *hate* to be pressured. Deadlines backfire. They react negatively if pushed. Their fundamental systems of consensus and group considerations take time ... often much time. To Americans, many North Europeans and others, time is almost a "tangible asset." You can save it, cut it, kill it, waste it, or use it. We feel that we have only a limited amount of it. Both the hour glass and the digital clock are continually reminding us how fast the seconds slip past; the sands of time keep running on—and each of us has only an allotted number, whatever that number may be. We operate in "time frames." These keep passing—and cause us pressure.

Asians, who think of Time as a continuum—a circle not a line—a merging from past, to present, to future generations—are not as pressured. We think in terms of a line. When we get to the end of the line, that is it. Their circle merges from the present into the future, with no breakpoint. They do not have anything like the sense of time pressure that exists in much of the West.

Pace

Pace is one of the subtle but most challenging adjustments that all of us have to make as we move from one country or culture to another. It is almost always a difficult adjustment. It affects every aspect of daily life. For each country it must be consciously "felt," for each one has its own metronome.

Stacey Simon, who lived and worked in Japan for some years, spoke of the difference in office pace between America and Japan: "We in America work at an exhausting pace all day, "she said. "Frequently we do not stop for coffee—just drink it at our desks. We often eat lunch while we are still working. The Japanese have longer working hours, but they are more relaxed. They have more breaks in the day; they do more socializing at each others' desks. Since the offices are 'open' they 'visit' with one another a great deal in the course of the day. They have long tea breaks in the mornings and afternoons, and would not think of working during lunch."

In fact not only the pace, but the whole concept of Time—its importance, its continuity, and its use—is viewed with great cultural differences throughout the world. It may be *the* most different, most difficult element there is in terms of cultural adaptation. One cannot by-pass it. It is woven inextricably throughout every person's life at all levels, *i.e.*, daily and long term; personal and working. Furthermore, we feel emotional about it if we are rushed, pressed, delayed, or thrown off stride from our norm— whatever norm that may be for each one of us. Let no one underestimate how crucial an element time is in each person's cultural pattern.

The Saving of Face

"Face is vitally important to the Japanese—more so than meeting a deadline, or being consistent, or being frank," says John C. Condon. "Frequently they will stick by a decision even if they know it is wrong, rather than *lose face* by admitting their error," he says.[4]

If, as the British say, you "drop a brick," or, as the French say, make a *faux pas*, or, as the Americans say, "you goof,"

4 *John C. Condon, With Respect to the Japanese, p. 32.*

your Japanese colleagues will pretend not to notice. They will not laugh at you or tease you about it, as might happen in other countries. That would make you "lose face," and they would never willingly cause that to happen. It would show lack of respect, lack of courtesy, lack of kindness.

For them, every individual is part of a group. Negative reflection on him therefore also reflects on the group. That being the case, they feel no one should ever be embarrassed—even slightly—or scolded publicly, or otherwise humiliated, since this would hurt the "face" not only of the individual but also of the group.

Westerners put their emphasis on the individual. They do not feel that people are woven into a web of interrelated relationships—as do the Japanese.

The Japanese are deeply and constantly concerned about what other people think about them. Condon writes that for them "Concern for *face* is a primary means of social control. Proper behavior," he says, "is ensured through outside social pressure. It is part of their vitally important interdependence; part, too, of the maintenance of their social harmony."

He points out that in Western societies pride, the desire for self approbation, the desire to excel, and other internal feelings— as for example, a sense of guilt—are likely to guide behavior a good deal more than concern for what other people think.[5]

"I just would not feel right if I did that" is, generally speaking, far more of an inner drive to Westerners than "What would my neighbors think?" But for the Japanese what other people think of them is tremendously important.

Most of us Westerners are individualistic. Most of us do not come from "group" societies, be we French, Swedish, British, Australian, or whatever. Most of us do not think of

5 *Ibid., p. 30.*

our personal behavior as being entwined with our company, or our club, or our neighbors. We do not (literally) commit suicide or immediately resign from our job if we feel we have either shamed or embarrassed others."Too bad about them," is a more normal reaction to us. Westerners understand "losing face," but it is not vital to them whether they "lose face" or not. We feel a bit guilty sometimes, or awkward, or embarrassed. We wish we had not done something, or that we had done it differently, or spoken differently. But the same events or comments that cause such mild feelings in Westerners are likely to cause deep and often lasting shame, humiliation or guilt in the Japanese. They are profoundly sensitive to anything that affects their dignity or pride. Disrespect, criticism, or any kind of humiliation are not passed over lightly. We say "Oh, forget it." But they remain hurt for a long period if they have "lost face," particularly in front of "outsiders."

If You Should Err

If you do something a little out of line the Japanese, as we have said, are likely to look the other way and ignore it. However, if the error has been serious, or if it has insulted them deeply, you will probably feel a palpable silence. They may not return phone calls; they may not speak to you in passing. They will rarely tell you what the problem is, or even hint at it. If, after a time, you feel this uneasy "silent treatment," look back over your actions to see what you might have done (or said) to cause it. You may have unwittingly made someone feel stupid or apologetic; you may have blamed someone for something in public, or spoken to them sharply in front of someone else. You may have made a sarcastic remark, or told a joke at someone's expense. Perhaps you made some teasing crack like "There goes good old Oshi, dropping the ball again." You could

have made some veiled or half-humorous—yet critical—
remark in passing, and thought nothing of it. You may even
have offered, in good faith, what you thought was helpful,
constructive criticism.

In any of these ways, intentionally or not, you may have
hurt and embarrassed him in public. Perhaps, unwittingly,
you did not mention someone equally "worthy." All of this
may seem "touchy" to us. However, it is a deep part of the
Japanese heritage to be extremely careful of other peoples'
feelings. This "carefulness" has been trained into them
through generations of close, crowded living. It is a key
part of their national psyche. If when you discover that you
have upset someone in any way you apologize deeply and
really *mean* it, they will forgive and forget. If you react
differently from that they are baffled. In their book *There
Is a Difference*, Fieg and Blair write: "When Japanese
terrorists caused an incident at Tel Aviv Airport, the
Japanese government officially apologized, expressing
the nation's deep regret. They did so in a sense of collective
responsibility. They expected the apology to be accepted.
However, they were much surprised when instead, some
people took the apology as an admission of legal liability
and immediately demanded compensation."[6] Two wholly
different views of an apology!

In dealing with the Japanese people, we need to understand that apologizing sincerely and readily for any fault—
large or small—is an important part of getting along well.
You cannot brush something off by saying, "Oh, for gosh
sakes, I didn't mean that," or worse yet, "Oh, don't be so
touchy. It was only a joke." If they seem to be hurt or upset,
one should make a formal, respectful, convincing apology.
Unless they feel you are truly sorry, there may be politeness, but forgiveness will not be there.

6. *John P. Fieg and John G. Blair, There is a Difference
(Washington, D.C.: Meredian House International, 1941)
p. 21.*

Nor will things blow over. The unpleasantness will continue to rankle and affect your relationship unless you "ring true" with your apology.

The hardest thing, however, may be to know when a Japanese is upset. Especially at higher levels, they do not like to show any emotions, especially not negative ones. They are very good at hiding their feelings. In their book *Hidden Differences: Doing Business With The Japanese,* Dr. and Mrs. Hall suggest some clues to help you recognize Japanese reluctance, anger, or distress: "The Japanese does not do what you ask. He says, 'I will do my best,' but then does not. He sucks in his breath and says '*Sah...*' He stiffens his posture; he grows more silent, more tight-lipped, more contained. He drops his voice, speaking very slowly and softly."*Dr. Hall suggests:*

1) Apologize—even if it was not your fault;

2) If it is a big blow-up, see if you can get a Japanese friend to intervene. Ask him to give you advice and counsel, and, if necessary, to handle the problem." (As noted earlier, they are far more comfortable having discord handled by intermediaries than by the principals themselves.);

3) A small gift may help to re-establish relations. If given, it should be given the next day, quietly and in private, with conciliatory words."[7]

Perhaps Dr. Hall's most useful suggestion was to "back off." He suggests that one does not rush in but allows time and leeway for the "harmonies" to be restored. If you give that urgent need for *Wa* (or harmony) a chance, it may go to work, to everyone's benefit. If it does not, however, you should not fail to pursue the subject and clear the air.[8]

7 *Edward T. and Mildred Reed Hall, Hidden Differences: Doing Business With The Japanese, p. 113.*

8 *Ibid., p.112.*

The Skill of "Not Noticing"

The Japanese are skilled at covering for one another so that they can help each other to "save face." They will "not notice" many things that would be embarrassing if mentioned. This is part of a highly developed Asian skill: that of providing "psychological privacy."

An American woman went with a Japanese colleague to call on a distinguished Japanese author. They arrived at his home at the appointed time. When the door was opened by a maid the host was sitting on the floor in the middle of the small family room right in front of them, clad only in very scant undershorts— nothing else. He was busily reading the morning paper.

The American's response would have been to apologize profusely, back out, mumbling that she would come back later when it was more convenient.

The Japanese colleague, however, handled the situation in a totally Asian way. A cloak of psychological privacy was immediately dropped over the writer. The ladies sat down on two stiff chairs on either side of the doorway, saying not a word to the host, not even looking at him as he quickly gathered up his papers and disappeared through a sliding door. Ten minutes or so later—minutes of total silence between the ladies—he reappeared, smiling and welcoming, fully and formally dressed. He greeted them as if they had just that moment arrived; the session proceeded as if nothing had occurred. There was no loss of face or embarrassment whatsoever, because "nothing had been noticed."

"Face-saving" Techniques

Westerners can learn "face-saving" techniques. Many of these lie in learning to phrase questions obliquely, giving the other person leeway, which is what the Japanese

always need. As for example: "I wonder what would happen if you treat it this way..." rather than saying, "See, you are holding it wrong"(or "using too much," or whatever). The one approach does not threaten "face"; the other batters it. Personnel evaluation reports need to be made in the affirmative wherever possible, rather than critically: "He is getting better at..." rather than "He is still poor at... "Everyone reading that will realize that there is still room for improvement, but "face" will not be lost. Evaluations should be written as much as possible with an eye to causing no embarrassment to the individual, nor to his Japanese superiors when they receive a copy.

If a Japanese asks for your "frank opinion," or says "please tell me if I am doing anything wrong," he is in fact *not* asking for you to point out his faults. Any fellow Japanese would understand that clearly, and none would answer with criticism. The man is actually asking for reassurances, positive reinforcement of some kind. So you should respond by quickly praising him for whatever he *has* been doing well—or even adequately. (If you were a foreigner in Japan, you too might welcome similar reassurances from time to time!)

John Condon suggests that "Americans (and others) who work with Japanese need to be more 'thin-skinned' (*i.e.*, more sensitive to feelings) and that Japanese need to be more 'thick-skinned' regarding what other people say and how they are treated."[9]

How to "Lose Your Own Face"

There are a number of ways in which one can "lose one's own face," without being aware of it:

1) *Saying "No" bluntly, or flatly refusing a request.* If you say "No, that is impossible," or "I would not think of

9. *John C. Condon, With Respect to the Japanese, p. 33.*

it," or in other words give any flat, all-out negative, you rob your colleague of "face." Any time you hurt or embarrass anyone else, for whatever reason, whether intentional or not, you appear in Japanese eyes to be "insensitive."

It is better to soften all edges. A Japanese will clearly understand you if you say:

"It would be difficult..."

"Let me think about it..."

"We must consider further..."

"Perhaps it needs more time ..."

He will know perfectly well that the answer is "No" — that nothing much is going to happen. However, he will not feel rebuffed.

2) *Criticizing your competition*—either domestic or foreign. This is just not done by the Japanese. They think poorly of it.

3) *Arriving late for an appointment or meeting.* To them this relates to lack of respect. They expect punctuality. If you are late, be sure to apologize profusely and explain the reason fully. Don't just brush it off with "I'm sorry I'm late." You have to be considerably more apologetic than that. You should not only explain the reason, but stress your very real sorrow at having inconvenienced or delayed the other person.

4) *Talking business at a first meeting*, or "getting down, to brass tacks" before exchanging pleasantries and general conversation at subsequent meetings. If you fail to do this—and in a leisurely, interested way—you will "lose face." You will appear to them to be insensitive-uncaring-impersonal-cold.

You will soon learn to adjust the degree of this. It depends to some extent on how "Westernized" your Japanese colleague may be, but if in doubt it is better to err on the leisurely side rather than appearing super efficient and rushed. You must ring true. Your colleague must feel that you consider business to be really secondary to your

relationships, before you get down to the matter in hand. It is worth the short time it takes to make this initial friendliness a habit. For most people it is only a matter of extending their normal friendliness a little longer than we tend to do in the West. No rush!

5) *If you attend a Japanese party* it is likely that you will be expected to perform in some way (if you are a man), *i.e.*, sing a song, recite a ballad, tell a funny story, do a trick ... or something. You will "lose face" if you do not contribute when invited to do so. Go prepared!

Different Drum Beats

Since East and West stem from profoundly different philosophies—different training—different behavioral roots—each naturally operates with a different kind of logic as well. We dance to the rhythms of two different orchestras. It is only natural, therefore, that we have periods of being out of step with one another sometimes. The marvel may be that we are as harmonious as we are across such massive cultural differences!

When you stub your toe on some phase of Japanese behavior that seems to you unpredictable—unfathomable—outrageous—shady (or anything other than familiar and therefore understandable), just draw a breath. Stop to explore where your colleague is coming from in *his* terms, and in *his* mind. The chances are that once you understand his point of view, you will also understand his action—whether you agree with it or not. You will find that things go far more easily and smoothly if you keep consciously remembering that we all start from different vantage points. We move to the beat of different drummers. When one remembers that, it becomes easier to give the other fellow leeway. Time and leeway are two of the most vitally important elements that spell "courtesy" to a Japanese. They are both crucial in making wheels go round smoothly.

Section 2:
Can Anyone "Read" a Japanese?

No one can really "read" any other person—no matter who it may be, or from what nationality. (One cannot "read" even one's own husband or wife much of the time!) But one *can* purposefully concentrate on getting to understand one another better. In dealing with the Japanese, this is well worth the effort. They are a proud people, and have much to be proud about:

There is virtually no illiteracy in their country;

99% of their students complete high school, as compared to less than 80% in the USA. Their school year is sixty days longer than that of the U.S. (240 as compared with 180). As a result of these two facts, the Japanese as a whole are better educated than many Americans—and many in other countries as well;

They have the world's highest life expectancy; their medical care is affordable and available for rich and poor alike, from cradle to grave;

They have (and need) only a third as many policemen per capita as does the USA;

They have the highest per capita income of any major country in the world.

These are but a few of their justifiable prides; some of the reasons why the Japanese consider themselves to be a "superior" nation.

No Westerner should assume that either they or we are "superior." What we are is: very different from each other.

The point is to understand the many differences that occur, especially in the assumptions and expectations on both sides. We need to recognize that what seems normal to them may *not* seem so to us, and vice versa. If we BOTH understand that clearly and keep it in mind as we work

together, we can avoid much misunderstanding, confusion, and even "hostility" on both sides.

Going Around a Subject

If asked to name a primary force in their own country, most Westerners would probably cite something like drive, initiative, or knowledge. We would not say "harmony." To many Westerners, directness is a major virtue. We like to "call a spade a spade;" we do not like to "beat around the bush," we like to "get on with it." Time is far less important to the Japanese. Many other things take precedence.

Since the Japanese are so deeply concerned with keeping the harmonies and so alert lest they upset other peoples' feelings, they often do something that most Westerners find hard to take. They frequently respond to questions with what they think you WANT them to say, rather than giving an accurate reflection of the facts. They are meaning to be polite and kind. They are intent on not upsetting anyone. They are NOT trying to be evasive or to misrepresent. It is simply that the priorities of their values and ours are different in this regard. To them politeness is more important than accuracy. To us it is not. We "come right out" with everything. We *ask* for a raise if we feel it is due; we ask for a job or a recommendation. We put agreements in writing in contracts, to be sure that they are clearly understood by both sides. We do not like "hidden agendas," or people who play what we consider to be "close to the chest." Open directness is very important to most Westerners. We are anxious to "get to the point"...and the point usually is to make a deal or arrive at a decision. Everyone quickly "gets down to brass tacks" and "puts their cards on the table." After all, time is money, isn't it? We like facts. The Japanese like suggestions. They *imply* rather than *state* a view. We are playing different ball games.

In their book *Managing Cultural Differences*, Moran and Harris summarize the Japanese character. They point out how basically different it is from the gung-ho, money-focused, "no time to waste" Westerner. "The Japanese character," they say, "is diverse with a sense of poetry and the ephemeral; there is a concern for the transitory, inconclusive qualities of life, for nature and its observation. It is actively curious, energetic and quick, with a sense of delicacy and wistfulness."[10]

This does not mean that the Japanese are in any sense "wishy-washy." They, too, love success. They are hard-headed as well as sensitive and extremely adaptable. They do not resist change, but eagerly make use of it as, for example, in their broad use of automation and their wide gamut of new technologies.

Moran and Harris say, "Although realists, they are like their island homeland—a floating world that changes course."[11]

Ambiguous Replies

The Asian method is to talk around a subject at length, so that everyone understands each person's point of view without anyone having to express it straight out. Otherwise someone might "lose face" if they had to back down, or were overruled. To avoid this, people talk obliquely—vaguely—indirectly around the subject. Gradually everyone knows how everyone else feels, learning it by implication-innuendo-indirection so there is no confrontation and no argument; no "loss of face" for anyone. One Japanese gave other tips for foreigners: "If you give us too many details and specifics it insults our intelligence; when you

10 Robert T. Moran and Philip T. Harris, Managing Cultural
     Differences (Gulf Publishing Co., 1987 Edition) p. 394.
11 Ibid.

want to put everything in writing, Japanese feel you are implying that our word is not to be trusted."

Japanese are so conscious of "saving face" that they try to avoid giving offense by any kind of negation. Some Asian languages actually have no word for "no." The Western bluntness seems to them to be intrusive—demanding—abrupt. Often we seem highly aggressive when we do not mean to be at all.

It is equally easy for Westerners to misinterpret and misunderstand the Asian's indirect way. We get impatient and annoyed. We frequently think we are being "lied to" or "manipulated." "Why did he say that?" we ask. "He knows perfectly well that..." The Western attitude generally is "Do you, or don't you?" "Will you, or won't you?" "Do you agree, or don't you?" Our urge frequently is to say: "Stop dilly-dallying around, and come out with it." Japanese silences, delays, hesitations, and roundabout approaches can be really infuriating to those whose goal is to "get on with it." Neither side means to annoy the other. Each does it quite unconsciously. (**See more on this in Part IV, Patterns of Communication.**)

In selecting staff to handle negotiations or to work with Japanese colleagues, therefore, it is important to choose people who have a calm equanimity about them, people who—though strong and firm—will not become agitated by a slower, more roundabout pace. They will generally be far more successful than will driving, aggressive personalities.

Even if delays and a leisurely pace remain annoying to those on a faster circuit, it becomes easier to understand *WHY* the Japanese react as they do if one takes the trouble to keep exploring how they think, and keep watching what is important to them. Anyone working with people from other countries has to keep reminding him or herself that those from different cultures inevitably (and understandably) approach life from different points of view. Priorities

are a key difference. Different things seem important—
and to different degrees. Values originate deep in every
nation's cultural roots. They are kept alive in succeeding
generations through different types of pressures and training. These many subtle—usually unrecognized—matters
make a tremendous difference in how each of us reacts to
the other.

Expressing One's Feelings

Self-Control

One of our most fundamental differences may be found in
the fact that Japanese are past masters at controlling and
hiding their feelings. For centuries they have lived in close
quarters. They cannot afford to let their emotions run
rampant. Rarely does one see a visibly angry Japanese.
Anger is expressed more by silence—clipped speech—a
look in the eyes—than by any explosive expression. They
have deep contempt for lack of control. If you lose your
temper and show your anger, you will gain absolutely
nothing. In fact, you may totally destroy your relationship.
Once you have lost their respect, it is a hard, slow, and often
an impossible job to regain it again.

They believe that it is possible to prevail over other
people only if you have real control over *yourself*. They are
also deeply concerned with what people think of them.
Hence the great emphasis on self-discipline and conformity, starting in kindergarten—or before. Only if you are
truly self-controlled and self-disciplined, they believe, can
you command other peoples' respect. They consider such
control—shown partly through refined manners—to be a
sign of spiritual stature. Manners for them are not something that one turns on and off. They are an expression of
one's inner strength. As a result, they rarely show anger;
they almost never interrupt. They stay in control of them-

selves—including their voices—even under considerable provocation or annoyance. Their quietness should not be taken as a weakness. It is, instead, very much a strength.

Another manifestation of their control lies in the way they show consideration for other peoples' feelings. They hide sorrow, for example, unwilling to make the listener also feel sad, unnecessarily. To them this would be foolish or rude—or both. If they do talk of something sad, they will often smile as they do so. They feel the sorrow will be lessened for the other person by this. The sadness will not be passed on to someone else. Do not take it as lack of feeling on their part. It is self-discipline instead.

Smiles

We outsiders often read a different message into Japanese smiles than is the case. Most people of the world smile to indicate welcome, good humor, agreement, affection, *etc*. Generally it is a spontaneous reaction. Although the Japanese often smile for all these reasons, they also have that smile of self-control, which is quite different. This, too, is taught them as children. Furthermore, they are likely to smile while you are taking them to task for doing something poorly or wrong. They are not showing contempt or insincerity, or lack of concern or bravado—as we would read it if a Westerner grinned while being reprimanded. With the Japanese it is a sign of embarrassment.

Smiles (or even giggles) are often caused by embarrassment or self-deprecation. For instance, if a maid drops a spoon and breaks a glass while she is serving a meal, she is likely to cover her mouth and giggle. This is to cover her embarrassment. She does not think it is funny at all. She is not being fresh. But a rule of life to them is: one presents the most agreeable face possible at all times. However you feel inside, it is your social duty to smile bravely to the world outside.

Anger and Irritation

No matter what one is feeling, one "keeps one's cool" in Japan. Showing anger is very much looked down on and considered as "loss of control." Since this is the case, there are rarely clear warning signs of impending disaster with the Japanese. Most Westerners, intent on driving home their own points hardly notice the reaction among the Japanese. We hammer on, often in a rising crescendo of voice and excitement as our frustration grows when we elicit no response. The quieter they are, the angrier we get.

Because the Japanese are so highly controlled emotionally, outsiders—especially any who are somewhat self-engrossed and lack sensitivity to others—often do not realize, as their own blood pressure mounts, that tension is quietly mounting in the Japanese as well. So they continue. They often press too far. Suddenly they find themselves facing a resolute, unswerving, albeit polite, rejection. The Japanese team may suddenly just gather their papers and start to repack their briefcases. Session is over. "So sorry." Once tension reaches a certain point within the Japanese, the jig is up. It can be hard—if not impossible—to rebuild respect, or to resume talks.

We could ask ourselves "How are we supposed to know they are getting to this point if they don't show it?"

The answer is: Keep yourself in tune with them. Don't get wholly engrossed in your own side. Watch their eyes. Allow silences. Let them speak. DON'T PRESSURE. Watch them closely. They show their tension by small movements of their feet and hands, small shifts of position, and particularly their eyes. If you do not keep yourself alert to these quiet, unintentional signals, you will miss them. They will be trying hard to act as if nothing is happening. They feel that if you ignore personality clashes and disagreements, these may peter out and disappear. Tomorrow

may be better. If you get entangled in them, they believe, things will only go from bad to worse.

Anger is one of many deep cultural differences. It takes varying lengths of time to arouse anger in people; different kinds of things bring it out; we all express it differently. Some of us come to a slow boil; others are explosive. With some, anger is like a rapier; with others it is like a blunderbuss.

The Japanese have been taught for generations to remain quiet. The word for their patient forbearance is *Nintai*.

Nintai

Japanese forbearance is more easily understood if one again remembers their feudalistic background, their overcrowded islands, and their fundamental desire for "harmony." It is one more expression of their national need to fit in inconspicuously, making no shock waves, submerging their own individual identities into the whole. They accept what is expected of them with great patience, whether it be crowded living space for their families, long, exhausting, sardine-packed daily commutes, late hours at the office, years of grinding subservience as they work their way up the job ladder—a difficult opponent across a negotiating table can also be "endured."

Because rules are nearly always obeyed in Japan, order prevails. If you know their rules you can pretty well predict what their behavior will be. But because we are so individualistic in the West, they do *not* know how to predict our reactions. This is one major reason why many of them tend to be quite ill-at-ease when they first come abroad.

The "Humble" Approach

Most Westerners learn early in life that they must speak up for themselves. In the USA, for example, even first grade

children have "Show and Tell Hour" in school. They learn early to stand up all by themselves in front of a class, in order to tell the group something interesting, or to show them something new, or to suggest an idea. Westerners are happy to "stand out." We like to give and receive awards and honors on an individual basis; we write "profiles" of individuals in the local papers; we encourage people to "make something of themselves." Libraries are full of biographies and—heaven forbid! —autobiographies! Our focus is individualistic and independent. We are rarely if ever "humble"; we hardly even dare be a little modest, lest someone takes us at our word!

Since the Japanese have always been interdependent people, they are extremely conscious of the OTHER person, and constantly downgrade themselves. This includes their families, their "stupid" wives, their "poor, unworthy" homes, *etc*. These are all considered to be extensions of themselves. One does not praise oneself. Therefore, one does not give outward respect or honor to any outside manifestations of oneself either.

In his book, *With Respect to the Japanese*, John C. Condon speaks of this "humbleness" and "deference." He says: "Both the deference which raises the other person and the humility which humbles oneself are basic principles of interpersonal relationships in Japan." He goes on to say, "Sometimes when two people attempt to out-humble themselves, or out-compliment one another, the attempt is actually comic."[12]

The Japanese scrupulously avoid anything that could be construed as self-promotion. They would never, for example, pull out some photos and say, "Here, let me show you my wife and family. That is my house, and that's my wife, and that is my dog, Towser." Most outsiders (espe-

12 *Used with permission John C. Condon,With Respect to the Japanese (Yarmouth, M.E: Intercultural Press Inc., 1984) p. 53.*

cially Americans) appear to them as embarrassingly boastful, self-promoting, self-engrossed. Again their crowded land...Training since childhood has been to "melt into the group"; to "flow with the traffic"; to cause no "shock waves."

Praise is almost as embarrassing to them as blame, if it means that they are singled out from their colleagues. They like to be modest and quiet; they patiently await their turn throughout life. Another of their proverbs says "The clever hawk hides his claws." No Japanese who tried to sell himself aggressively in Japan would be respected. When they come to other countries it is hard for them to "promote" themselves, their businesses, their products. They are not, generally speaking, strong in the fields of promotion, public relations, or advertising—although they are learning fast.

Those of us who work with Japanese people need to realize that this modesty (which can seem to us excessive) is a national characteristic, not merely a personal one. Once again, our value systems are different. Rather than standing out or excelling on a personal basis, the Japanese are seeking to develop *group* relationships, to build strong and respected positions within congenial contexts. They rarely, if ever, speak of their own personal accomplishments. "Let that come from other people," they say. They find much of the world to be what is, in their minds, "brash."

"Groupness"

Few people in the world are as "group-minded" as the Japanese, raised, as they have been, in their country's uniquely overcrowded, "pressed-together" land, reflecting their ancient feudal, agricultural heritage. For centuries each person was immersed in—as well as bounded by— his or her small rural world. One should never forget how

strongly the past affects peoples' national characters. **(See Appendix I, All Nations Stem From Their Historic Roots; So, Too, the Japanese, page 277.)**

Those of us who come from nations of space—Americans, Canadians, and Australians especially—feel pressured when we are in groups for too long, or when we feel ourselves to be too tightly "organized." We keep breaking away—on our own—from highly structured tour groups, for instance, often to the annoyance of the leader! We cut classes, or skip events at conferences if we feel we have had enough of "groupness" for a while. We champion the rights of every individual to live life in his or her own way—whether or not we like them—or even know them. We involve ourselves in other peoples' lives through a multitude of "causes" and community efforts. We rebel at—or poke fun at— what we see as excessive conformity; we break old traditions with ease.

The Japanese, on the other hand, do conform; they sacrifice; they yield their own rights to those of older family members, for example. One sees it frequently. A man will give up a scholarship and all the opportunity that it offers in order to help his father back home in his shop. One hears of a brilliant professor giving up her hard-won university post to look after the aging sister of her grandmother!

We of the West generally put more emphasis on present and future generations than we do on those whose lives are nearly over. We do not believe that an older brother or older—therefore more respected—member of any group to which we belong, has greater "rights" than we do. "Each man for himself," we say. The Japanese willingness to sacrifice themselves for the sake of a group—be it family, college class, army unit, corporate division, or what—has long made their social fabric strong.

This contrast between group loyalty and individual independence is often a fundamental cause of misunder-

standing between the Japanese and the people of any country where individualism is strong and admired. In Japan, individualism is actually frowned upon. They do not like people to "stand out." One of their proverbs says "The pheasant that flies gets shot." They prefer to have individuals blend in with others "like drops of water in a stream."

The Japanese derive real pleasure from doing things in big groups. Virtually the whole nation does calisthenics at the same moment each morning for example: all over Japan, old and young. Practically every able-bodied person in the country participates. They line up together in their offices, their plants, their schools. They even participate in their homes. The country becomes linked together, listening and responding to the same instructions coming to them over national radio, all moving in the same way, at the same time.

"Nothing is less characteristic of the Japanese than a charismatic leader," someone has written. They like wearing uniforms and do so a great deal. They live by a multitude of daily rules which they seldom question, following proscribed behavior. One sees this acceptance of "living by the rules" in their choice of clothing, for example. These accord with their age and social position rather than their preferences. You virtually never see a Japanese in off-beat clothing, or weird color combinations, or kooky hats, for example. They conform to styles "suitable" to their age, position, and status. They are comfortable "conforming." Who has not seen groups of Japanese tourists, wearing arm bands—or even identifying matching jackets—happily following their tour leader with his group banner, as they troop through museums and public places? Few of us would be comfortable doing that. But the Japanese are.

Inside-Outside

The Japanese have two important words: *uchi* literally meaning "house," but used to mean "inside"; and *soto*, meaning "outside." These words refer to those who are "In" or "Out" of the family, the school group, the club, one's division in a company, the company itself. There is a tremendous feeling of "Us" or "Not Us" at all levels of life. The family on the block is "Us"; everyone else is "Them"; the members of *my* school or university, or company are "Us"; everyone else is "Them." Competition *within* a given group or work unit would bring everything to a complete halt. However, beyond the confines of a given "in" group there is a constant sense of competition and "separateness." This remains true wherever the Japanese are. They are an intensely competitive people. In their eyes there are people who "exist" and those who do not. In other words: there are those with whom one has some form of relationship or "connection" and those with whom there is no relationship. You can expect that with any foreigners the "they" feeling will prevail—not "we."

There are clearly defined rules of conduct and courtesy relating to all those who in some way or another "belong." But for those who "do not exist," such as people on a crowded street or in a stadium, for example, anything goes. You can shove and elbow people aside with all your might, stepping on their feet, even on purpose. In Tokyo "pushers," identified by their white gloves, are, in fact, sometimes hired during the subway rush hours to push and heave masses of humanity together before the door can close. "Unknown" people can expect short shrift among the Japanese. It is every man for himself in that case.

The same distinction—which is essentially that of "public" versus "private"—is familiar in other countries as well, although it may show itself differently. We are all aware of people who are, for example, neat and tidy at

home, but think nothing of "littering" in a public park or in a bus or train. We recognize a sense of "territory" in birds and animals. We are often not aware that the same kind of territorial feeling exists in humans as well, though it is differently expressed, centering more on "public" and "private" than it does on actual territory.

Their deep "inside-outside" division can produce real stress in the Japanese. It also affects their point of view on many things, such as community service or welfare programs, for example. In their eyes, people in need should be looked after by their own families, not by outsiders. They rarely give money—or time—to community services. They find "volunteering" in the West a rather strange concept. Why do people do it? And for strangers? The Japanese tax system gives no deductions for charitable gifts. At death, money is nearly always kept within the family circle. As a result, private institutions are not strong in Japan. People will go to great lengths—even to lifelong sacrifice—to support their own relations. But not outsiders. One can count on them to be responsible and protective to those with whom they feel some "connection," but they rarely respond with any warmth on behalf of unknown people—such as Vietnamese refugees, for example, or even the disadvantaged in their own cities.

Connections

Connections, made through the good offices of friends and relations, are of VITAL importance. One simply MUST find ways to "be introduced"—to find "connections" in order to accomplish anything. These are the keys which will unlock doors that would otherwise be tightly closed. If one wanted to publish a book in Japan, for example, one would first have to find an intermediary who knew the publisher. Otherwise chances of publication would be

slim. That door, like many others, would rarely be un-
locked without a personal contact.

Many of the business acquisitions Japanese make in
other countries are made with a view to what is more
important to them than profits: entree, introductions, *connections*. They are looking for sales openings and channels. Profits can follow later. They look for a toehold, a
ready-made plant and workers, a distribution system. All
of these provide starting "connections" from which they
can build.

Once they have been accepted in a group (or class or
company), the Japanese are not likely to be thrown out,
flunked, fired, black-balled or even made to feel unwel-
come. This, of course, makes them cautious and slow to
accept new people into their groups. Once they have
admitted them, they may be "stuck" with them indefi-
nitely.

The need to fire someone can be anguishing for a
Japanese. A Britisher tells of a situation that occurred in the
Japanese firm in which he was working. A division manager was caught stealing. Clear, incontrovertible evidence
showed that he had been doing so for some time. In the
average Western firm he would have been fired immediately, in no uncertain terms.

The Japanese executive officer of the company, however, was in a misery of indecision when the facts were
made evident. He called three or four members of his staff
into his office while he thought it all over, out loud. He did
not ask their opinion. He merely used them as a sounding
board while he mentally worked through the dreadful
situation in which he found himself.

The staff members sat quietly in his office for a solid
forty minutes while he talked aloud, more to himself than
to them. Then he dismissed them. That same day he took
a plane all the way back to Japan to confer with his superiors. When he returned three days later, he did, in fact, fire

the man. The point was that the culprit was *one of his group*. He could not fire him easily, nor without pain.

A strong national group psychology is fundamental to the Japanese. It gives them close inner ties, a binding sense of belonging, a needed form of cohesion in that over-crowded land of pressure, jostle, and push.

When the Japanese Go Abroad

Understandably the various loyalties developed through-out their lives at home become very strong and sustaining to them. When they leave Japan, they feel all the more bereft and lonely without their supportive groups. It is one reason why they tend to cling so strongly together when outside Japan, choosing to live in close communities—even in the same apartment houses when they can, cer-tainly in the same neighborhoods as much as possible. They have established Japanese hotels in all major cities of the world; they buy in Japanese shops—also now found all over the world. They find it hard to relate to people of other cultures. They surround themselves with a kind of "mobile home," as someone has described it, of "portable, mental, self-sufficiency and separation," wherever they go. It is difficult for them to partake of other peoples' lives, whether these be in Brazil, Australia, the USA, or wher-ever.

One reason is that they purposely try to keep their "Japaneseness." It is vitally important to them to be able to fit back immediately into Japan's homogeneity when they return home. If they are considered to have become "West-ernized" on their return, they may find themselves "out-cast"—"different"—no longer accepted as part of their home groups. To be complimented on "how Western" they have become, is not a compliment in their eyes. It is some-thing worrisome to many of them.

Because this could be a problem to them on their return

home, they feel the need to hold themselves separate (at least to some degree), while they are abroad. They keep their own close family patterns. Some Japanese men prevent their wives from mixing with foreign women or learning the language, lest they get "wrong ideas" of female freedom. They send their children to Japanese schools whenever possible, since young people must be able to qualify for Japanese universities on their return home. Schooling in other countries is never adequate preparation. The children require extra tutoring and special preparatory courses. Children must keep up with the Japanese language also, so that they can slip right back into their home environment without dislocation. Hence Japanese "Saturday Schools" exist wherever a number of Japanese families are living and working—no matter what the country. This need to "stay Japanese" constantly overshadows Japanese families. It frequently isolates them in varying degrees from people of the country to which they have been assigned.

Often, not understanding the reasons, local people think Japanese are being cold or unfriendly. We need to understand, however, that it is imperative for them to keep "looking back," constantly reinforcing their "Japaneseness," keeping their own identities firm. They are rarely allowed to stay outside their own country—no matter what their rank or expertise—for more than at most seven years, more commonly three to five years. Then they are rotated home, lest they lose that vital national identity. Writing in *Fortune Magazine*, Brian O'Reilly says: "More than 95% go back. Men bid their Volvos goodbye, women worry about squeezing back into a tiny apartments, youngsters bone up furiously on their Japanese. Then they all pray that no one notices that they once lived in America."[13]

---

13 *Brian O'Reilly, "Japan's Uneasy U.S. Managers," Fortune Magazine, 25 April 1988.*

No Easy Access

A foreigner remains a *gaijin* (a foreigner) in Japan however long he lives there, or however much he adjusts to the language and life. In most of the major cities of the world—as well as in Japan—there are many "Japanese Only" hotels and clubs. The Japanese quickly establish their own shops and restaurants wherever they have gathered in any numbers, throughout the world. This is partly because of language difficulties, but in large part also, because of their need to feel "In" instead of "Out," wherever they are.

It is difficult for an outsider ever to become a Japanese citizen. Their past history of global isolation (**See Appendix I.**) shows through at every turn, despite their current global expansion.

The Japanese are polite, generally very kind, often very generous to people whom they know. But few foreigners ever feel they really "belong" in a Japanese community.

When working with the Japanese in your own country, you need to remember that they are often quite homesick. They are often groping for a substitute for the great sense of stability they have at home because of the interlocking way their society works. They miss it sorely when they become isolated foreigners in someone else's land. This unaccustomed insecurity may show itself in different ways. We need to remember that it is not easy to be uprooted, especially if your life has always been closely interwoven in a variety of support groups at home. It is hard for the Japanese to face the fact that they are now on their own, they are now the *gaijin*—the "outsiders"—in their new and strangely unfamiliar settings.

Furthermore, it is a far harder adaptation for them than it would be for most of us. Change and upheaval have been part of most of our lives from childhood onwards. Most of us can shift from one school or college to another quite readily; we may take a year off before going to work,

unconcerned that our classmates will "get ahead of us" in terms of climbing the traditional job ladder. We hop from job to job for experience, for better pay, or maybe just to "try something new." We may change jobs for no other reason than simply to see another part of our own country or to explore the world. In our Western systems we look for freedom, excitement, openness-chances to expand our experience. In their system the Japanese look for loyalty, caring, and security, with a multitude of lasting ties.

Sensitive to Being By-passed

Another by-product of the group mentality is a delicate sensitivity about being by-passed in the chain-of-command, or being left out of a gathering where they feel they belong—or even something as simple as not being introduced to casual visitors who come to the office.

Inclusion becomes extremely important. Those of us who are not group people are often quite relaxed about this "need to be included." We have our own lives. If we were not invited to some gathering we figure that the hosts may have had too small a space so they could not invite many people, or they may have wanted to talk about something special, or whatever. It does not worry us. We may like to be "one of the boys," but if we are left out of some conversation, or meeting, or gathering, we do not brood about it.

But to a Japanese it can be a real misery to be "excluded." One form of teenage punishment in their country is to be sent outside the house or out of class. We do the opposite. We "ground" our teenagers at home, or keep them "inside" after class for a period of time. *We* restrict their freedom. *They* exile from the group. These are two fundamentally different approaches.

In order not to hurt their feelings, one has to become sensitive to this whole matter of "groupness" when work-

ing with the Japanese. They can feel excluded, for example, if one individual is singled out for praise or credit when they thought the project was, in fact, a group effort. They can easily feel by-passed, also, in the making of a decision if, in their view, their job level entitled them to be consulted and they were not. They will be silent. But they will be hurt. And you will have lost ground with them.

Things are Changing

There are signs that this nameless, conforming retreat into group life is changing, especially among Japanese outside Japan. Fred K. Boren has long been working in Ozaki, Japan. He believes the Japanese are coming to recognize that "the reluctance to foster individuality could be a big problem in the future." He quotes a Japanese colleague as having told him that schools are now "encouraging children to be a bit more oddball—a little less conformist." He said that because the Japanese want increasingly to be innovators, especially of technology, they realize they must develop more individuality. "It is the only way to foster innovation and creativity," said Mr. Boren.[14]

Rank, Respect and Level

These three words, "rank, respect, and level" mean only a limited amount to most of us except in formal settings, whether business or social. They are, however, vitally important to the Japanese.

You may—or you may not—want to follow the ex-

14 *Fred K. Boren as quoted by Wil Lepkowski, "Americans Living In Japan Describe Life and Work There," as abstracted with permission from Chemical Engineering News, 2 January 1989, 67 (1), p.13. © 1989 American Chemical Society.*

pected courtesies of rank and respect when dealing with Japanese people in your own home office or plant. However, when *Mr. Important—san* himself comes to visit your operation, or if you are anxious to make Japanese people (at any level) feel more comfortable, it is helpful to be at least aware of what seems normal to them.

Clearly you will generally follow your own natural customs when in your own land. However, you can often help reduce—or better yet avoid—awkward, disturbing or confusing moments if you understand what social relationships, what individual obligations will feel comfortable or uncomfortable to them. Even if you carry on your own regular routine, you can ease it for them by a kindly explanatory word or two if you know what they are thinking.

Rank

How do you determine rank? How do you tell where, in the hierarchy of this vertical society, any given individual belongs? How much respect will each one of them expect?

The best answer is: Just watch them.

Bowing is so ingrained in the Japanese psyche that even while shaking hands with Westerners, Japanese will usually bow unconsciously. Of course, they normally use that form of greeting with each other. Watch them carefully in any formal, or semi-formal setting, and you will pick up helpful clues as to each other's rank:

The younger person bows to the older;

Both younger and lower-ranking people bow first to the older, ranking person. There may, in fact, be two or three bows to a man of considerable rank;

Bows will be shallower or deeper, according to their perceptions of rank.

Visiting dignitaries are likely to arrive together as a group when coming as guests to your office or plant. If you are anxious to handle their ranks politely, but are not sure which of them is the most senior or most important, watch their *own* precedence. They will almost surely sort themselves out instinctively—but visibly—by their own ranking system. Watch as they:

Enter or leave a room;

Get on or off an elevator;

Introduce each other (precedence is based on a combination of both rank and age);

Present their business cards (these will go first to the senior or ranking man, then to the others, generally by rank).

Train yourself to observe such procedures carefully. It can become quite instinctive to watch for and read useful signs of this sort. Actually the whole concept of rank is similar to the courtesies observed in our Army, Navy, or political circles, where the General, Admiral or Ranking Member of the Parliament, Committee, Congress (or whatever) is given his appropriate level of ruffles and flourishes. It is just that the Japanese carry these formalities and courtesies farther down into the ranks than do most of us.

Once the Japanese move outside their own country, they, too, have difficulties in terms of *our* courtesies. John Condon raises the point: How much respect should be shown if a 59-year old Japanese vice president of a bank meets a casual 31-year old Westerner, who is, however, at his same level or rank in the same bank? Should the greeting reflect their difference of age, or should it reflect their equal professional rank?[15]

15. *John C. Condon, With Respect to the Japanese, p. 23.*

Will the older man *ever* really respect the younger one? Suppose, of all things, the young Western vice president turns out to be a woman? What then?

In its true sense, respect is one of the most intangible of human relationships. People of different countries show it differently. Furthermore, there is "decreed" respect—as to a man of high position, or the flag, or a ceremony; and there is "felt" respect. This latter can show itself by formal means (bowing, curtsying, taking off one's hat, *etc.*), or in its deepest sense it is shown by one's manner: how intently one listens, for example; how much weight one gives to a person's opinion; how one defers to greater knowledge, or skill, or understanding, or ability.

The Japanese have a multitude of conventions and visible levels of respect. Many Westerners seem to them to be "breezy" and rude because the Japanese do not recognize that there can in fact be an entirely different way of showing respect. They do not realize that even when Westerners feel tremendous admiration, even when they gratefully accept a man's or woman's wisdom and judgement, they *still* can be casual, informal and easy with them on a personal basis. Westerners do not metaphorically "Exit Backing" from people whom they admire, as people do from royalty in some countries. *Reserve* on the one hand, and *relaxation* on the other, do not necessarily have anything to do with internal respect.

Bowing

The Japanese bow is multi-purpose. It is the normal way in which people greet others, pay respect, express thanks, apologize, ask favors, or say "goodbye." You see it everywhere in Japan—in shops, offices or classrooms; on railroad platforms and airports; in the home. Don't try to copy them. Bowing is a real art form among the Japanese. Westerners will virtually never get it right. Incline your head and

body politely as you shake hands—as you might if you were meeting somebody's grandfather or even a chief of state. But don't try to copy their depth of bows, numbers of bows, or any of their traditional rituals. You will only look foolish and be embarrassing to them.

John Condon writes: "A student bows to his teacher in respect. If years later that student becomes Prime Minister, he would still bow to that teacher. Respect is not a matter of power and fame. It is a matter of *acknowledging one's proper place*. It is part of a system that helps to maintain harmonious human relations in a crowded land."[16]

This matter or rank and respect is yet another area, however, where customs are in the process of rapid change. As the Japanese excel increasingly, as they move more widely throughout the world as economic leaders, their former sense of inferiority and "modesty" is turning into a growing sense of superiority...sometimes seen as arrogance. Within their own circles some are beginning to ridicule those outsiders, foreigners, non-"in-group" people, whom they feel to be inferior. Many of them have started to give sloppier service than they once did; to take a more aggressive approach; to show feelings of their own rank and precedence more clearly.

This is by no means universally true. The old system of courtesies and manners still prevail as well, especially among older, top leaders. However, it is clear that new winds are beginning to blow around the world. A reordering of priorities and precedence is taking place in Japan— as it is in other countries.

16. *John C. Condon, With Respect to the Japanese, p. 22.*

Section 3: Working for the Japanese

"The Japanese have surged into the mid-eighties like a rocket rising from a launching pad, fueled by its $100 billion per year trading surplus."[17]

Naturally the Japanese handle situations differently depending on whether they are establishing their own company in another country, establishing a joint venture within another country, or acquiring an already existing firm that *belongs* to another country.

Joint Ventures

Dr. Lester Thurow, Dean of the Sloan School of Management at the Massachusetts Institute of Technology, says: "If you look at American-Japanese joint ventures, I think you can say two things. First of all, most of them are a failure. Secondly, most of those that are a success have evolved into a position where they really are not joint ventures. One side is a silent capital partner, and the other side is the managing partner."

He suggests that questions on which joint ventures often flounder include such matters as: "What do you pay people? Who gets to decide? Who gets to decide what the work force is? Who can you hire? Who can you fire? There are a whole set of questions like that," he says. He further points out that no country wants some other country to come in and pay wages above the local level, thereby getting all the best employees. "However," he says, "that is exactly what any foreign joint-venture *DOES* want to do."[18]

17 *Newsweek, 6 February 1989.*
18 *Dr. Lester Thurow, Economist and Dean at Massachusetts Institute of Technology, quoted by Richard L. Wentworth, The Christian Science Monitor, 4 April 1989.*

Acquisitions

In the case of acquisitions, the Japanese are generally looking for access more than profits. In that case they buy a company—for the least possible amount of money—but then do not generally upset the existing management to any great degree. These "acquired" companies tend to have minimal Japanese impact. They are run along much as they were before—at least for a time. They are bought for their entree—their sales and distribution potential, their plant, their location—but not necessarily because the Japanese expect any great financial profit directly from them.

Their Own Companies

When the Japanese buy up companies in other countries, they are apt to take on a far greater managerial role than do most European companies. When Europeans have bought out a company many of its customers and clients are quite unaware of it. Europeans generally look for local management, allow local decision-making, and keep a low profile.

Said a *gaijin* working for Mitsubishi, "The Japanese rarely, if ever, do this. In most cases everyone is clearly aware of the Japanese ownership. Non-Japanese who are ambitious will find that—generally speaking—they are unlikely to be given top level responsibilities in a Japanese company. However, such companies do provide excellent training grounds for early stages in a person's career."

Sharing R & D (Research and Development)

While the Japanese invest increasingly abroad, so too are foreign enterprises setting up more and more R&D centers in Japan. The flow is not all one way.

Many foreign firms are developing their own research centers in Japan, partly to take advantage of Japanese expertise in applied research, but partly also because it has

become increasingly difficult to import foreign technology.

In the two years between 1985-1987, about 160 private R&D institutions were built in Japan. Many of these were in the pharmaceutical and biotechnological areas; others in electronics and new materials. At first these clustered in and around Tokyo, but increasingly other prefectures are also welcoming such centers, pleased to have new technology entering their areas, and promoting local industries.

One of Japan's strongest research centers is Tsukuba Science City, in Ibaragi Prefecture. Fifty national research institutes and laboratories have been established there, not to mention eight industrial parks, in which more than a hundred Japanese and foreign companies are setting up research institutes. These include such well known companies as American Upjohn, British ICI, and French l'Aire Liquide (the world's leading company in industrial gas sales).

International companies that are keenly aware of the tremendous growth of the Pacific Rim and Asian markets, and are also aware of its highly competitive nature, are using these new R&D centers not only for scientific studies, but also in large measure to explore Asian needs, tastes, and requirements. They are coming to realize that you cannot compete in that vast potential market without knowing what sizes, styles, and desires there are in the region.

One example of the magnitude of this trend is that of Bayer, the West German chemical maker. They are investing $500 million in Japan during the next five years. Their President, Mr. H.J. Strenger, explains: "We need to have that R&D in order to maintain our competitiveness. Japan is scheduled to be Bayer's third major development base, after West Germany and the USA."

The Western world is making moves in these directions.

However, in terms of R&D the Japanese are bounding ahead of other countries like sprinters rounding the last lap. They provide budgets as much as three times larger than their American counterparts for research and development; they file a tremendous number of new patents every year—even with the U.S. Patent Office. In fact, in the year 1987 it was reported that the three companies holding the largest number of U.S. patents were all Japanese. It is clear that the Japanese are no longer merely copying other people, or adapting work that originated elsewhere, as was once widely alleged. They are out in front; they are surging towards the 21st century.

What Foreigners Say about Working for the Japanese

(A number of people of different nationalities, working at different levels in a variety of Japanese firms, were asked for their comments about working for Japanese managers. For obvious reasons—and at their request— their names are not given, but this is what they said:)

1) *The Japanese Presence*
"No one should resent the Japanese presence. Workers—in whatever country and at whatever level—should adapt to it, remembering who is signing their paychecks. Be grateful that jobs are being created in your home country. The jobs are there because the Japanese are there. They should be welcomed."

2) *The Impact of Nationalities*
"One can assume that—as with anything else—some individuals will get along well both personally and professionally together across national differences; others will not," said an American working in a major Japanese firm in New York. "In our office we provide the expertise and the Japanese learn from us— at least they try to. But pride

and the awkward situation of the hired hands teaching the bosses how to run the work inhibit this process—as does their constant rotation back home."

3) *The Mingling of Nationalities*

When asked if the nationalities mingled well at work, a vice president in a Japanese company in Chicago said: "There is no separation; they mingle well. However, the Japanese usually eat together in the dining room so they can relax into their own language for a while." Another person who worked in the same company added, "They do tend to eat by themselves. It is partly to relax, but partly also, in my view, there *IS* a sense of separation. I think it may also be because their table manners are so different. Slurping, burping, and spitting are all okay in Japan."

4) *Their Way Is the Right Way*

A human resources vice president with one of Japan's big companies said: "To my mind the most difficult thing about working for a Japanese firm is their insistence that the Japanese way is right—even when common sense dictates otherwise. The good thing about working for them, though, is that there is such a strong corporate sense of family."

5) *Cultures Collide*

"The cultural clash is unbelievable," says a marketing manager who worked for a Japanese pen company for fifteen years. "I am not passing judgement on who is right and who is wrong, but the Japanese think and act differently than we do, and they are not about to change. Most Americans leave Japanese firms out of utter frustration," he says. "Americans make quick decisions, one on one. What my marketing director and I decide on in minutes would take nearly a week in Japan with five or six people involved ...When push comes to shove," he continued, "their contempt for Americans is thinly veiled ... they consider us different and deal with us at arm's length. At

the same time they seem to fear us. Consequently they make a lot of costly mistakes."[19]

6) *Group Pressure*

Even Japanese who have been in an overseas country for five years or more remember, first and foremost, that they are Japanese. That bond remains strongest forever. However, some—especially those who do not have families with them—do develop strong bonds with local people too. This depends on:

...How long they have been in the host country;

...The size of the Japanese group. (The smaller the group, the more quickly those who are there "bond" with the local community.)

...Whether or not they are isolated from other groups of Japanese.

A few of them, off in the hinterlands, get to be a real part of the community. This often does not happen, however, with those who have easy access to other Japanese. Then they tend to stick together. Many of us do the same when we are in countries other than our own. National "enclaves" always form quickly among overseas business people from different countries. We should not be surprised when it happens in our lands, too.

7) *What Changes? What Stays the Same?*

Overseas Japanese are apt to loosen their work ethic, relaxing a bit after they have been out of Japan for a while—especially the younger ones. Their company loyalty often becomes less strong too. Other fields look green. However, they do not usually change their method of making decisions. They still look for a group consensus, rather than for individual votes or decisions. They still talk in nuances and relate better to quiet than to flamboyant approaches.

19 *Daniel J. McConville, "Pilot's Occidental Pilot," Northeast International Business, April 1989, p. 28.*

8) *Don't be Fooled by a Western Exterior*

Someone has said: "In some ways the Japanese are like steak—crispy on the outside but it takes a long time to cook through. Many appear to become Westernized, facile and adept....but the "westernization" may not have "cooked through" very far—especially in the older ones. One has to explore this. Do not necessarily take "western veneer" at face value.

9) *They Sometimes Use the Direct Approach*
In negotiating they *can* be direct!

a) If they feel urgency is on their side;

b) If a good relationship has already been established between both sides they grow increasingly direct; they "insinuate" or "imply" less often. After a while the problem of "indirection" becomes infrequent. However, it never goes away. You have to be ready for it and always alert to overtones, undertones, hesitations, and to what these subtle signals *might* be meaning.

10) *The Japanese Are Learners*

The traffic manager of a New Jersey firm said that in his experience language was "almost the only major problem." Otherwise he found the Japanese extremely cooperative and easy to work with. "They are learning hard and fast all the time," he said. "They ask an enormous number of questions. I wish our Americans were trying to learn equally hard. We need to look at the Japanese with respect and to learn from them."

11) *Unspoken Communication*

"My advice to anyone starting to work with the Japanese is to be sure you never forget how skilled they are in masking their feelings—especially the older ones. You have to train yourself in a whole new language—being really sensitive to nuances—omissions—

silences and the like. You need to become really
observant; to watch and listen with your inner eyes and
ears. Most of us are not too good at that—we are in too
much of a hurry. But it pays to slow down and take a deep
breath, and to really LISTEN—both to what is being said
and what is not being said. Watch their eyes. They talk to
each other a lot by glances."

12) *Innovative More Than Creative*

The Japanese are very bright and extremely innovative.
But most of them are not very creative. Creativity comes
from individuality and from exploration. It is a quality that
rarely comes from patterns of conformity and "consensus."

However, once given an idea, the Japanese can use it,
develop it, produce it, and distribute it with enormous skill
and vitality.

The tale is told of a young boy who could not possibly
have invented or created a word processor. However, when
his father brought one home, the boy went crazy with
delight over the concept. He adapted it in all kinds of
ingenious ways, and in the end made their house an almost
fully electronic house—based on the capabilities that that
one word processor possessed.

One of the good things about working with the Japanese
is the chance to watch their innovative abilities at work.

13) *On the Way Up*

A European who has worked with a Japanese company
for 27 years talked about the young Japanese: "They look
for people to latch onto so as to help their careers," he said.
"They look especially to people higher in their own company. You might say they are looking for *coat tails*. When
the upper echelon (older) man is promoted, he may well
take two or three younger men with him in the Japanese
system."

Management Style

14) *Working for Japanese Bosses*

"Two things bother me about working for the Japanese," said an American vice president in a Japanese bank. "One is their lack of consistency on issues. For example, regardless of carefully worked out personnel policies, tables of reference, *etc.*, a Japanese executive will suddenly ask for a 10% raise for a particular man one week. However, the very next week he will ask me to fire that same man! In meetings they will take one tack one month and another tack next month. ...."

"The other problem," he continued, "is that I find you have to keep starting all over again with each change in Japanese management. Since all their officers are transferred home at least once in seven years—often earlier—there is a great deal of re-adjustment going on all the time."

15) *Long Hours*

"Hours are getting shorter in most parts of the world, but shorter for the Japanese still means at least 8 A.M. to 6 P.M.—which is long for many of us.

These hours are not exactly required, in many cases, but one is made to feel guilty if one does not comply. Their work ethic is *so* strong. One does not go home until the boss leaves. They are all work-centered to a large degree. They do not like it if you are not equally focused on work. "If you turn down an invitation to 'have dinner and talk work' more than once, you may find it takes considerable time to recoup your standing with the boss."

On the matter of working late, another man said: "Yes, they do work late—often up to midnight, but they understand if foreigners go home about nine. 'After all,' he quoted them as saying, 'You people have families here...' "

16) *Discrimination*

"They discriminate against women a good deal. Raises are smaller—usually less frequent than they are for men doing equivalent work. The Japanese tend to feel that women cannot be trusted with difficult responsibilities or assignments. They are given to judging people by strictly superficial externals—even when faced with a preponderance of contradictory evidence." When asked about the Japanese attitude towards women in their offices, one older, high-level Japanese executive smiled somewhat condescendingly. "We look on women as flowers in our business offices," he said. "This means they need to be replaced frequently." That attitude is changing, but it has not disappeared.

17) *Promotions and Responsibilities*

"They hire American and European engineers, and others with good experience and reputation, then pick their brains hard and constantly. However, they then frequently leave them out of decision making. They lose a lot of good men that way.

Another irritation is that since upper management is usually Japanese, they often hold their executive meetings in Japanese. Important memos are often written in Japanese too. Rarely is a good translation provided."

Another man suggested, "They do not promote Americans readily because they do not trust their loyalty. They expect them to job-hop at any time."

Many foreigners in Japanese firms feel that they do the bulk of the actual work, yet get no credit. This leads to a cog-in-a-wheel feeling that is not good. "It does not wear well," said one man wryly.

A Britisher explained this by saying: "Japanese resent working for *outsiders*. They look on any overseas assignment—in any country—as being merely a springboard for their careers."

Another European said: "You have to learn to suppress your feelings as to any goals you may have, any sense of power or decision making you may *wish* you had. However, you make a decent living. If they trust you, they will let you handle a certain amount of business by yourself, but it takes a *long* time before you get recognition or trust."

18) *Young Westerners Move On*

"Any bright young person is likely to get frustrated by the slowness of Japanese decisions, let alone promotions. Decisions often take literally months. Many foreign staff leave after about three years. The Japanese do not care—there are plenty more where they came from!"

19) *Desire for Status*

In whatever country the company may be, the Japanese look mostly to 'name' universities in filling executive jobs, just as they do at home. They will seek out Yale, Harvard, Stanford or M.I.T.; Oxford or Cambridge; the Sorbonne; the University of Bologna... Status is vitally important to the Japanese in all phases of life.

20) *Reasons for Their Success*

When asked how he explains the great economic success the Japanese have had in recent years, an American executive high up in the Bank of Tokyo explained: "One reason is that their government supports their businesses. It does not let them down as ours frequently does (as for example, refusing to grant a cooling off period when needed in a major airline case). Nor does their government keep changing the rules on Japanese business-shifting tax burdens, or making other changeable financial rulings.

The Japanese government also does not allow companies to fire people by the thousands, as U.S. companies are free to do. One U.S. firm can lay off 2,500-5,000 people in a matter of months, with no regard to the hardship caused.

This could not happen in Japan. A country like the U.S. is profit-minded, not socially-minded. Companies have very little regard for their social responsibility to people."

He mentioned another major Japanese strength. "This lies in the fact," he said, "that their companies collaborate together. Instead of firing workers, for example, they will 'loan out' parts of their work force to each other. They do a lot of retraining. Often they share this—and similar services—between companies."

In his book *More Like Us: Making America Great Again*, James Fallow says that living in Japan for three years highlighted for him many things that U.S. residents (and many other Westerners) casually take for granted. He says: "I just want to say to people: Look, it *is* unusual here [in the USA]. It's unusual that women can compete for jobs with men. It's unusual to think that you can have a society that is made up of different races. It's unusual to think that you can marry someone of a different background or class, and that you could change your job at age 30...That's worth recognizing." [20]

20 *James Fallows, More Like Us: Making America Great Again (Houghton Mifflin, 1989) as quoted by Catherine Foster reviewing Fallow's book in the Christian Science Monitor, 12 May 1989.*

What Japanese Say About Working in Foreign Lands

1) "It is hard to communicate well. The language is difficult for us, so it is hard to make our ideas known and equally hard to be sure we understand others correctly."

2) "Especially the older people still bear grudges from World War II. Some of them spread these to others. So do many films and television programs. We are often still portrayed as untrustworthy—and the enemy."

3) "For whatever reason, we are singled out like scape-goats. I think you call it 'Japan-bashing.'" When asked how he handled this, the speaker replied: "By introducing good things; by never trying to make excuses; and by reminding people that we are *creating* jobs—not taking them away. When things work well, everything is okay. But if something goes wrong, hatred quickly rises. It is difficult for us."

4) "If more people who work with us learned the Japanese language, it would help their understanding. When you learn a language you start to know how other people think; you learn to respect how they think and you feel better with them."

5) "As more of us Japanese come out into the world it will help. We need to know each other more. Most people do not know the Japanese well. It is a pity. It will help when we meet each other more, socially."

6) "At first I thought family life in the West was very unfeeling; it was too casual, too cold, too distant. We have very close family ties in Japan, with great respect for our elders. But after a while I have come to see that the West-ern system gives more individuality—there can be more free thinking; each person is himself, not just a small, in-significant part of a large family."[1]

7) "I thought it was very cold when I saw that most people in the West do not know most of their neighbors—even in the same apartment house. But then I realized that that has its good sides. There is less gossip—more freedom. In Japan everyone worries what other people will think. We must pay attention all the time. I see that Japan's way is nice if you are peaceful with your neighbors and are happy with them. But it can also be difficult."[2]

8) "A group is more comfortable to me. I am not used to being by myself so much. In Japan there are patterns. It is easy to be part of a pattern. But—especially in the U.S.—everything in the West is always moving, always changing, everyone is always going and coming. It is hard for us—and lonely. Here one cannot predict what people will do. My country is so small, so compact that people are, you might say, all part of a unit. You can predict what they will think and do. That is a lot easier to live with."[3]

9) "At home I am all the time constrained by the rules of etiquette and position. Here is a chaos, but it is more carefree. No one worries about what other people do."[4]

10) "After you have been away from Japan for some time, you look for a middle road between Japanese serenity (which comes from a sense of security) and American individuality. We find that individuality exciting, but also harsh and sometimes even hard to bear. Then Japan seems comfortable."

1 *Comments adapted from John P. Fieg and John G. Blair, There is a Difference (Washington, D.C.: Meridian House International, 1941) p. 25.*

2 *Ibid., p. 26.*

3 *Ibid.*

4 *Ibid.*

PART IV

PATTERNS OF
COMMUNICATION

Tori-no-ichi Fair at Asakusa, Tokyo

(photo by Kenji Arai)

Section 1:
How the Japanese Do—
and Do Not—Communicate

Japanese on foreign assignment have usually been well-prepared for the new job, including years of learning English (or whatever language is spoken where they are to be). Nevertheless, communication still remains a major problem in many, if not most, cases.

It may be helpful to consider how the Japanese communicate with one another, as well as with us foreigners, for our patterns are often different. Their many uses of silence, their indirectness, their verbal cues for what they are NOT saying—all these are languages in themselves—ones that non-Japanese often find more than perplexing. We have trouble communicating with them for other reasons, too. They like suggestions—we like facts; they imply—we specify; we announce our conditions, then argue and defend them—they begin cautiously, in generalities, then gradually refine their statements working towards their point.[1]

More People are Learning Japanese

Increasing numbers of foreigners are scaling the language barrier these days, which is good. Language has long been a kind of prison for the Japanese, part of the country's isolation. Without it, foreigners have not been able to study at Japanese universities or read their publications. Until recently it has hampered Japanese travel abroad as well.

1 *For much of this chapter I am indebted to Edward T. and Mildred Reed Hall and to John C. Condon. As mentioned in the acknowledgements, I have absorbed their work gratefully over the years.*

Current figures announced by a Japanese survey state that in 1984 more than 600,000 people were enrolled—worldwide—in Japanese language courses. In 1989, estimates put the number at more than a million. If the number of people studying privately or following Japanese course by radio and television are included, the numbers would rise dramatically. An estimated 25,000 foreign students are currently studying at Japanese universities. Once "insular," Japan has now embarked on a massive "internationalization" program. They want to expand their view of the world. This necessarily includes expanding the world's view of them as well.

Young people in the USA are preparing for careers in the next century. Especially along the West Coast of Canada and the U.S., the focus is increasingly on Pacific Rim countries.

The Minister of Education for British Columbia, for example, has received a grant of $11 million from the government with a mandate to construct a "Pacific Rim Initiatives" program for the schools of that province within three years. This was to include emphasis on strong language programs.

In the USA an increasing number of even high school students along the West Coast are tackling that difficult language. A boom for it has developed. In the State of Washington, for example, sixty public high schools and a few private schools now teach Japanese, according to Barbara Lloyd McMichael. This is the highest secondary school level for any state in the USA, she says. Oregon has programs from preschool through high school. California has yet to catch up with either of these states, but, like the others, is hampered by a lack of teachers. To help offset this problem, Ms. McMichael reports that Atsumi McCauley, a college instructor in Spokane, Washington, began teaching Japanese by satellite television in 1986. Her course includes homework and biweekly exams. Today she is

teaching 300 students in her "electronic classroom," ranging from Alaska through Washington, Oregon, Idaho, and Montana.[2]

Unfortunately, too few of the people now studying the Japanese language are American business people.

Robert Ellis, an international business consultant and author, wrote in *The New York Times* on January 11, 1989 saying:

"In the course of research for a book on the failure of American business to penetrate foreign markets, I discovered that among the dozens of Fortune 500 vice presidents in charge of international marketing, only three spoke any foreign language. None of the managers in charge of Japanese markets spoke Japanese."

"Of the dozens of negotiations I have done for Americans in dealing with the Japanese, nearly *all* their Japanese counterparts spoke English. I have met very few Americans fluent in Japanese and even fewer who recognize a connection between this and our trade deficit."

"Japanese businessmen have taken the time and trouble to learn English, and have also studied the American market and American culture. The near total failure of our executives to do the same accounts for more of our problems than the closed nature of the Japanese markets that we hear about from non-Japanese speaking representatives of American business. United States companies need to make a substantial investment in language-capable international management if American business is to become competitive."

The same is true, of course, for other nations as well. Since business relations with Japanese people are strongly based on personal relations, the lack of language really hampers Westerners.

2 *Barbara Lloyd McMichael, "West Coast Schools Learn Far East," The Christian Science Monitor, 31 May 1989.*

Of course one *can* establish a reasonably good personal relationship without knowing the language. But it means that if you ever go to the country, everything you do or say has to be filtered through somebody else...a Japanese counterpart. You cannot strike up a casual conversation with people that you meet; you cannot browse through newspapers or business periodicals to pick up new slants or ideas; it becomes difficult to relate to clients, suppliers, competitors, or government officials. It is even hard to catch people's names and titles if you have no facility at all with the language.

Furthermore, foreigners who make an effort to deal with Japanese people in their own tongue—however haltingly— make an important statement about their own values and trustworthiness. To the Japanese, even a stumbling effort to speak is a very real courtesy. It portrays a positive attitude and a much-appreciated sensitivity to them as a nation. Again, the vital concept of "respect" is involved. They do not *expect* foreigners to speak their language, but those who even *try* to do so, immediately create a warmly positive impression.

There are few Japanese subsidiaries in any country across the world that are not run by Japanese *who speak the local language*, be it English, French, Chinese, Thai, or whatever. The somewhat arrogant idea that English is the international language—"let them speak English"—is widespread in the English-speaking world. But it is very limiting, and there is a growing reaction against it in many areas.

Companies serious about their future with Japan should be actively recruiting some of the increasing number of to-day's young people who are currently putting the necessary years of full-time effort into learning Japanese.

It may be of interest to recruiters to know that at least three American universities—Temple, the University of Nevada at Reno, and Southern Illinois University—have

established branch campuses in Japan. Many more are hoping to follow suit. Stanford University, for example, is planning to open a branch in Kyoto in the autumn of 1989. This will serve not only its own students, but also those from Yale, Princeton, Harvard, Brown, Columbia, Cornell, Michigan, Chicago, and possibly others in the future.

Temple was reportedly the first American institution of higher learning to establish a branch campus in Japan (in Tokyo) as early as 1982. It currently has about 500 Japanese undergraduates, plus some 1,200 others who are enrolled in intensive English-language courses. As industry and finance proceed, the need intensifies not only for English-speaking Japanese, but equally for Japanese-speaking people in other countries.

In the years ahead, companies with good language facility on their staffs will have a decided edge over those who do not. So far, however, many of the young people who have made themselves fluent in Japanese are ending up in Japanese companies, rather than in Western ones. The reason is that the majority of Western firms still have the outmoded idea that "English will do."

Courtesy Phrases

Even though few of you reading this book are likely to embark on learning the Japanese language, nevertheless, it is frequently an important help in developing a congenial feeling on both sides if you can say at least a *few* courtesy things in the tongue of those with whom you are working. There is likely to be mirth and merriment as you experiment, but it will be a kindly, helpful kind of merriment, with much encouragement. It will make for greater friendliness and be well worth the effort.

To get you started, here are some simple, everyday phrases, written phonetically, so you can give them a try.

It makes it easier if you remember that each syllable is given equal weight.

Good morning: *O-hayo gozaimasu*   (often *O-hayo*, [like Ohio] for short)

Hello: (when meeting someone during the day) *Kon - nichi-wa*

Good Evening: *Komban-wa*

Good bye: *Sayonara* or "Bye-Bye"

Good night: *O-yasumi nasai*

How are you?: *O-genki desu ka* (*ka* at the end of any sentence means a question)

Very well thank you: *Genki desu*

I am pleased to meet you: *Hajimemashite* (pronounced: Ha-ji-may-mash-tay)

Thank you: *Arigato gozaimasu*

I'm sorry, excuse me: *Domo sumimasen*

I beg your pardon (more formal and deferential): *Osore irimasu*

Excuse me (in the sense, I have to leave now): *Shitsurei itashimasu.*

Excuse me (meaning also "Hello, I'm here at the door—sorry to bother you"): *Gomen kudasai* (also used to say "good bye" over the phone)

Please (when offering something): *Dozo*

Please (when requesting something): *O-negai shimasu*

How much is it?: *Ikura desu ka?*

Do you understand?: *O-wakari desu ka?* or: *Wakari mashita ka?*

I do not understand: *Wakarimasen*

Hello (when answering the phone or calling out to someone): *Moshi moshi.*

"Yes" and "No"

The words for "yes" and "no" need special attention. It is very important to phrase any question you ask affirma-

tively. Sometimes this takes a bit of real thought and practice. However, if you ask a question that has a negative in it, you are very likely to create confusion. If, for example, you ask "Doesn't this bus go to Osaka?" you may get the answer "Yes, it doesn't." We would expect "No, it doesn't" so we become a bit perplexed. "Aren't you going to breakfast?" may well be answered "Yes," but that could quite possibly mean "Yes, I am not going." It is negative that throws them—and us. So one should be careful to ask "Are you?" or "Does it?" with no confusing negatives involved!

When used by a Japanese, the word "Yes" rarely means "Yes, it is," or "Yes, I agree" in the way that we commonly understand it. More often it means "Yes, I hear you," or "Yes, I understand you"—neither of which necessarily mean "I agree with you." It may simply mean "Yes, I am listening." It is *our* mistake if we assume that it means an affirmative answer. With them, it may not mean that at all. If you *think* it does, or are in doubt as to whether it does, reaffirm what you think you understood with another exploratory question, or offer some comment that makes it clear to them that you understood it as an affirmative. It is not at all unusual for them to say "Yes" when they actually mean "No"! In their terms they are merely saying "Yes, I hear you." If we assume that because "Yes" means assent to us it means assent to them, it is *our* error. They use the word differently than we do—or they *may* use it differently. One needs to be sensitive and aware of both possibilities.

The word "No" is seldom used. It is considered too blunt. One needs, therefore, to attune one's ear quickly and consciously to the various softer ways of saying "No" that the Japanese commonly use: "Maybe"; "Perhaps later"; "It is possible" (sometimes the voice will give you an added clue to the unspoken "But not likely"). It takes practice and conscious effort to alert yourself to these

various signs and signals, but it is quite possible to catch the subtleties of "No" once you are aware of the ways in which it is avoided. One very common form of negative answer is "Let's think about it." Another is the taking of a long breath, followed by *sa* —which really often means "I don't want to say."

Often you have to guess at what they are thinking. They do not readily express any negative opinions for fear of offending, or of causing arguments, which they abhor so will avoid at almost all costs. You are left having to "sense" the other position. You may need to come at it from several different angles. If you keep getting polite roadblocks, you can realize that the answer is very likely "No."

In his book, *Getting Your Yen's Worth,* Robert T. Moran warns: "If in business negotiations or talks you are kept waiting for an exceptionally long time, be wary. Japanese are normally punctual. A long delay *may* be a polite way for your colleague to let you know that your request or proposal has not—so far at least—met with approval. It can presage and warn of the final 'no'." [3]

It is obviously important to concentrate on learning to read other varieties of *non-verbal* negative signs. These can be such signals as:

   a questioning expression, with the head cocked;
   a very deliberate, hesitant, careful speech;
   a little hiss of in-drawn breath between the teeth;
      what we feel to be "beating around the bush," *i.e.*,
      unwillingness to be specific;
   any of the multitude of delaying phrases, such as
      "That may be a little difficult" or "It may take a
      little bit more time."

Westerns need to become keenly alert to all such signs, tuning their antennae to new shades of phrasing and to

   3 *Robert T. Moran, Getting Your Yen's Worth: How To
     Negotiate With The Japanese (Houston, TX: Gulf Publish-
     ing Co., 1985) p. 21.*

subtle forms of negative communication. These gentler phrases or uses of body language replace the blunt "That would be impossible," or "Absolutely not," or "We would not consider that" which are commonplace in many Western business conversations. It is, in fact, possible to be just as adamant but far more gracious, less abrupt, less negative. In dealing with Japanese people—and actually with most people of the world—it is more effective in the long run to consciously avoid head-on negative replies. Many of us do not even try to avoid them, however. We look for speed and/or clarity rather than grace.

Negative Feelings

It is often hard to tell when a Japanese is reacting negatively. They tend to retreat into one of their silences, or smile, or—and this is far the most difficult for the uninitiated—to say what they think will please, *even if they know it is not true*. It is again a matter of values. One has to remember that to them harmony is apt to be more important than accuracy. That is not true for us.

Mr. H.F. Van Zandt, in his article "How to Negotiate in Japan," gives an example of this: "I recall well a case where a visitor obtained a commitment from a Japanese concern to take some action. But after the visitor had boarded his plane for Honolulu, the president of the Japanese company told me: 'I know, of course, that we cannot carry out our promise, but I did not want to hurt his feelings and spoil his trip. Now you must cable him and explain it can't be done.'"[4]

Similarly, a number of Japanese and American executives went to Japan to meet with the top brass of their com-

4 H.F. Van Zandt, "How to Negotiate in Japan," Harvard Business Review, December 1970 as quoted by Robert T. Moran, Getting Your Yen's Worth.

pany in the Tokyo office. Before they took off, they were briefed by the Japanese Director of their international branch office: "Be very accepting of whatever you are told," he said. "If it has nothing to do with what we are actually doing—or planning on doing—in our office, it does not matter. We will listen, and agree—I will handle it later. All you need to do is just agree to whatever is said."

"They will 'Yes' you to death," said a Britisher, "then do whatever they want. It is part of the whole matter of saving face—the other person's face. They do not want to disagree or argue, or make anyone feel badly, so they just keep all the pleasantries affirmative, no matter what."

It takes considerable time to learn to read this kind of "indirection," but it is of vital importance to remember that it relates to their emphasis on "face" and harmony, and to their perception of priorities. It is *not* the intentional "deception" that foreigners often take it to be. It is just that they and we put different values at the top of our priority lists— harmony for them; accuracy for most of us.

How Do You Handle That?

It has been suggested that if you really want to get some facts or honest reactions, the best way to deal with this Japanese tendency to say the pleasing, accepted thing, is to avoid inadvertently indicating in advance the answers you hope to hear. For example, don't use a phrase such as "Wouldn't it be a good idea if..." He will almost surely agree verbally, whether he really agrees or not. A better approach would be to ask "Would it be more effective if we did A, or would it be better if we did B?" That way you give him no courtesy clues. He can answer what he really thinks. Another approach is to bring the issue up in several different ways, at different times. The answer will gradually become clear to you that way too.

Easing the Edges; Removing the Personal

Another helpful guideline is to avoid blunt, direct questions of the "Do you—or don't you"…"Will you—or won't you"…"Is it—or isn't it?" variety. The less direct you are in your questions, the easier it will be for them to answer frankly and honestly. Instead of asking "How do you like American parties?" for example, you will get more of an answer if you give them their needed leeway. It would be easier for them to give you a real answer if you phrased the question more loosely, as for example, "How do American (or Canadian or British or French) parties differ from the ones given in your country?" This removes the question from the realm of the personal. They will therefore, be more comfortable in answering it.

Polite and Real

Japanese are very conscious of the difference between "real" feelings and those which are simply said to give a pleasant surface, or because of polite conventions. There is for them a major difference between *tatemae* actions and words (*i.e.*, the polite, the formal, the expected, the surface) and *honne*, which is the real, the inside, the honest self. We outsiders, however, are often left feeling quite unsure as to what the actual facts are, or what is mere politeness— something said because they think we expect that answer or would prefer it.

We Do the Same

It helps to realize that, in fact, we do exactly the same thing, only in our own context we find it familiar and recognizable! We say "You must come to dinner sometime." Is that a polite, surface comment, or is it meant? Are we really going to invite them? Or is it merely a convention that one says something like that after spending an evening with a

couple, or a person? We say "I hope to see you again," when actually we may not hope so at all. These are *tatemae* words for us too—the polite, the formal, the expected, but not necessarily the real. All countries do this to a greater or less degree.

The Setting Matters

In judging whether the Japanese are—or are not—meaning what they say, one needs to take into conscious account the situation in which the conversation takes place. If you are in an informal setting—after hours—in front of a fire—having a drink together—you can expect that you are hearing the Japanese "true voice." This is one reason why it is so important to "socialize" with Japanese people. If you see them only in official, or semi-formal settings, you will see their formal, polite, "outside" self most of the time.

Talking without Talk

A great deal of communication goes on without words. This naturally increases where there is a language barrier. Since most of us do not speak Japanese, it is all the more important for those who work among Japanese people to concentrate on learning to recognize their many non-verbal signals. You can be sure they will be watching yours. They read our faces and body language carefully. Postures, finger-drumming, the shuffling or tapping of feet, hand gestures—all these things are watched with care and are interpreted—whether rightly or wrongly.

Many Westerners for example, slouch comfortably in a chair. We believe that looking relaxed gives a comfortable impression to others—that it is somehow contagious. We assume that if we look and feel relaxed they will feel relaxed too. Not necessarily so.

In Asia there is great emphasis on balance. If your body is sprawled out carelessly they feel the spirit cannot be alert

either. Body and spirit are "in harmony" if the body is upright, the feet are on the ground, the voice is quiet, the person is "in control" of him or herself.

In watching them, we need to be constantly aware that the cock of the head, the quick drawing in of breath, the expression of the face, the depth of the bows, all are part of the language among their many non-verbal ways of expressing themselves.

It is, of course, easy to misinterpret non-verbal language. Take eye contact, for example. We tend to be on guard with someone who never looks us in the eye. We think there is something "shifty" about it. "What is he trying to hide?" we wonder. We teach our children: "Look at people when you speak."

There is, however, much less eye contact among the Japanese than among most other people. One old Japanese explained the reason for this. "Eyes are the windows to the soul," he said. "You do not look into another's soul." In this the Japanese are just the opposite from people like, for example, the Arabs. When Arabs are walking together you see them stop, turning to face each other directly, so that they can see into each other's eyes while they talk. Most of us use our eyes in communicating more than we realize.

Silence

"Silence is a form of speech; don't interrupt it," say Lennie Copeland and Lewis Griggs.[5]

Silence is one major area of communications in which Westerners and Japanese often have considerable difficulty in understanding one another. Most Americans, Canadians, Australians—among many others—look on silence as something rather negative. It is read as anxiety—

5 *Lennie Copeland and Lewis Griggs, Going International: How To Make Friends and Deal Effectively in the Global Marketplace (Random House, 1985) p. 110.*

or shyness; the lack of anything to say; a form of fumbling; sometimes as a sign of hostility or anger. We quickly fill up any silence with words—often rather inane ones like "Nice day today," or "Hot enough for you?"

Or we assume that the person has not understood, so we say our piece again, sometimes—but not always—in different words. One of the worst things we frequently do is to decide they just did not hear us. So we say it again, but LOUDER. This is rude. It makes people feel uncomfortable. They "lose face." They heard you alright but they did not quite understand, or they may be deciding how to answer, or perhaps they are sorting out their own halting English before answering. In any case, they become embarrassed if you rush them.

For the Japanese, silences are quite different. They are respected; often they are companionable sharing. Silence to them is frequently a matter of respect for the person who has just spoken. Silence following his words gives weight and due appreciation for what he has said. It can also be that silence means disagreement with what has just been said. As they are not prone to argue, they often let silence reign when they disagree.

The Japanese distrust words. A favorite proverb is "Hollow drums make the most noise." They like quiet people.

In feudal times—not so long ago in Japan (**See Appendix I.**)—one could literally lose one's head for "speaking out" (*i.e.*, not fitting in, or not being adequately subservient). Today they still consider that speaking "too much" means you are empty-headed or immature; they think women talk too much. The Japanese character for "woman" also means "noise."

To them silence is not an emptiness, a void, the absence of speech. They say—and firmly believe: "Words separate; silence bonds." In his excellent book *With Respect to the Japanese*, John Condon suggests that to them silence is

to words what "white space" is to painting or calligraphy. "As in art," he suggests, "having no space confuses; it detracts from what is there."[6]

Those of us who talk quickly—and often—are likely to fill gaps almost as soon as they occur. We elaborate on a point, make a joke, repeat the idea yet again. If we read the silence as disapproval, we often start to backtrack and yield ground—still talking: "Well, I did not mean it really quite the way it may have sounded…" or (making unasked-for concessions) "Well , if that price seems a bit high, perhaps we could…"

Non-Japanese must learn to expect long silences. The Japanese may be buying time; perhaps they are thinking of the next step; they may be hoping to unnerve the Westerner, for they have learned that compromises or concessions often follow in that case. Perhaps they are giving their own colleagues time to contemplate the discussion, or are doing so themselves.

The thing to do when such silences occur is to relax, not fidget. Wait quietly. Watch their body language. Think of something else, or mentally review what has just been said. But DON'T feel a compulsion to "break in" or to "fill" the silence; don't wriggle around uncomfortably, tapping your pencil or looking at your watch. If the silence goes on so long that you cannot bear it, it is always possible to get up quietly and wander over to the window, or poke the fire, or pour yourself a glass of water. But do not feel you must *say* something. Some people get quite good at staring into space as if they, too, were contemplating. They become as "enigmatic" as the Japanese themselves. That can be a very good ploy. With practice you can learn to handle—and even to enjoy—silences.

A point to realize when dealing with Japanese silence is that they are basically not a verbal people. Most of us are.

6 *John C. Condon, With Respect to the Japanese, p. 40.*

They are so homogeneous and have lived so closely together in their island world, that they understand each other without words to a far greater extent than most of us do. Furthermore, being poor communicators, they prefer to operate by what they call *haragei*, which means "gut feeling." Anyone who has worked around a Vermont farmer, or a rancher, or a deep sea fisherman knows about that! No need for words.

In the business world this can lead to a variety of difficulties. Nonetheless, it is part of the Japanese pattern. Furthermore, if they realize that you do not "feel" something, that you have not "read" it from their non-verbal communication, they are not likely to try to explain it to you—lest you "lose face" or be embarrassed. "It will become clear in time," they will feel—another example of their sense that there is no hurry—things will "unfold." A direct, assertive, "take the bull by the horns" approach is repugnant to them. They are far more comfortable with suggestion and subtlety. It is part of that precious element of "leeway." "Getting right to the point," which seems so valuable to many of us, does not seem to them to be a great virtue. They prefer to ease into a subject. They will go to great lengths to avoid answering at all if that might cause the other person to "lose face"—and thus be embarrassed.

Conversely—and it is important that we never lose sight of this—any time we give *them* a straight, flat-out negative response, they tend to feel rebuffed. We must remember that our precise, linear, direct, Western speech is like hob-nailed boots to them.

Speaking "Around the Corner"

Those of us from the Western world assume that one communicates basically through words. If an idea is not put into words, we generally feel it has not been really communicated. We feel that if someone has something to

say, he should say it! In meetings we are expected to "speak up." This lets people know we are paying attention; it shows we have ideas; we are thinking; we are "with" it.

But the Japanese culture is not the same. We should not judge Japanese in business situations by our same yardsticks. Quick, clear, direct answers or questions are not necessarily the signs of an alert listener to them. The quiet, thoughtful, silent participant may, in fact, be the *most* alert mentally. As John Condon says: "It is lines and points with us; circles with the Japanese." We are familiar with *lines* of argument, of reasoning. We know about "bottom lines" and "base lines." We also understand about *points*; "Come to the point"; "Make your point"; "The point of the exercise"; "No point in that…" Mr. Condon says "The Japanese rarely go 'straight to the point'. In their view it is better to go 'around' a subject. Points might injure someone."[7]

We of the West, on the other hand, tend to see circles as "ambiguities," as a "cover-up," a way of avoiding what we really mean. To us "going around in circles" or "beating around the bush" are negatives. We believe, instead, in "calling a spade a spade," or in the vernacular, "telling it like it is." We expect to take words at their face value.

"Yesterday you said…but today you are telling me…" We tend to be highly critical if there is any variation between what is said, what is felt, and what turns out to be true. We read it as a "lie," or a "manipulation," or a "shading of the truth" if something turns out to be different from what we considered had been agreed. However, what we often do not realize is that in their terms it may *not* have been agreed at all. Their "Yes" may have meant "Yes, we understand that is how you feel." We jump on what people say and hold them to it. Things are far less rigid with them.

An American woman had been trying for months to make travel arrangements through a gentle old Chinese

7 *Ibid., p. 43.*

travel agent. Finally she exploded with anger and frustration. "Last week you said that the papers would definitely be complete today," she bellowed at him. "Isn't that true?" He looked at her with dignity. "For the time that was then, it was true," he answered. "For the time that is now it is not true." To him that was a complete, accurate and satisfying answer. In Asian terms it was.

The Language of Space and Touch

Another noticeable difference among people of different nationalities and backgrounds, relates to the their use of space. We all are comfortable at different distances from each other. North Americans normally stand instinctively about 21 inches from each other, researchers say. Japanese need almost twice that space to be comfortable. This feels "distant" to us, so we instinctively move in closer. They tend to step back—just as we do when South Americans, Arabs, and others move inside what are "comfort zones" for most Europeans and North Americans. We feel they are breathing all over us when they get so close. The Japanese have the same feeling when we move in closer to them than they like.

No Asians like to be touched, patted, kissed, or poked. They do NOT like a friendly arm around the shoulder, or anyone to take their arm as they cross a street. An *abrazo* —the warm greeting, with both arms outstretched and kisses on both cheeks, that is common in South America, Greece, Italy, and other parts of the world—really distresses Asians. This definitely includes the formal Japanese.

Effusion Versus Restraint

Many of us—Americans, French, Greeks, Brazilians, for example— seem really effusive to people who come from

societies where emotional restraint is expected—or indeed required. Watch a family meeting a relative back from a long trip. In most Western countries there is great excitement, loud calls, much kissing and hugging, eager chatter, sometimes tears of joy. In Japan there is quiet bowing—at considerable space from one another—a restrained greeting. The family quickly melts away, out of public view.

If you give a compliment to a Japanese, he or she will deny what you say. If they were to say "thank you," as is the familiar response in many countries, they feel it would show they were accepting the compliment. This would seem presumptuous to them. So they deny it.

Finesse

It is true that many of us find it hard to know what the Japanese are really thinking. They, on the other hand, find it hard to handle what they consider to be our blunt forthrightness, especially in situations where they feel "finesse" is needed. Japanese conversation is tempered when there are "outsiders" present. They are also carefully circumspect in their speech when top level, senior-ranking people are present. When we Westerners talk freely and easily, under almost any circumstances, with little visible regard for rank or status, they often cringe inwardly. Being outspoken, "calling it like it is" no matter what other peoples' feelings or awareness may be, are all jarring to Japanese sensibilities.

Perceived Lack of Respect

The American's immediate use of first names feels very comfortable to him. It seems to him friendly, relaxed, egalitarian, democratic—. To him, using last names with a title (such as Mr., Mrs., Doctor, etc.) seems formal and stiff. He therefore, assumes that "Call me Joe—and what

is your first name?" will put everyone at ease right away. It does not. It makes most Asians—and certainly the Japanese (not to mention British, French, and others of many nations) "uptight." Much of the world reacts to it as "presumptuous," "insincere," "fresh," "rude," "a bit arrogant," "crude."

In the business world of today, younger Japanese are taking first names in stride, when they are among foreigners. They adopt a foreign name—usually a single syllable one, such as Pete, Sam, Ken…(or in Europe, short names like Jose, Pedro, Pat). They easily adjust to that, although few—if any—would think of using their own real names in such a casual way back home. Older Japanese men do not usually go so far.

Non-verbal Disrespect

Disrespect of a non-verbal nature can be shown in many ways: by sitting with one's arm behind one's head, slouching in a chair while talking, wearing untidy clothes, crossing the legs widely, or putting the feet up on a desk, a chair, a train seat, a radiator. The message given by such sloppiness is one of "not caring," or "no respect." We do not mean it so, any more than they mean "disrespect" when they spit, "hawk" loudly, or slurp their soup. Both sides need to give the other leeway in interpreting what are generally unconscious, unintended, and often misconstrued "messages."

Service

What seems "democratic" in some countries often seems "impolite" to the Japanese.

Servants and service people are subservient in Japan. The barber is not friendly and talkative; there he—and the shoemaker, the television man, the delivery man—are extremely polite, even servile in Western eyes. They are visibly and constantly aware of the servant/master roles.

This is gradually changing as people in Japan are coming to feel more equal too, but especially older Japanese often consider service in the West to be "too friendly"—to the point of impoliteness. They feel respect is lacking.[8]

Section 2:
The Written and Spoken Language

The Japanese language with its special sentence structure and its system of writing has little in common with any other language in the world. Nevertheless, it is a world language if measured in terms of the number of people who speak it, or the range of countries where it is currently heard and widely spoken.

The Written Language

Ideograms were first used in China over 2,000 years ago—pictograms and signs, such as the sun, or a tree, or a man. There are said to have been about 50,000 characters in wide use in the 5th and 6th centuries. The system spread to what are now Japan, Korea, and Vietnam.

Obviously a system with that many characters was cumbersome, so about 1,000 years ago two much simpler phonetic systems (called *Hiragana* and *Katakana*) were devised, each with just 46 symbols, representing the 46 sounds of Japanese. The word *Kanji* refers to pictograms of Chinese origin which are still widely used. It is estimated that some 2,000 *Kanji* are needed for daily use; pro-

8 *John P. Fieg and John G. Blair, There Is a Difference (Meridian House International, 1941) p. 24.*

fessionals may use twice this number.[9] Also the Japanese are increasingly using Romanized letters, especially in advertisements and place names.

As if this were not complicated enough, one needs to realize that one can also read or write Japanese in three directions: left to right; right to left read horizontally; or right to left read vertically. For centuries the writing was vertical, but is currently being written horizontally more and more, in order to accommodate Arabic numbers, passages in foreign languages, Western names, *etc*. However, since it remains easier for most Asian readers to as similate sentences vertically, most papers, magazines, and popular books are still printed in that form. (The first line is on the RIGHT of the page; succeeding lines follow to the left.)

Despite the complexity of the language, there are Japanese typewriters! A single key moves over a large grid which has many of the basic *Kanji* characters. Word processors are coming into wide usage. They can store, display, and print *Kanji* characters and are rapidly changing the work place in Japan—as they are in the USA and other countries. Not surprisingly, fax machines are also sweeping Japan, playing a big part in office automation.

Complex though the language is, Japan has one of the world's highest literacy rates—considerably higher than the USA. It is estimated that 99.7% of the Japanese can read and write their own language. Only Finland is said to have a higher percentage.

The Spoken Language

It is far easier to learn to speak Japanese than it is to either read or write it. Modern *spoken* Japanese is not any more

9 *The Economist: Business Traveller's Guides: Japan (The Economist Publications Ltd. and Webster's Business Travellers Guides Ltd., 1987) pp. 98-99.*

difficult to get along in than are most European languages. The grammar has few exceptions to its rules, and the language has a flexible structure. One does have to get used to simple but unfamiliar differences, such as the fact that the verb often comes at the end of the sentence—as in German—or that there are no singular or plural forms. When clarity is desired, the speaker uses numbers. Any sentence—no matter how long and complicated—becomes a question simply by adding *ka* at the end.

It is not the structure of the language itself that is hard for foreigners, as much as the emotional, "honorific" and sometimes poetic nuances. Since the Japanese often leave much unsaid, or never state the subject, or only hint at a meaning for fear of being too direct, the whole matter of speech can sometimes become a guessing game for foreigners. Indeed, a professor of language at Tokyo University said he estimates that even the Japanese understand each other clearly only about 85% of the time, because they speak so much in figures, allusions, and ambiguities.

A former American IBM executive who lived in Japan for eleven years writes: "Many times when two Japanese are having an intense discussion, one of them will write *Kanji* characters 'in the air' to clarify a point, since even his Japanese friend cannot understand the word he is trying to get across. I have seen this many times in subways. Also in restaurants one will take out a pen and write on the place mat to clarify a word or a point."

Nevertheless, most of the time they are far happier and more comfortable with their suggestions, carefully chosen implications, innuendos and allusions than they are with what they perceive as our blunt, direct, often "cold" facts.

Pronunciation

Japanese words are not hard to pronounce, though they look as though they are going to be. For one thing there is

little accent or stress. If you stress every syllable equally you will come out quite well. Most Japanese words have a number of syllables, nearly always ending with a vowel (sometimes an "n"). To help yourself pronounce their words, divide them into their syllables, as in *"ki-mo-no"*, or *"Hi-ro-shi-ma"* for example.

Sounds of the vowels are constant and phonetically simple:

> **a** as in f**a**ther (ah)
> **e** as in r**e**d (eh)
> **i** as in p**i**ano (ee)
> **o** as in c**o**rd (aw)
> **u** as in fl**u**te (oo)

A bar or ^ over a vowel means "hold twice as long." Otherwise the stress is even for all syllables—which is very helpful. If you see "u" at the end of a word (as you often do) you pronounce it very lightly—if at all. Long and short sounds can change the entire meaning of a word. This means that one needs a good ear both to speak and to understand the language. One can, for example, confuse "aunt" with "grandmother" just by the length of syllable. So watch those little bars over the vowels!

Subtleties

The greatest difficulty with the Japanese language—predictably—is its infinite use of subtleties:

…There are often many words for the same thing—or what seem to us to be the same thing. Just as the Eskimos have some fifty words to cover all the different kinds of grains/wetness/hardness, *etc.*, of snow, the Japanese often have numerous words for the same thing, each with a shade of difference. Take for example the word "you." There are several different words for it depending on the status, sex, age, occupation, *etc.* of "you." There are nine different words for "I," depending on the relative status of both

speaker and listener, *i.e.*, standard form, used by both men and women; informal used by women; informal used by men and boys; vulgar used by men; used by elderly men….You can also talk of eating, using the standard form (*taberu*); the polite form (*meshiagaru*); the humble form (*itadaku*); or the vulgar form (*kuu*).

…Japanese is a highly refined language. For example, there are six words to express varied aspects of Truth. Verbs also often have careful nuances. There are varying verbs to express exactly *how* one "carries" things, for example.

…There are variations in usage depending on whether the sentence is being spoken by a man or a woman, by an adult or a child. Furthermore, one must choose words not only appropriate to the speaker but also in relation to the person being spoken *to* (similar to the French use of *tu* or *vous* depending on who is being addressed).

Despite these various fine points, learning to speak workable, understandable, passable Japanese is by no means an impossibility. Many foreigners do learn to speak a simplified form of it reasonably well within a year. This is, of course, very different from being able to conduct business in Japanese which, experts say, takes a minimum of two years, full-time, in school, and should be started before one is thirty. This means that corporations should be planning ahead and training up young executives.

Japanese start learning English by the 7th grade—sometimes before. They continue through college. Many now working in English-speaking countries have studied it for twenty or more years.[10] Actually the language includes some 25,000 English words. It has a lot of Dutch words

10 *Reprinted by permission of Bantam Doubleday Dell Publishing Group. Edward T. and Mildred Reed Hall, Hidden Differences: Doing Business with the Japanese (Garden City, NY: Anchor Press/Doubleday, 1987) p. 106.*

as well, left in the tongue from the strong trade relations in the 17th-19th centuries, and many Portuguese words from the same period. A good many Italian words have also come into the language—most of them related either to music or to food. There are, in addition, quite a few French and German words.

…"Polite" language indicates "distance" in personal relations. When two Japanese argue, for example, the language often gets more and more formal as emotions heat up, even if the surface remains polite. We tend to do the opposite. We get less and less polite as our emotions rise.

"Gairaigo" (or "Japlish")

An English-speaking person who goes to Japan has fun trying to read any of the signs that are written in Roman letters. English words have been modified as they have been taken into the Japanese language. (In using them remember that "I" is always pronounced "EE.") Once a person gets the hang of *gairaigo* they find they can read many sighs, or menus, or notices. But one has to read them out loud first in order to catch the meaning, because they *look* very different from the original.

This hybrid language is called *gairaigo*. The word *gai* means "foreign"; *rai* means "come"; *go* means "word." So it is literally "words that come from the outside." There is considerable debate as to whether this will impoverish or enrich the language. Actually, however, most languages have a tendency to merge and flow with other ones over a period of time.

Examples of "Gairaigo"

escalator—*eskareta*
whisky—*uisuki*
glass (cup)—*koppu*

wine—*wain*
hot dogs—*hotto doggu*
cake—*keiki*
ham and eggs—*hamu-eggu*
spoon—*supun*
fork—*hoku*
knife—*naifu*
taxi—*takushi*
waiter—*boy-san*
night ball game—*naitah*
strikes and balls—*sutoraiku and boru*

Another clue to their melding of English with Japanese lie in their passion for abbreviating words as for example:

television—*terebi*
department stores—*depato*

If You Go to Japan

You will find the people try to be very helpful to foreigners. Bear in mind that although many of them read foreign languages, the spoken word is harder for them. If you are in trouble, therefore, it may be a good idea to write your questions clearly. When choosing someone to help you, look for a young person. They are more likely to be conversant in English than are their elders, and often welcome the chance to practice. In talking with them, remember that it is often hard for them to distinguish "b" from "v"; or "l" from "r." Remember the famous phrase, "I'd like flied lice" instead of "fried rice!"

You will be pleased to find that place names and directions are being translated increasingly into English at least in Tokyo, Osaka, and Kobe…and also on highways, subways, and railroad stations.

If you feel the need of an interpreter when in Japan, you

can contact them through your agent or firm, through the Embassy, through major hotels, travel bureaus, or interpreting agencies. You can get either students or professionals (at widely varying rates, of course). **(See page 214 for more on Interpreters.)**

Communicating Is A Two-way Street

What about our own communications? Do we "get to" the Japanese?

They have a really hard time with Americans. Not only must the Japanese know the English language, but they must also cope with slang, frequent sports references, professional jargon, and "alphabet soup," not to mention a variety of local differences and accents.

"This man is picking on me." (Picking on me does not translate well into Japanese!)

Slang: "The important thing is to keep your nose clean."

"That was a real dilly."

"Let's make an end run around the old man and get moving."

Sports: "He threw me a real curve."

"What you need for that job is a man who shoots from the hip."

"Let 'er rip."

Other nations do the same thing too. "That was a sticky wicket," for example, a Britisher might say when he's "had a hard row to hoe."

Alphabet Soup: "I asked the SEC but they said the IRS would do it. However, when we took it to the OBM they bucked it over to GAO." (Washington, D.C.)

Localisms: "Hi, honey. You want a little scrapple this mawning? Or maybe you feel like a few grits or some nice cawn mush?"

"Y'all come for another visit, hear?" (The Japanese will probably think this Texan means: Come back with more people next time.)

"It won't play in Peoria."

Any of the following could trip up a person who has learned English out of a book, or in a class:

"What's the synergy here?" or "There's too much down-time," or "Did ja notice we were just sandbagged?"

"Will it float?" or "That won't fly."

"He's lost his marbles."

"Let's run it by him tomorrow."

Imagine the bewilderment of a Japanese waitress when an employee who had mistakenly ordered both french fries and potatoes, looked at her and said, "Scratch the potatoes." This story was portrayed in the excellent, amusing , and highly recommended study *The Tower of Business Babel.* Its moral is: Be merciful! Speak to the Japanese in language that they *might* understand.[11]

---

11 *From The Tower of Business Babel (Parker Pen Company, 1985).*

PART V

DOING BUSINESS
WITH
THE JAPANESE

An old traditional temple
(photo by Masashi Yanagihara)

Section 1:
How the Japanese Operate at Home

Two Different Working Worlds

There is a vast difference between the high profile and
well-known "empires"—such as Sony, Honda, Hitachi,
Matsushita, or the other "giants"—and the majority of the
country's six thousand businesses.

Approximately one-quarter of the whole Japanese work
force works closely with MITI (Ministry of International
Trade and Industry). These workers have long benefitted
from a highly paternalistic system which provides substantial lifetime benefits, including housing, schooling, full
medical care, and much else. Currently, for example,
though real estate prices are out of sight in Tokyo, increasing numbers of companies are providing new housing for
their workers. Toshiba Corporation, for example, is planning to build 2,700 apartments and 1,800 houses for their
newly married employees.[1]

However, what is often not understood by outsiders is
that roughly 75% of all Japanese businesses have, in fact,
less than 100 employees. These employees have never had
the security of lifetime employment. For them life has
always been precarious. They still continue to have a far
lower standard of living than those in the big international
firms—not only in pay levels, but also in old-age security,
"perks," working conditions, and social status. Some of us
think that the paternalistic system we hear about applies to
everyone in Japan. This is by no means the case.

The "Big Giants" wheel and deal in a somewhat intimi-

1 *Wall Street Journal, 14 March 1989.*

dating way behind the scenes. Their weight affects stock markets and government policies around the world. The ten largest of them employ more than 40, 000 each; however, only 1% of Japan's businesses employ more than even 500 workers; more than 98% employ fewer than 300.

It has been said that one of the greatest strengths of this least understood world power may lie in the endless hours of hard work and the patient skill of those millions who work in the small and medium-sized firms. These are the people who provide the millions of small parts that the giant companies must have in order to send their goods around the world. It is important to understand this as one looks at the country as a whole.

Inside Networks

Open competition has never been a real part of the Japanese heritage. Being "group" people, not individualists, they have long been accustomed to "collective action" (which, as a matter of fact, often seems to Westerners very close to "collusion"). This "collective action" is often under the leadership of the government itself. Cartels are deeply woven into Japan's business life. They are usually legal and legitimate. Leaders in industries such as the automotive industry, for example, often get together to make agreements with each other regarding supplies of raw materials, prices, distribution channels, or whatever. Outsiders have no chance to participate—nor to benefit from the agreements.

When Japanese managers come to other countries, it is, therefore, understandable that they frequently find western regulations in these regards to be hampering and restrictive. Both sides need to understand that the other is coming from a totally different set of attitudes about freedom and restraints.

Trading companies, known as *shosha*, play an enormous role in the country's international trade. A trading company is a marketing organization that not only participates in several types of manufacturing, but also acts as a wholesale distributor of the products. In addition, it will often have direct interest in both wholesalers and retail stores; furthermore, it is often its own exporter, even providing its own ships in many cases. Beyond that, it may supply the necessary raw materials as well, often importing for distribution within its own ranks.

This means that the small to middle-sized manufacturer may have in one organization (the trading company) a built-in banker, exporter, importer, purchasing agent, and local Japanese marketing agent!

For foreign businessmen this can prove totally frustrating. They must often fight miles of red tape rather than deal directly with the manufacturer. This can be a great frustration for Americans and others who like to go directly to the source for products that they like.

The Japanese are beginning to operate in a similar way in other countries.

William Glasgall, writing in *Business Week* says: "As Toyota Motor Corporation and other major Japanese companies enter the heartland (of the USA) Japan's financiers come not only as lenders to them but also as bankers for their affiliated suppliers. They are helping Japanese parts-makers to find places to build their own U.S. factories— and then financing them. In other cases, the Japanese banks, brokers, and trading companies are acting as matchmakers between U.S. companies that need capital and technology, and Japanese companies that are seeking access to the U.S. market."[2] **(For a list of major trading companies, see Appendix V)**

2 *William Glasgall, "Japan In America," Business Week, 14 July 1986.*

Japan's Distribution System is under Attack

The Japanese market is the second largest in the world and is fiercely competitive. Japan's internal distribution system causes considerable grief to the rest of the world, and increasingly, to the Japanese themselves. It is unique, and in no way designed to help an outsider *gaijin* company penetrate Japan with a new product.

To begin with, Japan has always been a nation of small shop-keepers. They still have more small retailers than any other major industrial nation. The announced figure is 1.6 million small stores in the restricted island area that is Japan.

Beyond these little stores are layers of wholesalers, each with their own varied types of controls. A manufacturer from abroad may have to pass his goods through three or four layers before reaching a single sales outlet. In addition, many of the "Big" companies have their own private systems of wholesalers and retailers. The huge electronic firm, Matsushita, for example, has no less than 27,000 of its own stores. Try penetrating that for competition!

Naturally such a complex, fragmented system makes it extremely difficult for foreign goods to get a toehold in Japanese markets. Furthermore, if they do, it is often at costs that make the product almost unaffordable.

In addition one can never forget that their group society is closely interwoven. Distribution of goods is frequently based on close personal networks of family, friends, and colleagues. Sometimes these networks go back for generations, with interweaving obligations, long-term trust, and clearly defined expectations. No wonder it is difficult for outsiders to break into such a closely-knit system.

Things may be changing fairly rapidly nowadays,

however, because it is not only foreign companies that are locked out. So, too, are new Japanese firms that are trying to get started, or to open markets in new areas, or to increase their exposure through such devices as discount stores, all-night stores, malls, and the like. The Japanese are themselves looking to expand distribution outlets in new ways.

Furthermore, Japanese people are going overseas by the hundreds of thousands these days—to study, or to visit or tour, as well as to work. They see for themselves, more and more clearly, that they are paying phenomenal prices at home compared with those of other countries. So they, too, are looking askance at their own situation.

As one might expect, the whole system is under the powerful administration of MITI. It is based on a 1974 law that tangles the whole system up in red tape. MITI provides "administrative guidance"—with its own goals in mind, of course.

The American Chamber of Commerce in Tokyo recently studied the system carefully. It reported tremendous frustration on the part of foreign companies who are stymied by layers of barriers to entry, and by an almost impenetrable thicket of regulations. Some of them may be having difficulties also because the Japanese are sophisticated buyers. Products must not only be of top quality and good design but also need to be adapted to Japanese needs and preferences. The Halls say, "American's biggest single problem in the Japanese marketplace is the uneven quality of American products."[3] Some foreign companies, such as West Germany's BMW, for example, or the Mars Candy division, have set up their own direct sales networks. Others, who have been in Japan a long time,

3 *Reprinted by permission of Bantam Doubleday Dell Publishing Group. Edward T. and Mildred Reed Hall, Hidden Differences: Doing Business with the Japanese (Garden City, NY: Anchor Press/Doubleday) p. 135.*

such as Proctor and Gamble, have simply doggedly stuck it out until finally they have become part of the system.

But most are frustrated. However, changes and reforms are thought to be on the way. MITI says they are in "a process of dynamic change." They admit there is a "price gap" due to lack of competition, and they also admit—under pressure from abroad—that there is in fact need for more imports.

One step, namely that of reducing the number of retailers, is underway, partly because today's young people are no longer interested in following "Mom 'n Pop" into running the little store. But that is a slow, evolutionary process.

MITI talks of changing the laws to limit the roadblocks. However, since MITI itself has a vested interest in the status quo, it is not likely to be quite as dynamic a change as they currently claim.

The best hopes lie in pressure from abroad and pressure from the Japanese people themselves, as they realize with increasing clarity what obscene prices they are paying for goods, as compared with people in other countries.

Trade Unions

Unions are a comparatively recent concept in Japan, brought in after World War II, under the terms of the new Constitution. Article 28 of that Constitution established the "right of workers to organize and to bargain and act collectively." This freedom to "act collectively" was new and exciting to the workers. It was legalized as part of the policy of "democratization," that U.S. authorities pursued. Although not an integral part of their heritage, workers responded with enthusiasm. From 1946 onwards, union membership grew rapidly. By 1980 there were nearly 73,000 unions with a membership of 12.3 million. Of

these, more than half were in the large corporations (*i.e.*, those with over 1,000 workers).[4]

Early on, a deal was struck by which unions accepted the control of management, as well as the need for high productivity. In return, they were guaranteed no layoffs (except for temporary workers). At first, this looked like solid security to the workers. Actually, however, it turned out to benefit management quite as much—if not more—than it did the workers, for the system, being static, provided virtually no alternative possibilities of employment. Furthermore, at each plant, workers had to work long, hard hours in order to make their employers successful enough to pay them!

Since most unions in Japan are federated by industry, not organized by job or occupation, the employees were soon bonded rather permanently and tightly to whatever firm paid their salaries and allowances.[5]

On the whole, the workers trusted their companies. They were used to lifetime employment, welfare benefits, a wide range of family-oriented facilities, and a system of seniority. Workers were, therefore, linked more closely to the company than to the unions. Furthermore, all people in supervisory and management positions were themselves union members—often even union leaders. As a result, managers and unions had a close understanding, a "feel" for one another. Therefore, although companies and unions often had different views as to the distribution of profits, they were basically on common ground as to the overall prosperity of the company on which the profits were based. **[See also section on "Japan's Internationally Important Power Lines," paragraphs IV and V. p. 172]**

4 *Nippon, Land and People, 1982.*
5 *Malcolm Trevor, Japan's Reluctant Multinationals: Japanese Management at Home and Abroad (New York: St. Martin's Press, 1983).*

Japan's Internationally Important Power Lines: Six Major Organizations[6]

Although for the most part readers are likely to be working with Japanese colleagues outside Japan itself, it is, nevertheless, important to know what some of the major business power lines are back in the home country, as one will hear their names, and need to be aware of their influence.

Six major organizations have real influence on those Japanese firms that are working in the international arena:

I Keidanren (The Federation of Economic Organizations)

This is the most powerful of the groups. It acts as a kind of focal point for the business community. Its members are the major trade associations and nearly all the prominent companies in practically all fields of both industry and commerce. It has a full-time secretariat or roughly 180 people, and works through 18 Standing Committees which address a variety of specific problems.

The Federation's *primary* role is to be a pressure group for the business community. With its broad spread of influence and its high level of organization, it exerts a formidable lobbying power within Japan itself, as well as working to ease trade frictions with other countries. Domestically it is interested in working for cuts in corporate taxes, lobbying for cuts in government spending, trying to ease government pressures, anti-monopoly moves, and the like.

Its *secondary* role involves international problems. Working closely with similar business organizations in other countries *Keidanren* carries on a tremendous amount of private-level diplomacy.

The Federation's *third* role is that of providing an

6 *Information in this section is derived from The Economist Business Travellers' Guide, Japan Power in Business (Prentice Hall Press) pp. 46-47.*

energetic and effective Public Relations office for the business community. It works through all available media and channels to inform not only the Japanese public, but also opinion overseas. The public relations function is centered in the **Keizai Koho Center** which conducts extensive surveys; organizes seminars all over the world; places worldwide advertising skillfully and widely; sponsors television programs; organizes speakers for international conferences; and publishes a great array of magazines and booklets in Japanese and also in other languages.

II Keizai Doyukai

This is the *Japanese Committee for Economic Development*. Its members are not corporations, as in *Keidanren*, but are individuals. Most of them are the CEO's of big corporations—Directors, Chairmen, or Presidents. Many of them wear two hats, since they are often also officials in *Keidanren*. These are powerful men!

This group is oriented towards the actual making of policy. It has long-standing ties throughout much of the world; its members are often part of study missions sent abroad on various projects. Members are deeply concerned with management philosophy and the growth of their own economy. The group provides an experienced, knowledgeable forum along these lines. They strongly advocate free enterprise and stand firmly for the liberalization of trade and capital in Japan. They are concerned with decreasing the frictions that exist in international trade, and are well aware of possibilities for real hazards in the future if these tensions are not resolved. The present Chairman (who is also Chairman of Nissan Company) says that he sees his primary task as that of "revitalizing" and "sparking" the organization which was founded in 1946, but which has been losing momentum over the most recent years.

III Nikkeiren

This is the *Japanese Federation of Employers Association*. It speaks for the *employers* in labor and wage nego-

tiations, and represents over 10,000 companies. These, in the aggregate, employ about 30% of Japan's work force (1987 figure). One of their chief goals is to improve management-labor relations. They work on this by educating employers along social lines, training workers, and developing wide publicity for employer policies (such as targeting inflation as "Public Enemy No. 1").

Nikkeiren has a respected advisory role in the country regarding wages and working conditions. It may be under considerable stress in the years ahead. Because of the appreciation of the yen and the nation's huge trade surpluses, Japan may be pricing itself out of a labor market that feels growing competition from such places as Taiwan, South Korea, and Singapore, where labor costs are less than a third of the $12.06 an hour average rate paid by Japanese manufacturers (1988).

Both management and labor in Japan (which until recently have had very cooperative relationships) are feeling the heat of these new pressures.

IV Rengo (Japanese Private Sector Trade Union Confederation) and **V Sohyo** (General Council of Trade Unions of Japan)

Until recently, Japanese trade unions have been willing to accept relatively modest increases in wages and benefits. However, the rising cost of living and the fear of inflation are creating considerable new pressure for higher wages. Although *Rengo* was created as recently as 1987, it has 5.4 million members. It is, in fact, a federation of the biggest enterprise unions of Japan. *Sohyo*, with 4.5 million members, is the smaller-though older-counterpart of *Rengo*. They, too, are seeking higher wage increases, and are also pressing for greater job security protection.

These two labor federations are preparing to unite—*Sohyo*, which represents mostly public sector employees, will dissolve and merge into *Rengo* (the Private Sector Confederation). *Sohyo*'s clout has been reduced over the

past years by rising prosperity, falling unionization, and the increased use of part-time workers.

"If the unions break into various groups instead of consolidating, they will continue to lose power," said a spokesman for *Sohyo*. The merger is not expected to have great immediate impact since most workers continue to be represented by individual unions, which deal with only a single employer. But as regional and international shifts occur, and as the Japanese continue to move their operations overseas, the whole union picture may change.

The shift of production overseas, in order to reduce labor costs and acquire favorable trading positions, naturally is creating increasing restlessness and uneasiness among workers back home. Huge companies, such as Fujitsu and Sanyo Electric have recently made substantial investments in new manufacturing facilities in Spain, for example. Labor is cheaper there, and—vitally important—Spain provides increased access to the European Common Market. As is well known, many auto manufacturers, taking advantage of their favorable currency position, are also investing heavily and rapidly in facilities in various parts of the USA, as well as Wales, Ireland, and England. Nissan, Honda, Toyota, and Minolta have all been building American plants to reduce their cost of selling in the U.S. As we have seen, the same process is going on in various industries throughout Europe and other parts of the world. Japan is definitely on the move. As this well-designed and long-planned "globalization" of production continues, the number of plant closings rises at home. These have put added pressure on both *Rengo* and *Sohyo* to protect their members. The current situation jeopardizes the entire basis on which labor-management harmony has prevailed over the past years. Management also watches South Korea with considerable concern. In the past few years, there has been a wave of union militancy in that neighboring country, with many long and bitter strikes throughout the

1980's. These have resulted in substantial wage increases and massive bonuses in order to bring settlement. Japan's new economic moves are also creating strong pressures on the relationships between Japanese business leaders and the nation's trade union leaders. The full impact of these new stresses is yet to unfold.

VI Nissho

This is the group which most non-Japanese business-men know best. It is the *Japanese Chamber of Commerce and Industry*, a federation of 481 local Chambers. It is Japan's oldest and biggest business organization, with 11,000 staff, and branches spread widely around the world.

Nissho operates primarily on behalf of small and medium-sized firms. It is active in strengthening ties with foreign businessmen through liaison with Chambers of Commerce of other countries, as well as through their own Japanese Chambers of Commerce established overseas. *Nissho* is also linked with a number of regional bodies, such as the Pacific Basin Economic Council.

Among them, these six groups exert tremendous power. Their names and global purposes should be familiar to all who work closely with Japanese "bosses," wherever they may be.[7]

Section 2:
Management Styles Vary with Cultures

One might think that the Japanese management style would not work well in another culture. Experience has indicated otherwise, however. A good example is the Toy-

---

7 *New York JETRO (Japan External Trade Relations Organization), 1989.*

ota-GM venture in Fremont, California. The highly union-
ized work force of the General Motors plant had long been
famous for its absenteeism and for poor quality control.
When the Japanese came in, however, that same plant was
soon making as many cars in a day, with 2,500 workers, as
had been produced previously with more than 5,000.[8]

Management and Culture

The more one looks at management styles arising out of
different cultures, the more one realizes that although
management must be compatible with a country's culture,
the two are not really too closely interwoven. Management
is not necessarily deeply culture oriented. It can, therefore,
adapt readily to changing circumstances. Business schools
in many countries are teaching large numbers of students
from other countries. High speed economic growth, not
only in Japan but also in South Korea and Taiwan, for
example, have almost nothing to do with those countries'
cultural backgrounds. Mainland China was also following
other Asian countries towards considerable gains in labor
productivity before its 1989 crisis.[9]

It is in day-to-day operations that cultural differences
show themselves most clearly. As Johnson and Ouci observe: "Americans will disagree with their boss rarely but
violently; the Japanese disagree often, but politely. Americans will say 'I could not get a thing done today—I was on
the phone all day.' Japanese managers, who feel themselves to be facilitators and shapers rather than activists,
would feel that a day spent on the phone was quite
compatible with their own self image as a manager."[10]

8 *Chalmers Johnson, "Japanese Style Management in America," California Management Review, Summer 1988, p.40.*

9 *Ibid., p. 41.*

10 *Ibid., p. 42.*

Decision by Consensus

Perhaps the most fundamental difference in management style between the Japanese and most other countries lies in the area of decision-making. *Westerners* often find the Japanese method of making decisions to be aggravatingly slow. Few realize the very different thought processes and procedures that are going on.

Westerners tend to make major decisions at the top, in board meetings, among department heads, and the like. They then "pass the word" down the line to managers and others, to implement and carry out the decision. The *Japanese* do the opposite. Their system, commonly know as *ringi* is the corporate version of "government by consensus."

Decisions are not made "on high" and handed down to be implemented. They are proposed from below and move upwards, receiving additional input and approvals after deliberation through all levels of the company.

"One should think of the system as a filter through which ideas pass," says Robert T. Moran. "The whole process, as it winds its way through various levels of the company, can last from two to three weeks to a matter of months. Each level takes its own time to go over the details. If the matter under consideration is complex or sensitive, it can take even longer."[11]

Ringi is naturally not used for every transaction. However, it is virtually required for major negotiations over a certain value. It is used also for transactions that involve advance payments, or high-risk investments, or major changes within the company. Only a few top level foreigners are likely to find themselves involved with *ringi* decisions, and only if they have been co-opted into the system.

11 *Robert T. Moran, Getting Your Yen's Worth: How to Negotiate with Japan, Inc. (Houston, TX: Gulf Publishing Co., 1985).*

This would include primarily upper level foreign management and/or those top foreign staff who are able to communicate in Japanese.

Since the Japanese are comfortable when working in teams and groups, they do well with this process among themselves. They have been trained to depend on each other; to have a strong group loyalty. They tend to look to seniors as respected mentors.

For decisions that are not of really major importance, approvals can be given by various individuals (or by groups of them). But when any decision is a matter of great importance, the Japanese look for broad consensus. *Ringi* should be seen as a "process" rather than a system. It gives management the choice of a broad selection of pragmatic options. Often the initiator is a section chief. He proposes an idea (which may well have been suggested to him by one of his workers). He gets his section members to research it; they all discuss it. When satisfied, he passes it up the line. Even junior members take part in all this deliberation. It is considered part of their training and a means of developing their company motivation. The idea is considered all the way up until it reaches the president. If he approves it, it will have been seen, considered, and passed on by virtually everyone who could be in any way involved in the final implementation. One can imagine the bargaining, persuasion, trading of favors, seeking of support and general "lobbying" that goes on throughout the process! All of this is known as *nemawashi* which means "binding up the roots." (The image is that of a tree that will survive only if everything is properly prepared in advance.)

Actually, of course, managers can do a great deal to bring about whatever "consensus" they want by "suggesting" to subordinates that they study certain matters, or by "planting" ideas in their minds over a period of time. But the skill lies in making the lower echelons feel that it was they who came up with the idea. Often it can, in fact, turn

out to be a camouflaged "top down" decision, rather than a true "bottom up" idea. "Consensus" frequently can mean that the subordinates have caught the drift of what the superiors have already decided. Generally speaking, however, the normal *ringi* process does end up with a reasonably true consensus, reasonably broadly based.

It is important not only that all those "properly" involved be consulted, but that they should also be *known* to have been consulted. Anyone left out would (or could) feel that if he was bypassed, a potential threat to his career was intended. Such a one would suffer what are referred to as "wet" feelings of unhappiness if he felt he was being excluded from a decision in which he thought he should legitimately have been involved.

One of the major benefits of these *ringis* is that it avoids the possibility of anyone being marked as "personally responsible" for a decision. Where responsibility can be diffused, potentially embarrassing "loss of face" can be avoided. No fingers can be pointed.

"Delays in making even simple decisions can become almost unbearable at times," said a fast-moving American executive who works with a worldwide hotel chain. "Everybody has to be involved with *everything*," he continued. "It takes forever. As far as I am concerned, this is without doubt the very hardest part of working for a Japanese company. You feel as if you can *never* get a decision on anything, large or small." "By the time the decision finally does come through," added another, "I have usually lost interest in whatever it was and am on to something else. Interminable delays are deflating to one's sense of energy and drive."

If you try to hurry the process, it does more harm than good. The Japanese do not like pressure. Obviously, frustrated Westerners will be itching to know what is going on as the silence goes into weeks or months. You submit a proposal or an inquiry. Nothing happens. Who is holding

it up? What is happening? Did the message ever get through?

If the decision you are impatient for relates to a new idea, perhaps something you have initiated, you can count on a really long delay. If, on the other hand, the company is merely talking about some refinement of an idea they have already agreed to in principle, then it may take considerably less time to come up with a reply.

But you can take it for granted that you will rarely get quick action unless, as one veteran of the business world put it, "You have gold that is $7.00 on the open market and are willing to sell it for $6.00. Then you will get action without delay."

You may occasionally encounter Japanese who will try to foreshorten their normal time as a concession to Western impatience. But don't count on it.

In writing this book, I asked a number of businessmen who work well with Japanese colleagues, what they consider to be the *single* biggest factor in their success. In every single case the first attribute mentioned was "patience, patience, and still more patience." They all agreed: "If you lose your patience or your cool, you are likely to find yourself empty-handed."

In his book *Japan's Reluctant Multinationals: Japanese Management at Home and Abroad*, Malcolm Trevor quotes a British manager: "The Japanese are—so far—willing to pay the price of slowness in order to maintain their traditional system. The maintenance of organizational cohesion," he says, "is worth the occasional loss of business, *especially in non-Japanese environments* [italics added]."[12]

Although the *ringi* system is undoubtedly slow, no one

12 *Malcolm Trevor, Japan's Reluctant Multinationals: Japanese Management at Home and Abroad (New York: St. Martins Press, 1983).*

can complain afterwards. Harmony is served. Factional-ism and power struggles are at least minimized—if not eliminated—for once the process has reached a certain stage, no one feels he can "buck the tide." So, he goes along with it and initials it. After that, he is effectively silenced. Direct opposition is rarely effective among the Japanese. One achieves more with them through the kind of persua-sion and negotiating—one might say "lobbying"—that is sanctioned and made broadly possible through *nemawashi*.

Actually, the length of delay before achieving the ulti-mate goal may not be as great as it sometimes appears when compared with Western systems. Where the Western "top-down" approach to decision-making is used, the original plan or agreement is frequently made relatively quickly at the top in the board room. However, delays of weeks or months may subsequently follow while staffs and workers are first apprised of the decisions and then persuaded to give their cooperative support. Both steps are necessary before a plan can actually get moving with any momentum. When lower levels have not participated in making the decision, misunderstandings, snags, balks, or other delays frequently occur.

In Japan, in contrast, once the decision is finally and actually arrived at, all relevant staff members understand it thoroughly. They are familiar with its various ramifica-tions. During the talking stages, they will have pretty well mastered the "what-when-how" of their own responsibili-ties vis à vis the project in question. So, although it may take a long time to arrive at the decision, once approval has been given they can put it into practice rapidly and smoothly. The final time difference between the two systems there-fore, may not be as far apart as it can sometimes seem.

Furthermore, in the Japanese system, those in low echelons feel they have been involved. They have been able—often urged—to suggest proposals, projects, or refinements. Japanese bosses believe in encouraging sug-

gestions from the rank and file. The idea of creating a consensus that incorporates the whole organizational hierarchy is at the heart of Japanese business philosophy and methods.

Even if the *ringi* process is not practiced in your own company, it is helpful to know what is going on when one encounters what seem like uncommonly long delays in doing business with Japanese firms. Should the Japanese "bosses" in your company be outside Japan, it is probable that they will still be using the *ringi* method at least to some degree, since it is their familiar and normal style of management.

Ringi through Western Eyes

Westerners frequently find problems of various sorts in dealing with the *ringi* consensus system.

1. Unseen Relationships

Western businessmen are nearly always focused primarily on maximizing profits. In Japan business relationships are far more interwoven. For them, business involves a considerable amount of reciprocity with their suppliers and others. These relationships are enduring and more important to them than immediate profits. It would be most unlikely, for example, for a Japanese company to disappoint or let down a major Japanese supplier, even if by doing so, they could secure a new foreign contract. A company that did this could easily lose all future business with that supplier. It would also put the company's good name for reliability at risk. Most Westerners would be after the best price and the new customer. They would have little concern about the supplier's feelings or sensitivities.

One needs to be constantly aware that a multitude of complex relationships exist among and within Japan's

major industrial groups. These frequently include cross shareholding. There are also complex hierarchical relationships, which the outsider does not understand, dealing with the control of smaller supply firms by the large companies. The whole power structure is closely interwoven with political and business elites whose power goes far and deep into the very fabric of Japanese life and business.

2. Precedents

Another problem which men of the West sometimes find tedious and irksome lies in the fact that cases which already have clearly established precedents are often treated as if they were brand new. Therefore they are assumed to require full discussion all over again, from the bottom up. To the Japanese this makes sense. It is a new case; there may be different shadings of thought about it; new attitudes; slightly different conditions may prevail, so they start again from scratch. Westerners make assumptions based on previous cases, and adjust later for whatever changes are necessary, in accordance with whatever variations may have occurred. They consider that starting all over again from the ground up is a terrible waste of time. However, time is less vital to the Japanese than is absolute thoroughness and precision. Again, we see the impact of different cultural priorities.

3. Control from Japan

Head offices are seldom prepared to give their "branches" a great deal of autonomy. Once a decision has been announced at the top level, there is usually little room for compromise or adjustment to suit local conditions. Japanese managers operating abroad are often unaccustomed to taking independent action—or perhaps are not allowed to do so.

4. Split Loyalties

Since loyalty among overseas Japanese tends to be first to the Home Office, Japanese managers are subject to a

kind of double allegiance when they are overseas. This can add another hampering and delaying factor in taking necessary action or in making needed decisions. Needs and conditions on the overseas front—wherever it may be— are not always represented strongly at headquarters.

5. Loss of Momentum

Western businessmen generally have a quick eye out for ways in which to take advantage of unanticipated circumstances—changes on the stock market, rising or falling currency valuations, new real estate possibilities, the collapsed sale (or merger) of a rival firm... . Whatever it may be, such opportunities are often lost during a long, tedious wait for some major decision from the Home Office. This can be highly frustrating for those involved.

It is hard to achieve consensus unless there is certain basic ethnicity and a relatively similar educational level on the part of participants. The homogeneity of both the Japanese people and their educational system allows for consensus agreements far more than is possible with the ethnic and educational diversities found in most other countries. In these more diverse nations, "one man, one vote" seems to be a more effective system.

Nor is a consensus system readily compatible with entrepreneurial approaches. Even in the *ringi* process, not everyone is *really* able to speak out because of basic Japanese conventions, and the unspoken, but very real, awareness of each individual's "role" or "place." The Japanese are not a people accustomed to challenging authority. They rarely ask questions of their teachers or professors when in school or college, for example. They are taught to follow precedent; to keep closely to the chain of command without skipping any steps; to listen; to bow silently and show respect for their seniors. Someone has made the comment: "In Japan the little man has his say, but it better not be 'no'."

Labor Relations

Countries that have come late to industrialization have had a favorable break in that they are able to avoid some of the mistakes and rigidities of early industrializers in other parts of the world. They have been able to by-pass some of the road blocks that others have encountered and to see alternative approaches from the start. For example, the Japanese have avoided much class conflict and labor discord over the years by looking on labor as a form of capital. Being as short as they are of raw materials, they have seen the productive power of their nation as being almost totally dependent on the quality of their labor force ... in other words, their "human capital."[13] Therefore, their labor relations have been remarkably harmonious and a major factor in their "economic miracle."

Training in Japan

The Japanese method of promoting and training workers internally over a long period of time, keeping them as employees throughout their full working lifetimes, made it economically possible for them to expend considerable amounts of money, as well as time, on developing each man to his fullest possible productivity. Until recently, Japan's basic system was that of what could be called "tenured" employment. It was based on job rotation, on-the-job training, coupled with workers' identity with (and pride in) their own company. Much of their school training has always been rote; much of it at work is based on "learning by doing." This generally included a regular job rotation schedule during the initial years of a worker's life.

13 *Kazuo Koike, "Japan's Industrial Relations, Characteristics and Problems," Japan Executive Studies, Autumn 1978, p.46.*

They believed this rotation contributed markedly to organizational performance. Teamwork, competition, and team loyalty have always been strongly emphasized throughout their training systems. They consider participatory learning to be much more effective than the one-sided approach of "being lectured at." Out of this system came a widespread development of those high level skills that are essential for work in modern high-tech manufacturing.

However, it is economically less feasible to follow that pattern in countries, where worker mobility is great; or where newly-trained workers can easily be bought off by other companies; or where a man can voluntarily and quickly find himself another job—often at a higher salary—with a rival firm. All these factors now exist in Japan.

Robots

These matters may soon become academic. By the fast-approaching year 2000, the whole question of handling and training personnel may be radically different. Japan is light years ahead of the rest of the world in its use of advanced robots. Of all the working robots in the world, two-thirds are said to be in Japan. Furthermore they are manufacturing new ones at a tremendous rate, estimated by some at about 10,000 a year. With an eye to the future, they are engineering many of their new, sophisticated, high technology items in such a way that they can be assembled by robots, no longer laboriously by human hands.

Robots can, of course, geometrically increase the pace of productivity. Japan's level of productivity is already thought to be roughly three times that of the USA. The increased pace of production capacity will be the plus side of a "robot revolution." The question-mark side will be: What will happen to the level of employment? What will happen to all the workers replaced by robots?

Moving to Other Lands

Now that the Japanese are moving so much of their production into other countries, it is interesting to look at their management style, at what they are importing into other countries, and how much they are adapting from other countries.

When they take over the management of another company, the Japanese understandably look with keen eyes at cutting costs and improving quality. They pay great attention to quality; they are strong on "just-in-time"deliveries to keep costs down. They have also learned to adjust quite adroitly to the priorities of the workers in whatever country they are working. They prefer—and still work hard to attain—high employee loyalty rather than the traditional adversary relationship found in many countries, between management and labor.

Wherever they are, the Japanese concentrate on what they consider to be "human capital." Mr. Haruo Shimada, Professor of Economics at Keio University, refers to this as "humanware technology." He considers this to be the third important ingredient of modern technology, together with hardware and software. He describes it as "the way people and machines are combined so as to integrate peoples' creative potential as closely as possible with the production system."By focusing on "humanware" techniques, the Japanese manufacturing industry has made its extraordinary progress in the last few decades.

The essence of that approach is to give workers real responsibility so that they care about—and therefore catch— mistakes. They will do this, of course, only if they trust management. Management naturally has to be able to trust them too, as it is always easy for workers to foul up or "sabotage" management if they want to do so.

The Japanese go to great lengths to discover the causes of defects in whatever is being produced, preferring this to

eliminating defective goods later. They concentrate on having everyone concerned with the production of the item focussing in on problems that could even *potentially* occur. Through Quality Circles and other means, they encourage workers to think also of protective maintenance from every possible aspect. Workers are kept deeply involved. Their views and suggestions are not only solicited, they are also heeded! They work together in flexible "teamwork" settings. They are given a chance to discuss how their own jobs could be better set up. Often they come up with excellent ideas that save time, or money, or fatigue. Quality Circles are taken very seriously. In these groups people are made to feel that their opinions are worth something.

Under Japanese management, categories of jobs are often cut to fewer numbers. In this way, work can be spread out more evenly than is possible in countries, where multiple, tight job categories make for rigid divisions of work. As the Japanese move into management roles in other countries, their "team" approach has, for the most part, been welcomed by workers.

When they go abroad, Japanese managers study the new country carefully and try to fit into its work patterns. In the United States, for example, they take full account of the American imperative for individualism and for "equality." As they do back home in Japan, managers present themselves as reasonably "equal" by avoiding such special and visible "perks" as special dining rooms or parking lots for upper level managers. American workers like that greater sense of equality. Far more important in their eyes, however, is the fact that layoffs are kept to a minimum. In Japan, workers are shifted to other jobs—other plants or even sent "on loan" to other companies if necessary—but they are kept on the payroll to the greatest extent possible, even in hard times. Overseas, the Japanese modify this system, but nonetheless, their focus is on training, then *holding*, and using to the best advantage, the skilled,

flexible, and innovative work force needed to handle today's advanced high-tech manufacturing and service. A sense of job security is obviously a strong component in helping to build company loyalty. The Japanese care about that.

They make it clear that people are important. Japanese workers do not feel themselves as "impersonal" objects hired merely to press buttons and make machines work. They do not fear mass firings; grievance systems work quickly; their cases do not drag on over months or get lost in red tape. Bonuses are given frequently—often twice a year. The result of this "worker-oriented" approach is that in most Japanese-run plants, there is a high level of worker harmony.

Overseas Transfer: Not without Problems

However, when working in other countries, Japanese managers often feel frustrated. "Workers in the USA come for eight hours of work and eight hours of pay," says Tanemichi Sohma, a Sanyo V.P. "As long as they get that, they don't care what happens to production. One does not find sacrifice here."[14]

Outside Japan older workers often resent being moved from production lines to lesser jobs in order to make room for faster, more productive workers. "Here is Mary's chair," says Charlie Green. "Mary has sat there for fifteen years, and she'll be damned if she's going to move from that spot."[15] Charlie Green was coping with one of the countless human problems that occurred when his company, Warwick Electronics, Inc. in Arkansas, was taken over by Sanyo Manufacturing Corporation. Frictions such as this, and different ideas of precedence occur with great

14 *John A. Byrne, "At Sanyo's Arkansas Plant the Magic Is Not Working," Business Week, 14 July 1986.*
15 *Ibid.*

frequency, of course, as totally different priorities collide all over the world, in factories, offices, and work places as different as Tokyo and Forest City, Arkansas, or Yokohama and Upper Burlington-on-Sea, Kent (England).

Stumbling Blocks

Trust in the Japanese is not necessarily strong in Americans, Australians, British, Filipinos, and others who once "hated Jap. guts..." The Japanese often feel wary too, particularly of trade unions. They often try to by-pass or undercut them. Japanese managers frequently think U.S. medical and other benefits are too high, so they try to reduce them. U.S. workers are not necessarily enchanted with "work-rule flexibility," nor with the speeding up of assembly lines. Board meetings in Japanese-run companies may merely be formal ceremonies to acknowledge and report what has already been decided elsewhere by the inside *ringi* method, rather than being the lively, open discussions and deliberations that Westerners expect. When minutes are read, everyone is expected to say politely, "No objections." Non-Japanese board members are rarely happy when this state of affairs occurs.

Japanese often establish new manufacturing plants a distance away from major cities. They look for areas where they can find space and a potential work force; rural land where costs are lower. Their impact on such areas can be tremendous. Chrysler and Mitsubishi, for example, have jointly established a new plant, Diamond Star Motor Corporation, in an area that was, until recently, open farmland. It is expected to provide nearly 3,000 jobs and to be producing 240,000 cars a year by 1990.[16] Such a project would disrupt *any* rural countryside, regardless of where it might be.

When you add the collisions of cultures and styles

16 *Chicago Tribune, 18 January 1989.*

which are inevitable (no matter what the country), adjustment is bound to be difficult. The Japanese do not always appear to be friendly and are often considered aloof. Many speak other languages only with difficulty. Often they have been trained to read and write, but find a spoken language difficult. If they swarm into a community in large numbers, they necessarily make a jarring impact on the local schools, the restaurants, the whole life of the community. There have to be adaptations on both sides. But those who have always lived in that community—and often their fathers before them—frequently expect the "adjustment" to be all one-sided—on the other person's side. That never works. There has to be give and take, a willingness to go part way, on both sides.

It is Hard for the Japanese too

Adjustment to any new culture is difficult for everyone. Many Japanese have extra problems:

They often have to leave their families at home, if their children are of the age to be preparing for arduous university entrance exams;

If they find themselves in small towns, urban Japanese often sorely miss the crowded, bustling, familiar environment they knew back in Tokyo or Yokohama;

Many must consciously "hold back" lest they get too westernized and thus be rejected when they go home;

Many Japanese suffer racial and ethnic indignities—large and small, intended or not intended—in many of our countries;

They are, of course, visibly different from most other people when they come to the West. This sense of "being different" is never easy for anyone in any country.

Trade frictions are growing stiffer too. Resentment of competition can make the overseas life of Japanese people very difficult. As they take a more and more commanding position in global economies, other peoples' noses start to

get out-of-joint. Wherever Japan is seen as an awesome, unstoppable economic power, resentments and fears grow.

These resentments take their toll on both sides. None of this is helped by the fact that Japanese managements often play very close to their own chests. They do not give easy access to researchers or journalists, for example, for serious research or analysis.

"They do not like to explain the implicit norms, rules and practices which shape their behaviors and objectives even to those who work with them," admits Mr. Shimada of Keio University. "They are reluctant to engage in frank and open dialogue with trade unionists and other outside interest groups. They are also reluctant to participate voluntarily in community activities." This lack of openness, as it seems to many Westerners, is another manifestation of Japan's age-old "homogeneous society." In that society, protected and regulated as it was by the government, open discussion among different people and groups was not necessary—nor was it encouraged. Silence was safer—as in China today.

The Japanese are currently in the process of learning, for the first time, how to work, live, and communicate with widely different types of people. This is new to them. What one needs to understand about all nations, as the world continues to shrink, is that "they" and "we" (whoever "we" are) operate on different wave lengths. As we have seen, the Japanese gather consensus slowly. Americans (and others), on the other hand, thrash things out, often in direct confrontations, heated arguments, and vigorous debates. The Japanese believe that successful decision-making does not generate heat and confrontation. They merely raise an eyebrow and can understand each other. Some of us pound the table to achieve the same result, or we raise our voices, or turn red with emotion.

Management styles clearly differ. Both sides need much patience and the real desire to understand each other. Given

the Japanese diligence and dedication, it will not take them long to adapt. They are doing so already, with incredible speed. Some of the rest of us may need to make more effort to catch up with them.

━━ ━━ ━━ ━━ ━━ ━━

Questions On Their Minds

Roberta Seret is a New York consultant in corporate relocation and cross-cultural relations. She has worked with many Japanese managers relocating to the United States. In Mobility Magazine she writes: "I find their questions fit into a pattern. To them, the American way of life is an enigma.*

Some frequently asked questions are:

How can I motivate my overseas staff to work harder?

What should I do when an employee is late?

Should an overseas manager in a Japanese company have the right to fire and hire subordinates?

What should I do when a Western woman invites me for lunch? Who is to pay? Can I order beer?

Can I expect my secretary to arrive at the office before me and leave after me?

What should I do when my secretary tells me she does not want to serve me tea?

How can I discuss business on the phone when my English is not good?

What are some differences between foreign and Japanese office procedures?**

* Roberta Seret, Mobility Magazine, Summer 1988.
** [Editor's note: The same is true of other countries as well.]

Section 3: The Business Environment

(A)   Relationships

How much each individual will need to adapt to Japanese customs will, of course, depend on his/her own circumstances and the situation of his firm. Those who are part of a small foreign minority in a primarily Japanese firm will naturally be expected to conform to a considerable extent. In a firm that has just a few Japanese people scattered through it, however, it is the Japanese who, in all probability, will do most of the adjusting. However, both sides will work better and feel more comfortable if they are at least *aware* of the other's major customs, preferences, and company relationships. In that way, they can decide what adjustments are necessary, and talk with each other about their perplexities. As a general rule of thumb, if the Japanese company's policy is made in Japan and a Japanese is superior to the Western manager in the overseas office, the decisions will clearly be Japanese.

Trust

It takes considerable time before things really start, when you first make contact with the Japanese people. Before they enter into any major business dealings they (like all Asians), need to establish a relationship of trust. There is no shortcut to this for them. They want to know what KIND of person you are before risking a business relationship of any importance. That is why there are often several meetings before anything of real substance is discussed; it explains the many lunches, dinners, and golf games in Japan's business life.

Westerners, with one eye on the clock, often feel restive with this. Our "quick action" way is to read a resume, or a proposal or report—ask a few questions, maybe make a

few phone calls, judge the situation rapidly, then be all set to go.

Japanese, on the other hand, customarily test people during the small talk of a first meeting. They like to meet more than once, preferably in different settings. You do not press for decision, for action, or for any kind of substantive comment at a first meeting. You will not get anywhere if you do, and you will, in fact, lose ground if they feel pressured.

Never be misled into thinking that their polite—often genuinely warm—hospitality means you are "in". It only means that they are feeling you out—finding your weak spots; gaining confidence in your strengths. While this process is going on, your cue is to be quietly at your best, i.e., no undue familiarity, no loud boasting or displays; no first names, no instant friendship. Be cool and quiet, respectful, attentive, unhurried—these are qualities to exhibit clearly in any first encounter with a Japanese businessman.

Equality

Much of the world is growing more sensitive these days to what they consider to be human rights—civil rights—minority rights—workers' rights—women's rights…

Not everyone agrees with what these—as yet mostly unachieved—rights should include. But there is throughout much of the world a widely observed desire for greater equality. That urge is being expressed in Korea … China … South Africa … Poland … Hungary, and many other countries of the world. Ideals and reality are often far apart, of course. Political stands dictate the suppression of some people by others. Everyone recognizes that not all individuals are equally capable. Standards of equality often seem to be impractical or, for various reasons, do not work out. However, the ideal of equal *opportunity* is a growing

concept throughout much of the world, however far off it may still appear to be for many millions of people.

The Japanese have always walked to a different drummer in this matter. In fact "equality" has always been contrary to their value system, as it has in many countries. The Japanese view has always been that everyone had his "proper" place. He or she was expected to be content with whatever role in life corresponded to that status level. A North American brand of individuality or efforts towards egalitarianism, are still alien to most of them. Equality does not fit readily with their values, although among younger Japanese—as in so many things—the picture is beginning to change.

Gaijin Responsibility

In most Japanese firms it is still rare for foreigners to be given real decision-making power. Thomas McCraw, a professor at Harvard Business School believes that Japan's success abroad (at least in the U.S.A.) may eventually hinge on how successfully its companies delegate real responsibility to local host-country managers and workers. Failure to do so, he thinks, is debilitating to morale.

The current perception that foreigners can rarely obtain positions of power understandably hurts Japanese firms when they go outside their own country. Competent and able managers are hesitant to work for a company if they feel that upward mobility is limited. This—like much else—may be in process of change. Japanese learn quickly and respond to situations as they perceive the need.

At present, however, "local" staff are very apt to be excluded in decision-making, and therefore by-passed throughout the preparatory *nemawashi* lobbying and persuasion processes[17], no matter how well their social skills with the Japanese may have been developed.

17 *See Section 5 Negotiating*

International Staffs

Basically all multinational companies, of all nations, are building their global corporations in terms of a world where money is power—not people. Capital is moved across national borders today in a matter of seconds, at the touch of a button. Questions as to the nationality of personnel when the corporation has become really global, grow less and less relevant. Any globe-circling firm becomes part of the total economic landscape—whether it be Siemens, IBM, British Petroleum, or Toyota. Personnel are becoming as global as are the world's products. This "globalizing" and "homogenizing" trend is obviously growing rapidly. **(See Part II, Section 1, "Globalization" Page 30)** Multinational companies are already a reality. The trend will inevitably accelerate in the years ahead as larger regional groupings, such as the European Community, Pacific Rim, Caribbean Basin, and others continue to develop worldwide. Students are studying more and more in each other's countries. World mobility is accelerating. National boundaries are ever more porous in terms of human interest, awareness, flexibility—and jobs. Color differences, tribal differences, the roles of women—are all under scrutiny and change. We are in a period when the world is clearly re-structuring its human relationships and when, through television and satellite, we all are able to watch what is happening across the world, whoever it may be or wherever we may be.

Seniority

Most western countries take people as they are, to a greater or lesser degree, regardless of their age. Not so the Japanese. Age to them is closely allied with wisdom. It has always been deeply respected. If you work for them you do well to show visible respect for age, whatever rank and position you may hold yourself. Small courte-

sies—like standing when older people enter, letting them through doors first, not arguing with older people or interrupting them, letting them speak first, are all important to the Japanese. The lack of such courtesies is noted immediately, though not a word will be said. Such small habits are easy to cultivate and are well worth the effort. Anyone who treats older Japanese as most of us were taught to treat our own grandparents, will gain big dividends.

Minorities

Having always been such a markedly homogeneous people, the Japanese are not accustomed to ethnic and racial mixtures. They do not find them easy and are not flexible about them. There is a definite feeling in some areas that they are "antiminority." Most other races and nationalities are at the bottom of the heap in Japan's own vertical concept of society. The more visibly different they are, the further down the line they will be, and therefore the less easily acceptable to the Japanese. As they move out to other countries, the Japanese are becoming aware of this failing in themselves. They are trying to cope with it. However, it does not come easily to them to mix with people of other races and lands. Their sense of superiority has always been strong, and it remains so in today's world.

In Japanese companies pay and respect are likely to be good for white males, but women or blacks (of any nationality) are likely to have a harder row to hoe.

As the Japanese have moved into other countries, a number of their managers have found themselves enmeshed in other peoples' customs and laws in these matters. In late 1988, for example, Japanese and Korean firms were involved in no less than six *major* anti-discrimination case law suits in California alone. Some were for racial and

others for sex discrimination. In most western countries people are protected by law from discrimination and unfairness. The Japanese, however, operate differently in their own country.

There is no legal defense in Japan against unfair treatment. When company questions regarding discrimination become legal issues in other countries, therefore, the Japanese find themselves treading on unfamiliar ground. According to Chalmers Johnson: "Some Japanese firms operating in this country (USA) have become so shy of being caught in the cross-fire of America's gender and ethnic struggles, that they will not promote any Americans, men or women, into their executive ranks, even when they know that by doing so they could improve their performance."[18] **(See also Section on the Law, Section 5: Negotiating: The Meeting of Business Minds, Page 250)**

Women

There is no code of chivalry towards women in the Japanese heritage. They were never taught to "help a damsel in distress." You do not find that theme running through their mythologies as you do in much western literature. There is no Sir Galahad, no Knight in Shining Armor.

Men go first, women follow. This is part of Buddhist teaching. Many Japanese are aware of the custom commonly known as "Ladies First" *(Lay-dee-zu Fah-su-to)*. They may attempt to follow it when in other countries, but it may make them giggle a bit—a sign of their discomfort. Western women should pay no attention to the giggle, just accept the courtesy gracefully.

"It isn't that men expect to go first", says Ruth Owades, head of a San Francisco mail order company, "but more

18 *Chalmers Johnson, "Japanese Style in America," California Management Review, Summer 1988.*

that in Japan women are expected to pull back." That is a subtle but very real difference.[19]

You will find that Japanese men do not generally help women carry suitcases, grocery bags and the like. Nor are women welcome at the evening after-work parties that are prevalent with the men. They are expected to wait at home, ready to welcome and pamper the husband at whatever time (and in whatever condition) he returns.

Japanese men working in Western countries also tend not to include women when they go out after work.

"They often go out to 'girlie places'," says one American woman who works in a Japanese firm. "They think nothing of leaving you alone in the hotel to have dinner by yourself." With glee she told of taking the wife of one of the Japanese executives out one evening. "I kept her out far later than the husband," she said. "He was astounded and perplexed that we could have a good time. We went to a horse show."

Of course when they are in a western country, Japanese men adapt to the customs of the land, in varying degrees. Their wives, however, often remain quite shy and retiring. This is their nature. Furthermore, most are not used to being included in the same easy sociable way that is usual for wives in many countries. In addition, many of them are not familiar with foreign languages.

Aiko Leeds is a Japanese woman who married an American and is active in Japanese-American groups. She says overseas Japanese families fall into two very unequal groups:

"I would say 90% want to socialize just with other Japanese", she said. "It is easier for them; they can relax; they have no language problems. The other 2% want to mingle with the people of the country where they are. But

19   *Paul Farhi ,"In Japan Women Are No. 2" , San Francisco Examiner and Chronicle, 7/4/87.*

they cannot, so they wind up joining the first group."[20]

She explains how the difficulties for the latter 2% relate to each country's culture. In America, for example, there are likely to be few women of her age around the neighborhood because they are all working. She cannot ask couples over to dinner—no matter what country she is in—because her husband comes home so late. He cannot make friends in the community (except on the golf course) because he generally works so late. So most Japanese wives outside Japan retreat into a Japanese expatriate community... if there is one. Otherwise they lead lonely lives behind closed doors.

In the suburb of Scarsdale, New York, a normally kindly, nice American lady said firmly, "We don't like having Japanese in our town. They are not friendly. Why, I took a cake I had baked over to our new next-door neighbors (who are Japanese) after they first arrived. They never even asked me inside the door."

What she did not realize was that two cultures were quietly colliding on that doorstep! It would not occur to the Japanese wife to invite her into her "poor, miserable house"—especially if it was not in apple-pie order, ready to "honor" such a visit. The Japanese are not casual, informal people. The women are not accustomed to the easy "visiting around", or even the more formal "calling", they encounter in other countries. Therefore they are apt to remain retiring, shy ... and very lonely ... in their large, unfamiliar-style homes. This can be read (mistakenly) by their neighbors as being "aloof" or "unfriendly." It is not.

What the American lady could better have done would have been to ask her new neighbor if she would like to drive around the town; whether she could help her find her way through the overpoweringly large local grocery store; did she need help in finding local service people? *etc., etc*. This

20 *Quoted by Brian O'Reilly in "Japan's Uneasy Japanese Managers", Fortune 4/25/88.*

would all have been on neutral, impersonal ground, until they came to know each other. *Then* they could have exchanged visits easily in their homes and become real friends.

Women in the Work Place

In Japan, home still comes first. The honorific word for "wife" means "inside the house", which of course fits well into that chauvinistic scene. Except for those many thousands who work in menial or assembly line jobs, women in Japan are not encouraged to work outside the home. This is true partly lest they take good jobs from men, and partly because it is firmly believed that juvenile delinquency stems in large part from children not having mothers at home. A poll taken in 1987 by a leading newspaper, *Asahi Shimbun*, said that 60% of the population believe women should stay home and raise children.[21]

However, younger and increasingly well-educated Japanese women are no longer willing to be so meek and mild. Their desire to be part of the working world, to take part in Japan's growth, to take a more important (and more interesting) role in society is becoming stronger all the time.

Dr. Shozaburo Kimura says: "In the next ten years the term *shufu* (housewife) will fall out of use. Even when they get married, Japanese women will not have the burden of housekeeping that their mothers had, nor will they devote as much time and effort to raising their children. More and more women will be taking part in creative cultural activities, as well as finding jobs suited to their talents."[22]

Even now many of them are no longer accepting this "inside-the-house" characterization. Nor are they remain-

21 *Paul Farhi, "In Japan Women Are No. 2", San Francisco Examiner and Chronicle, 7/4/87.*
22 *Look Japan p. 6 Japan Information Service.*

ing content with low-level, menial or part-time jobs. Increasing numbers of them are coming out of universities these days, highly trained and educated, with useful skills. Furthermore, as in other parts of the world, many are being pressed into outside jobs through economic necessity, and the need for a second income in the family. Many go into politics, which is considered less "important" than business in Japan. As a result, politicians in local prefectural jobs are very often women.

The increasing extent to which women are beginning to assert their own independence was made clear in Japan's 1989 elections. Women played a considerable role in the overthrow of the long-entrenched Liberal Democratic Party. They were vocal in their rebellion against the hated 3% consumption tax that was levied by that Party. They also let themselves be heard loud and clear in reaction to sex scandals in the political and business worlds. Takako Doi, a woman, is a strong leader in the Japanese Socialist Party and may one day be Prime Minister. She is having a tremendous impact on the women of Japan. They already hold 13% of the seats in the Upper House of their Parliament (the Diet), although as yet there are only 2% in the Lower House. As Japan's women see themselves in a new light, and as rapidly increasing numbers of them graduate from universities, both in Japan and across the world, their impact is being felt with greater and greater strength through all phases of Japanese life.

Nevertheless, many Japanese corporations are still reluctant to advance women beyond menial posts. The Labor Ministry proudly states that "the number of female managers has doubled in the past decade." However, when pressed, they have to admit that still only one woman in a hundred is as yet counted as "management." Furthermore, even that figure is open to question. One tally showed that "40% of women managers holding the title of 'Section Chief' had no staff to boss." Women in Japan

still earn slightly less than half of what men are paid (1989).

For foreigners it is lucky that the Japanese system is still not taking advantage of their women's ability, for, as a result, considerable numbers of excellently well-qualified Japanese women are currently going to work for foreign firms which *do* recognize their training and abilities, and which do value them. Especially in areas such as banking, publishing, and consumer products, women are rising rapidly to positions of real responsibility. Many who travel with their husbands on overseas assignments, are eagerly seeking courses, and looking for training in skills that will lead to—or enhance—jobs in the future when they return home.

Western executive women are generally accepted more or less readily as equals to males, even though this has so far been true for relatively few Japanese women. Nevertheless many Japanese men are not fully comfortable working for foreign women, either as equals or superiors. A woman lawyer, for example ,is an uncomfortable figure for them; nor are they comfortable, for example, if a woman client invites them to a restaurant and pays their bill. Similar situations keep arising from time to time, taking them off guard and making them uneasy.

Adjustment is often needed in terms of *non*-executive women, such as secretaries, computer operators, and the like. Japanese men are accustomed to asking their counterparts at home to do what western women often consider "unacceptable" tasks—such as helping the man on with his coat, brewing his tea, buying presents for his wife (or other people) and the like.

"It is not easy to work for the Japanese," admits a high-level woman executive who works with one of the Japanese hotel firms in New York. "You are always, *always* an outsider. Because the cultures are different, the *expectations* are constantly different—both yours and theirs. This

means you have to be on your guard and learn to move cautiously to be sure you stay on the right wave-length. This gets very tiring. But you must be continuously aware all the time that you are operating with a different set of starting points. You will find yourself forever making compromises, weighing alternatives, balancing judgements...You also work long hours. I am there every day until at least six; many of the Japanese are there much longer."

She described the very real "plus" factors as well. "Once you work with the Japanese," she says, "you become part of the family. You have a tremendous sense of job security. There is a personal feeling, a supportive feeling—although at the same time you are often 'not appreciated.' That can make you paranoid! If you do something they do not like, they simply ignore you. You might as well be invisible." Laughing, she added: "In our world we think bosses should not just quietly make you feel guilty and miserable. They should YELL at you and get it over with!"

"When top brass comes from Japan", she continued, "office relationships become very formal. Normally I am No. Two in the office, in charge of a major department. But when top Japanese management comes from Japan, I am expected to take a very back seat. Western women working for Japanese bosses have to be flexible, have some sense of humor, and not take themselves too seriously."

"We women have to learn to stand up for ourselves with the Japanese," she went on, "but in a pleasant way."

She gave two examples: "The very top brass of our whole company was coming from Japan to visit our various hotels," she said. "I was expected to rush on ahead and be at the door of each next hotel to greet him—bowing and so forth—in order to introduce him to that hotel's manager." I asked them: "Why? We are all here together. Why should I rush ahead? Anyway, I don't know how to bow properly." Her colleagues let the matter rest and all proceeded together.

Giving another incident she said: "My boss requires a good deal of attention. He wants me to buy presents for him to give (always expensive and always from the same prestigious department store). At first he ordered me to shop for him. I refused. I told him that he had to ask me pleadingly. If you say, 'Please can you help me?' I will do it, but otherwise I won't."

"Yesterday," she said, "he came to me almost on his knees. "Please", he said, "my wife is not here and I have lost a button from my coat. Can you help me?" "I have taught him not to *demand*."

Out of 240,000 Americans who went to Japan on business in 1987, a good many were, in fact, women. "When women are there for a legitimate business reason", says Elizabeth Andoh, Executive Director of the Association of Japan-American Societies, "there is not a problem."

"It all depends on the specifics of the situation", says Stacey Simon, "but usually Japanese men can deal with a woman in a given situation once they have established that she knows her business and is in a position of importance."

TV producer, Katherine Melchior (who works with Fuji-sankei Television) says, "I have found the Japanese will come to respect you as a woman and as a foreigner if you are worthy of respect. Clearly cultural differences will always exist, but they need not prevent firm and congenial relationships."[23]

In Chie Nakane's well-known sociological study "Japanese Society"[24] the author also points out that once a woman has attained status, gender ceases to be a factor. In other words, a woman who somehow manages to reach a management position may, in fact, faceless discrimination from the Japanese than numbers of women still do from

23 *Karen Croke, "Yen and the Art of Job Maintenance," Daily News, 5/19/86.*
24 *See "Recommended Reading" in Appendix.*

Americans, Frenchmen, British, or others in comparable positions.

Even strong and independent-minded foreign women can feel frozen out in negotiating deals, however. Japanese men are tough traders and negotiators. Women negotiators often find themselves dealing "with a double-edged Samurai sword."

(Note: Any woman going to Japan on business or working in a Japanese firm in her own country, should follow the Japanese lead in terms of inconspicuous clothing. Flashy jewelry and pants are both frowned on. Conservative suits of a quiet color are preferred. Skirts need to be reasonably long and reasonably full in order to be comfortable when sitting at low tables close to the floor, if one expects to be entertained in a Japanese restaurant.)

(B) Person to Person

Reserved, Conservative, and Undemonstrative

The Japanese are not in any way a demonstrative people. They are extremely low key and controlled. Their conservatism is clearly evident from their clothes, for example. In their own country they usually wear dark suits with quiet, inconspicuous ties.

Casual clothes, Reeboks®, or Nikes®, jeans, open-neck shirts in the office—or any place except the sporting world or the intimacy of one's own home—imply to the Japanese that the wearer is not "respectful" to the office, nor to those in it. Germans, Arabs, and many other people have the same reactions. That does not mean that they may not follow the example set in whatever overseas office they may find themselves. It does mean, however, that it will not come easily—at least at first—to most of them. Japanese will tend to be uncomfortable because they consider

"casualness" to be disrespectful. Furthermore, colorful, off-beat clothes call attention to the individual himself. This too bothers the Japanese.

Proper Form

For the Japanese there is a "right way" to do everything, whether this be greeting your boss; offering a drink; giving, accepting, or even wrapping a gift; presenting your business card...They learn all the various niceties of life "on the way up" from "older, wiser, more experienced mentors."

All of us stem from our own varied heritages. We must remember that in their relatively recent past, Japanese could be put to death merely for the disregard of manners. A Samurai could slash a man's head off with his sword if he was not providing adequate service, speed, or respect. For centuries everyone in Japan did what was prescribed "by rule" according to their position: the clothes they wore, how and where they walked, how they sat, how and where they ate, greetings that they had to use for people of different ranks gestures that were allowed ...*everything* was done "in proper form" according to one's class and one's position. It is no wonder that the Japanese are still extremely conscious of "form", no wonder that they continue to operate much of their lives according to clear "codes of conduct." People still are embarrassed if they find themselves in unpredictable positions. They are often uncomfortable with choices; they frequently do not like to be confronted with even simple ones like "tea or coffee?"—"with or without sugar?" They generally do not give guests choices. There is a "proper way." What choice does that leave? Although they like the variety they find in other countries, they are sometimes uncertain how to answer. What is the "right" answer? Choices are still often limited in Japan.

They still judge one another by the *manner* in which things are done. HOW a person acts is very important to them. Most Westerners are less concerned with the HOW, as long as what is necessary does in fact get done, and with reasonable dispatch. Few of us think that a man's way of operating reflects on his sincerity, his sense of respect, his training, his character... We do not think much about such things in the normal course of everyday life. But the Japanese do. Those of us who have grown up in other countries actually *do* most of the same things the Japanese do in the business world. We welcome people to our offices, for example; we take them to lunch, we express our condolences, or whatever it may be. But we do it in our own way, with our own form—or lack of it—and with very little thought about our "style." For most Americans, Australians, or Canadians, for example, this style is likely to be reasonably informal. The British are more formal; the French do things with *éclat*, the Italians with a genial, often noisy, warmth ... None of us are as conscious of our "manner of approach" as are the Japanese.

Day to Day Form in Japanese Offices

Most Americans—and many other Westerners as well— are advised to slow down the pace of their greetings with Japanese. Hurried greetings, such as "Hi there everybody," or "Nice to meet you. Now we are running a little late, let's just step into my office..." seem to nearly all Asians to be cold-aloof-rude. If rushed like this they are apt to start off the meeting outwardly polite, but inwardly miffed. It takes only a few minutes to be more warm and gracious, but it pays worthwhile dividends.

You will add immeasurably to your own impact if you have taken the time to learn a phase or two of greeting in Japanese, and if you use these greetings when you meet people for the first time. It clearly and quickly shows your

goodwill or, to use their word *Wa*. It does not hurt to learn "please", "thank you", "excuse me", and a few such phrases as well, and to use at least these few words as a friendly gesture. Seldom will you get more return for so little effort! **(See Part IV, Section 1: Courtesy Phrases p. 137)**

Introductions

In many lands it is quite usual for people to introduce themselves when groups come together. Sometimes, of course, in large groups this may be necessary, but when possible it is considered far more courteous for someone to make the introductions: lower to higher, giving the person's title and company, and, if possible, carefully the person's relationship to the situation.

"This is Mr. Hobson; he is Vice President in charge of engineering; he is here to discuss with us our water shortage problems in the new plant." In those few words the newcomer is identified; conversation can start easily on both sides. The Japanese particularly dislike being left in the air as to who people are. They need to know name, rank, and position as quickly as possible. They are uncomfortable and groping unless they know where everyone is on their vertical, hierarchical scale. This need for immediate identity makes the whole matter of business cards vital to them. Frequently they will present their *meishi* even before they speak. How can they know what language "case," what form, or what level of honorifics to use if they do not know the person's rank and status immediately?

Business Cards *(Meishi)*

It is hard for anyone, of course, to "catch" a person's name at first hearing, especially if it is in a different language.

Because Japanese is so different from western languages, this is particularly hard for us and for them. Business cards become all the more essential, therefore, in their eyes. To them a man's name is part of his dignity. Using it correctly is a sign of respect. They will always present their card to the ranking person first, proper side up, with the readable side facing him so he can look at it easily. In their book *Going International,* Lennie Copeland and Lewis Griggs describe cards as "…both a mini-resume and a ticket to the game of business. Gamesmanship is involved," they say, "in making the best use of the ticket."[25]

You "present" a card. You do not merely hand it over, toss it, or "deal" cards around a table, like a pack of playing cards. Furthermore, when given a card, you do not stuff it away in your pocket, or throw it casually in with your papers. You put it away carefully as if it had importance to you. In Japan, cards are frequently offered with both hands, with a little bow. Even outside Japan, time should be allowed for careful reading of the cards by both sides. It is important for everyone to take careful note of each name and title, and to connect them from the start with the proper face. In other words, one should practice really focusing on each person's information quickly and carefully, then using it correctly. Not to do so sends messages of "no respect" to a Japanese. Even though Japanese names may be difficult at first, it is important to make every effort to get them *and their pronunciation* right, from the start. If you do not know how to pronounce them, don't hesitate to ask. This will be taken as a sign of your real desire to show respect and to be correct. It may help to know that every syllable is pronounced, and each one is given the same weight or emphasis. Once you know that it soon becomes quite easy to read them.

25 *Lennie Copeland and Lewis Griggs. Going International. Random House, p. 161.*

Do not EVER let yourself run out of business cards. Since you may find yourself handing out 40 or 50 at a single meeting, you need to order *plenty*. Do not ever carry them in your back pocket. This is considered insulting. Cards should be in your coat or shirt pocket, easily and quickly accessible, preferably in a card case and treated respectfully. Copeland and Griggs say, "Not having a holder or case for cards is like making a business call with a shopping bag instead of a briefcase."[26] Think of a business card as the visible sign of a man's ego. Don't jot notes on the back of someone's card, for example, or even on your own. Such casual action indicates to them that you treat cards lightly.

Use of Names

In Japan the custom is for the family name to come first, as in our telephone books. However, in Western countries, and when they write in English, or other languages, they usually (but not always!) transpose them, to conform to our ways. Unless it had be transposed, Shimada Daisuke should be addressed as Mr. Shimada, for example. Or, if you are being especially respectful, you should call him Shimada-san. (Not Mr. Shimada-san. The *san* takes the place of "Mr.") Absolutely NEVER use *san* with your own name. That would be honoring yourself and would not go down well at all. Another suffix frequently encountered is *Kun*. This is sometimes added to the end of a name when being used by bosses to subordinates.

What we call "first" names (Daisuke in the example above) are virtually never used outside the home, except perhaps by young men to each other. So you can simplify life for yourself by concentrating on just learning what we consider the *surname* correctly at first. It is considered polite not to use even the last names of people who are

26 *Copeland & Griggs, Ibid.*

considerably older, or much higher rank, but to use their
title with *"san"*. In the workplace, for example, if talking
with top level people, the Japanese normally will use
Shacho-san (Mr. President), or *Bucho-san* (Mr.General
Manager), or whatever. This is similar to the German style:
Herr Doktor Engineer.

The Japanese do not expect foreigners to be "civilized"
in such matters—especially outside Japan—but they are
surprised and pleased if "outsiders " do understand and use
some of these customs. It is an easy way to please.

Appointments

Appointments, vital in the western world, are far less
important to the Japanese. They drop in and out on each
other, visiting amicably together among all the office noise
and activity. This is their way of keeping "in the swim".
They consider telephone calls to be impersonal and cold.
They prefer to gather information and to keep contacts
alive by many face to face meetings, often seemingly
unrelated to business, and certainly time-consuming. The
developing, keeping and building of "relationships" and
"connections" are the lifeblood of business to them; time
is of relatively little importance. Non-appointment drop-in
"visits" are a real part of their office pattern.

Using Interpreters

While the Japanese on overseas assignments—and many
of those at home—speak English (or the language used
in the country of assignment), it is still advisable for
you to provide an interpreter for any important meetings. It is proper to inform your Japanese colleagues in
advance that you are doing this, so they can feel free
to do the same. There are constant nuances and unfamiliar

connotations that may be important but can easily pass over anyone's head when dealing in an unfamiliar language.

When you choose your interpreter make sure that he (or she) is familiar with both cultures and the main cultural differences. You need someone who can deliver your message clearly in readily understandable and acceptable terms, *i.e.*, in the correct terminology, using the right form of address, the right names, making no faux pas or serious errors. Your interpreter should be able to help you understand what is NOT being said, as well as the spoken words. You may need help in interpreting silences, pauses, and hesitations—which among the Japanese are often pregnant with meaning. It is also helpful if there is someone there who can catch (and report back to you) the little asides and quiet comments that may be exchanged in Japanese.

If you get used to an interpreter, and he or she to you, they can be extremely helpful in steering you through many rocks and shoals of understanding. Be sure to take *ample time* before the meeting for a briefing so that he (she) will know the general substance of the discussions, the names and if possible "ranks" of participants, and the major points that are of particular importance to you. Give them any special vocabulary that may be used, if you can. Try to be well supplied with visual material, charts and the like, and see that the interpreter has enough time before the meeting so that he can understand them in advance. If important large numbers are to be involved, write them out for him. The more you can help ahead of time, the more he (or she) will be able to help you.

Don't take it for granted that you can pick up just anyone who speaks both languages to fill an interpreter's shoes. It is a highly specialized job, and difficult to do well. It is not easy to interpret other people precisely, even in one's own

language! Nor is it easy to be well versed in both sets of idioms or technicalities.

Of course, even with all the preparation in the world, you will still need to remember to speak slowly, quietly, and with ample pauses for the interpreter to use for both understanding—and then translating—your thoughts. *Never* interrupt when the interpreter is listening. Don't expect him to keep long paragraphs in his head. Sometimes you give a short statement (or request) and the interpreter may take what seems to you an abnormally long time to translate. Don't get agitated. He (or she) may be using the appropriate (often lengthy) forms of respect, or may be explaining some cultural differences. Conversely, if your opposite number makes a long speech and the interpreter gives you only a quick two or three sentences in translation, do not think you are being short-changed. He may have been able to condense a flowery presentation into its substance for you.

If the meeting is to be a long one, it pays to have two interpreters. If you watch at the United Nations, for example, you will see that interpreters are shifted at frequent intervals. It is an extremely intense, demanding job. If they tire, you are the one who will lose out, as their intensity and keen attention are vital to you.

One's tendency is to watch one's own interpreter as he or she talks. It is wise, however, to watch the faces of your opposite numbers instead. As they listen their faces quite often tell you more about their reactions than they may care to put into words ... especially if they are going to say "no", or if you are giving them an ultimatum, or are at some other critical point. You may catch revealing looks passing from one to another, for example, or detect a nervous tapping of a pencil. Japanese use facial expressions and "body language" to give signals to one another, much as a catcher communicates with the batter in a baseball game. You will not be able to understand those signals for

the most part, but you can watch for them and train yourself to be alert as to what seems to be triggering that kind of activity.

In short, while the interpretation is going on, have your antennae out to observe all you can about the reactions. You may not get a great deal of response verbally, so you need to use every clue you can pick up as you go.

Reprimanding

If it becomes necessary to reprimand a Japanese, NEVER do it in public. You will embarrass him deeply and are likely to find it difficult—if not impossible— to regain your relationship with him later. You will also lose face drastically with all who overhear the conversation and will find it hard to regain their respect as well. Humiliation is something the Japanese can hardly tolerate, for themselves or for their colleagues. Many have committed suicide rather than face a major humiliation. Failure to understand the extreme sensitivity of their feeling in this regard can lead to grave results. One should absolutely *never* embarrass or humiliate a Japanese in public—for any reason.

It takes a great deal of tact to cope with a disciplinary situation across cultural borders. Again, the best thing to do is to find a go-between if you can. If you cannot, then stress the positive to the greatest extent possible, rather than either tearing a person down or hitting out hard, and laying down the law. Remember that you must save the person's face and maintain the harmonies to the fullest possible extent, even as you sort out the problem and get your point across.

The best advice is to talk around the subject as diplomatically as you can, without personal, frontal accusation if possible, no matter how angry you are. Wait until you have calmed down enough to be able to do this. Then dis-

cuss the *issue* rather than the man's behavior. If it has been a serious offense, ask him to think it over and set a time when he is to come back and talk it over with you again. In most cases this embarrassment will be penalty enough.[27]

Office Space—Japanese Style

If you are working in a Japanese-style office, you are likely to find the physical arrangements quite different from those with which you have previously been familiar.

Similarly, if you have Japanese coming to work in your western-style office, they will probably find your set-up to be psychologically different from those they have been accustomed to. It may be a hard part of their adjustment at first. We need to understand that possibility, and do what we can to ease it. They are unlikely to mention it.

In accordance with their preference for group living and working (**see Page 101**) they do not like—and at home generally do not have—individual offices. Instead you will find a large open room—chaotic in the eyes of people accustomed to privacy. In it are desks, desks, desks; computer terminals; files; cabinets. The noise is almost palpable: phones ringing, loud talk, much laughter, the clatter of machines. Office space is exceedingly expensive in Japan and there is nowhere near enough of it to go around, so every square foot is used to the limit.

Although they work long hours, the Japanese actually spend much regular office time in socializing, wandering among the desks, gathering at the water cooler, chatting together, drinking tea...This is the way they like to work. Pressures are different. Many say they feel isolated and lonely in the individual offices they find in the West. Those who know the system know by the position of the desks

27 Edward T. Hall and Mildred Reed Hall. *Hidden Differences*, pp. 131-132.

where power lies. Desks are arranged in hierarchical order. The one farthest from the door is the place of honor; the Section Chief is often at the head of a long table. This general pattern is apt to be carried out—wholly or in modified form—in whatever country a Japanese style office is established.

This layout reflects the structure and social organization of their companies just as clearly as do the West's separate offices—of different sizes, "comer" locations, office "pools", varied styles of compartmentalization—or open and closed doors in Britain, Canada, U.S.A., or other countries.

Clearly this "open plan", in which Japanese staffs work in close proximity, suits their process of group consensus. It reflects their preference for teamwork, based on collective action. It is conducive to face-to-face communication, which they greatly prefer to the written word. It also provides subtle peer pressure to produce, in that land which, though careful of the harmonies, is highly and constantly competitive. Furthermore, managers have immediate access to one another. The fine gradations of position fit their vertical societal concept of ranks. They are clear and visible.

"The Japanese office operates as if it were a factory to produce decisions," says one Japanese manager.

Conversational Approaches

You are always safe in saying nice things about Japan—its culture, its art, its people, its food... Like all of us, the Japanese like to be liked!

Other good topics are golf, baseball (which they think is *their* game), travel, photography (which they love). What they do NOT like is conversation about personal matters. Don't ask about their families in any detail. Naturally they also prefer to avoid subjects like World War

II, trade frictions, politics, business scandals (theirs or ours), minorities, or other subjects that are likely to lead to arguments or heated feelings. They also have little interest in religion.

One needs to practice talking on general, non-controversial subjects, such as educational systems, the global greenhouse effect, music, wildlife or similar impersonal topics, at least as starters, until you know each other well.

The Japanese do not understand sarcasm well at all. It is best not to use it for, if taken seriously, it can be hurtful. As we have said, hurt feelings are particularly destructive to relationships among people who consider "harmony" to be a vital element in business and in life.

If you must at any time disagree, try to do it quietly, on an intellectual, not a personal level. Avoid arguing. Always remember: they do not like a "No". It is considered extremely impolite. They are themselves skillful in making their meaning clear without using a negative and without a direction confrontation. If they cannot do that, they are likely to remain silent, giving no answer at all, either in person, on the phone, or by mail.

Tea

Tea is a way of life—not just a beverage—to the Japanese. It is an integral part of their hospitality and appears virtually without fail whenever you go into a Japanese office. It is easy for Westerners to provide tea also—instead of (or as well as) coffee—when Japanese guests come to our offices. This is taken as a gracious courtesy which is much appreciated. (Use light teas. They do not like the dark Indian teas.)

Japanese Holidays

Although it is not likely that Japanese will honor their own holidays publicly when they are in other countries, an easy

way to show your interest in their country and your respect for them, is to be aware of their "special" days and to make some mention or recognition of them as the dates roll around.[It may also be useful to know when they occur so that you can avoid the major ones when going on business trips to Japan.]

It is interesting to note *what* they celebrate, for it gives a clue to their national character. With the exception of the Emperor's birthday, for example, not one of their thirteen national holidays honors an individual ... no war heroes, founding fathers, poets, political leaders... Nor is a single one of their holidays a date of religious significance (as is so often the case in other countries). Their thirteen holidays are:

January 1st
New Year's Day.

January 15th
Coming-of-Age Day. Ceremonies are held in all towns, villages, and cities to honor and to congraduate all those who are reaching their majority within the new year.

February 11th
National Foundation Day. This is the day when patriotic feelings are expressed—similar to the 4th of July in the USA, or Bastille Day in France. [It is interesting to note that the date of their founding is considered to be 660 B.C.]

March 20th or 21st
Vernal Equinox Day. (Date varies depending on the spring equinox.) This is the day set aside to praise and honor Nature, to show love to all living things. This has been a Buddhist festival day since early times.

April 29th

Green Day. Was the former Emperor Hirohito's birthday, but is still honored as a national holiday.

May 3rd

Constitution Memorial Day. The new Constitution was signed on this date in 1947. The holiday is meant to reaffirm hope in the growth of the nation.

May 5th

Children's Day. Combines with Mother's Day, and is often used as a celebratory day for boys.

September 15th

Respect-for-the-Aged Day. This is a day of entertainment, gifts, and ceremonies for the aged.

September 23rd or 24th

Autumn Equinox Day. On this day ancestors are honored and the dead remembered. It is another traditional Buddhist festival day.

October 10th

Health and Sports Day. This holiday commemorates the 1964 Tokyo Olympics, which opened on October 10th. It is a big sports day, aimed to "foster sound minds and bodies."

November 3rd

Culture Day. The Japanese Constitution was promulgated on November 3rd, 1946. The day is meant to stress love of freedom, equality, and culture.

November 23rd

Labor Thanksgiving Day. This day is a celebration of labor and production. The Emperor offers newly-harvested rice to the Gods.

December 23rd

Emperor's Birthday.

(C) Gift Giving and Favors—The Lubrications of Life: Western and Japanese Attitudes towards Gifts

Our western concept of "graft" and "bribes" reflects *our* culture. It does not in any way equip us to understand the uniquely Japanese gift customs. These have been pervasive in their culture for centuries. If we write off as "graft" or a "bid for favors" the elaborate system of entertaining and gift-giving expected of Japanese businessmen or office-holders, we over-simplify; we distort something that is ancient and complex in their society. It is not an area in which outsiders should be at all judgmental. It is too complicated for us to ever really understand, and it dates back for centuries.

There will always be much ritual about both official and personal giving when it is done in Japanese style. Gifts can be given as signs of appreciation and respect. They can be signs of power—especially in the political arena; and, since one is expected to return "in kind", gifts can also be used to put a person in another's debt.

In addition, as in all countries, gifts can come from the heart and be a sign of real affection.

When asked why the Japanese give so many gifts, the answer seems to be: "Japanese people are ceremonious. Living in tight quarters they must always be polite to each other. It is part of their harmonious group living, part of their close attention to rank and status."

Obligation

Mr. de Menthe, writing in *Japanese Manners and Ethics in Business*[28] says:

28 *Boye de Menthe, Japanese Manners and Ethics in Business. Phoenix Books, Arizona, 1981.*

"Given the Japanese emphasis on interpersonal relationships, it is not surprising that they are very sensitive to *obligation*. Their concept of obligation is much more complicated than our western version. Three types of obligation *influence* their behavior:

1) *On*—obligations that are passively incurred (son to parent, for example);
2) *Gimu*—These are on-going debts and obligations;
3) *Giri*—obligations that must be repaid in equal value.

The penalty for failing to meet these obligations is loss of face. Mr. de Menthe goes on to say:

"Emotion is the glue that binds the Japanese system together. If you want to get along with, influence, or lead a Japanese employee, associate, or client, see to his emotional needs..." In "Japanese Bearing Gifts" Shintaro Ryu writes:[29] "One remarkable fact is that, while Japanese are so nervously concerned with giving gifts, they have not the slightest inclination to consider whether there is anything wrong with the habit. At least half of the gifts given in Japan are a goodwill forced on the recipients," he says. "Part of their purpose is to create a vague sense of *giri* (Duty), consequently a consciousness of obligation on their part." He goes on to say:

"Gifts often serve as a subtle reminder of interdependence. They are sometimes unspoken 'contracts' to treat each other well, by engaging in what has been referred to as 'facework'."

Personal Giving

It is important not to confuse *personal* giving in Japan with "*giri*-based" giving. Like personal giving all over the

29 *Shintaro Ryu, "Japanese Bearing Gifts". Psychiatry, February 18, 1955.*

world, it is generally based on affection, rather than on obligation. Increasing individualism in Japan has made personal giving more prevalent of late than in the past. Most business giving, however, is still of the *giri* type. So, too, is entertaining. They expect to spend large sums of money in entertaining, especially in entertaining foreign businessmen. Even a clerk in a store may have an expense account for entertaining. The government encourages social spending as well. A certain percentage of company capital spent on social expenses is free each year; businesses can further deduct 50% of any business "lubrication" expense that exceeds the limit.[30]

From One to Another

In her excellent book *International Business Gift Giving Customs: A Guide for American Executives*, Dr. Kathleen Reardon suggests: "Do not 'out-gift' the Japanese. Gift-giving is more their custom than ours. Allow them to derive satisfaction from their giving and avoid obligating them by giving a more expensive gift than theirs."*

She also suggests that gifts be given when the recipient is alone unless there are gifts for everyone. Otherwise there would be great embarrassment on the part of everybody present.

Pointers for the Outsider

The Japanese give their gifts at the time, and in the way, that is "proper." Most of their ritual is well beyond the understanding of a *gaijin*. However, there are some pointers that may be useful to know:

* (Note: This of course does not mean "don't give anything." Dr. Reardon is only talking about not *outdoing* the Japanese in the gifts you choose.)

30 *"The High Cost of Lubrication"*, Japan Times, 1/19/67.

1) *Oseibo* is a big gift-giving time for the Japanese, to mark the end of the year. It more or less coincides with our Christmas, since presents can be given any time in December (though no later than December 31). Safe presents to give at that time are elegantly wrapped food packages, wine, or liquor. This is the time when businesses usually send gifts to people with whom they have business contacts. Presents given to you may be given in the form of fabulous meals, paying your taxi fare, providing some service (like a limo with a driver for a trip ...). In today's Japan, *Oseibo* gifts to families are often given as services. Since it is traditional to clean your house at this time (like our "spring cleaning" tradition) some department stores offer a year-end house-cleaning service, for example. Or one can give so-many miles of prepaid taxi service ... or other services that seem appropriate.

2) *Chugen* (mid-July) is another time when gifts and bonuses are given. In an article on gift-giving, the *Japan News* described *Chugen* gifts as "fraught with various significances; some are outright bribes, some are belated payments, some are acts of charity, while the vast majority are pure social amenities as between friends and lovers."

3) *Gifts for "Top Brass"*

A considerable amount of money is spent on gifts given to "Superiors" and much time and discussion go into the suitability of official business gifts. If such a gift does not have a fairly high value, it can be taken as an insincere gesture. A rule of thumb given by an American business-man was: "spend two or three times what you think is right". Good scotch and cognac are almost universally appreciated. In general the Japanese do not like bourbon (hardly anyone does outside the USA). Scotch is preferred, with Johnny Walker Black®, Chivas Regal®, and Haig®, not surprisingly, leading a list of preferences! If you are going to Japan, be sure to get all you are allowed from the duty-free shops in the airport, to use for special gifts. The

Japanese like to combine business with pleasure. In long drawn-out deals, this can become very expensive.

4) *Office Gifts*

If you go off on a business trip when you work in a Japanese environment, you may want to bring back small gifts for all your working colleagues. The Japanese nearly always do this for their office mates as well as for their families. The size of such a gift is not as important as the fact that you thought of them while you were away. It is easier—and socially wise—to select a "shareable" gift, such as cookies, a fancy cake, candies, or the like, so that no one recipient is singled out, and no one is forgotten.

5) *Family Gifts*

One takes a gift if visiting a home. Flowers are good in that case, though it is a good idea to check with someone over the customs in that regard. Certain kinds of flowers, and certain colors have specific meanings. You may—or may not—mean to give those messages.

A wedding invitation requires a gift, which is not surprising. However, so, too, do funerals in Japan. Money is the appropriate gift for both weddings and funerals. Ask Japanese friends how much it should be, if you should find yourself going to either event. Money must, of course, be given in an envelope—it can even be gift-wrapped.

6) *Presents MUST be gift wrapped.*

The wrapping is in itself important and should be elegant. This is another indication of "respect." Get the store to do it for you if possible. The importance of the gift *and of its wrapping* are related in their eyes; the more elegant, the greater the respect.

7) *Bow Now—Open Later*

Japanese do not customarily open a gift in the presence of the donor for a number of reasons—none of which is lack of appreciation, though Westerners often read it as such. They do not open them:

a) To show that it is the thought not the gift that counts;

b) To save the donor's "face" if the gift is not considered good enough, or if the gift is perplexing to the recipient;

c) If they are receiving several gifts, this avoids the "embarrassment" of comparisons;

d) There might be duplicates—another possibility for embarrassment for the donor.

8) *What You Do*

If they give *you* a gift, it is considered polite to refuse it once or twice before accepting it. This avoids your looking too eager for it.

When you have received a gift, be SURE to mention it again the next time you see the donor, even though you will already have thanked him (her) profusely, and/or written a note of thanks.

9) *If You Are a Visiting Businessman*

If you have been visiting a Japanese office for some period of time, it is an appropriate custom to give token gifts on your departure to any staff members (secretaries, junior clerks, *etc.*), who have been especially helpful to you. This should, however, be done privately as it will mean "singling them out" from the group. That would be embarrassing to them if done in public.

10) *Corporate Parties*

When Japanese businessmen give parties for their associates or clients, they often provide a small gift for each guest—anything from an attractive hand towel to a fairly expensive piece of lacquer, or something equivalent. If you plan to do the same at any time, it is advisable to choose the gift—even a small one—from a "name" store. If there is a first class Japanese store in your city (and these now exist in most major cities of the world) that might be a good source, particularly as they will also wrap the gifts in

magnificent style. A nicely printed small book of poems, or of photographs, or small art works, are all examples of acceptable gifts for such an occasion.

Favors

If you do a favor for a Japanese—get him his plane tickets, give him a lift, take a parcel to the post office for him—you can count on the fact that he will go out of his way to do a kindness for you shortly thereafter. This is called *on* (pronounced "own"). They keep careful track of their "kindness credits and debits." When working closely with them, one should notice and bear their favors in mind too, reciprocating also in some way whenever you can.

Think of this reciprocity as another part of *wa*, the harmony of life. It adds to the *Gemütlichkeit* or goodwill, or warmth of relationships. It is similar to our feeling that "we should invite the so-and-so's to our house because we have been invited several times to theirs." This feeling of give-and-take exists in all cultures, but it manifests itself in different ways, carrying different degrees of importance in various countries. With the Japanese, it is an extremely important part of life.

●●●●●●●●●●●●●●

The whole area of gifts and favors is a bit tricky for Westerners. It is best to get advice from a Japanese friend or colleague each time a perplexing occasion arises. They will be pleased that you care and want to know their customs.

In setting forth some of these details, their gift-giving may sound as if it is all "weighed" or calculating. This is by no means the case. The Japanese are a generous, kind people. They enjoy giving. It is just that they have customs that are sometimes different from ours as to *how* and *when* gifts are given, or what overtones there may be.

Some Ideas for Gifts the Japanese Like

Western belt buckles;

T-shirts (especially those with University logos. *Not ones with commercial slogans, or those in bad taste);*

Art or jewelry (or other items) that are special to your own country;

Tablemats, books, or handsome calendars of scenes or landmarks from your country;

Really nice desk accessories;

Intriguing, good, and well-made items from hardware or stationery stores. Look for something ingenious and useful—a novelty, but not a useless one. Look to be sure they were not made in Japan! Items related to golf or photography (if appropriate to the recipient);

Well-bound, well-printed books, especially nicely illustrated ones.

Warnings

Avoid giving four of anything. (Their word for "four" sounds like "death." Remember they have a superstitious streak.)

Never give personal items like ties, or lingerie, or shirts (except for T-shirts which they seem to like).

Do Remember

Have your gifts *wrapped handsomely.* This is very important to them.

(D) Drinking and Dining with the Japanese

After Work Drinking

In Japan, drinking plays a big part in establishing relationships. The Japanese do not talk business when they go out drinking. That is a time for getting to know each other, letting down the hair, and finally relaxing. What is said in an after-work drinking party is absolutely never to be brought back to the office and quoted. This is an unwritten law. They often get quite drunk (though it never shows the next day). The after-work drink session is for them a time to draw breath in their pressured lives, a way to let off steam, ease stress, and develop camaraderie. Our western pattern of rushing home directly after the office closes down leaves the Japanese a bit adrift. They find it hard to get to know their office colleagues when they do not drink together. Those who employ many Japanese in western offices should try to create a substitute outlet, providing some way for the "guest workers" to unwind with their colleagues somehow, if, as in much of the western commuting world, after-work gatherings are impractical.

If you are drinking in a Japanese bar or restaurant you will almost surely be offered *sake*. This is made from rice, and can be a very deceiving drink. You drink it—usually warm—from tiny cups. It slips down as if it were nothing. But it is, in fact, 16% alcohol. It hits the blood stream very fast.

There are three grades:

> *tokkyu-shu*—Best grade
> *ikkyu-shu*—Middle grade
> *nikyu-shu* —Ordinary grade

Japanese beer is *very* good. It often saves the day for foreigners.

The Japanese assume that everyone drinks *sake*. That and tea are the only beverages served at a traditional Japa-

nese meal. If, for reasons of health, religion, or preference, you do not want to drink it, do not fuss over it. Let your cup be filled and then just leave it. Don't ask for water or juice, or some other substitute. If a toast is drunk, just lift your cup to your lips. No one will care if you don't drink. The gesture will suffice.

Shochu is less well-known than *sake*, but also potent. It can be made from rice or from sweet potatoes, or from *soba* (buckwheat). *Shochu* is growing in popularity.

If Japanese women are present, it is all right to offer them a drink. They drink as western women do.

When you go out as guests of Japanese colleagues, there is a small nicety that is pleasant. It is their custom that no one should pour for himself. So you lift your cup while your neighbor pours for you, then take a sip before setting it down. Then you pour for him in like manner. It is a gracious touch, easy to conform to.

To avoid drinking more than you want throughout an evening, either keep your cup full, or turn it over when it is empty. It is quite all right not to drink if you do not want to. Just cover the glass with your hand and say "No more, thanks," as you would with anyone else.

"Going Dutch"

If this is something you and your friends normally do, you will have to teach anyone newly arrived from Japan. They are not used to it. In Japan, whoever suggests that you go out together picks up the full tab. Later, at other times, each person is expected to reciprocate, inviting this night's host to dinner or to drinks in return.

Chopsticks

Japanese chopsticks are lighter and more pointed than those of China. You will often be given wooden ones

wrapped in paper, in restaurants. If so, rub the sticks together a bit after you pull them apart, to be sure there are no splinters.

Many people feel apprehensive about using chopsticks, but it is courteous to at least TRY to eat with them, especially if the Japanese have invited you. They will enjoy showing you how to use them. Generally speaking, the food will be in small pieces and you will not find it difficult, once you get the basic idea. After all, Japanese children can handle them by the time they are three or four years old!

The Japanese will wince with discomfort if you flagrantly violate their normal use of chopsticks, however.

In a short article, "Table Manners on Tatami", Tomiko Shirakigawa gives the following pointers on what NOT to do with chopsticks:

1) Don't suck on them, or pull them through your closed lips.
2) Don't grasp them so they are held in your fist.
3) Don't use them to push food into your mouth·as if you were force feeding yourself!
4) Don't pick your teeth with them.
5) Don't poke around the food with them, looking for choice morsels at the bottom of the pot. That implies that you think the food on top is not good.
6) Never point or gesticulate with them.
7) Don't bite or lick off any choice morsels that may have stuck to them.
8) Don't lie your chopsticks across the top of your bowl. Although the Japanese do this at home, it is not considered "company" manners.
9) Don't break your chopsticks at the end of the meal. It looks as if you have a low opinion as to the cleanliness of your host or the restaurant.
10) Don't expect spoons. You lift bowls—with both hands—and drink from them, although the Japa-

nese also often use western implements when eating western food.

11) Meals are to be enjoyed with the eyes, as well as the taste. Do comment on the *look* of the dishes as well as the flavor.

12) Women should avoid short dresses or skirts if having a *zashiki* meal or, if caught in that predicament, should try to cover their legs discreetly with a scarf or jacket.

Mealtime Conversations

In America and some other countries, meal times are used to discuss business—often in considerable detail. This is not what the Japanese like. They will not be comfortable with it, though they will smile politely and take part if pressed.

In their view, however, meal times offer the opportunity for people to relate to one another, to enjoy one another, to learn about each other's tastes, opinions and characters; perhaps to learn background information that may affect their business, such as relevant political developments, for example. But they consider it out of place to carry on *specific* discussions of business details. These, they believe, belong in the office.

What is Polite in Japanese Terms

...You will be given a hot or cold towel (depending on the season) when you sit down at the table. Use it only for your hands and mouth. Don't go all over your forehead or neck as—especially in summer—some people do, to the great distaste of the Japanese. These towels are called *oshibori*.

...Don't start to eat until the host invites you to begin. Furthermore, if on some occasion, *YOU* are the host, do not

forget to invite your senior or most honored guest to start. (This should be when all the dishes have been put on the table.) Although the normal custom is for guests to start and host to follow, the Japanese may reverse this when they have invited foreigners so they can provide a guide to the action. If, as is increasingly likely to be the case outside Japan, the host is non-Japanese, he is expected to know the protocol.

...If you have been invited out, never order before your host. Then you can follow his lead, so the dishes you order conform to his choice. If you should happen to order food that is too simple for the occasion, your host will be made to feel uncomfortable.

...Don't finish one dish at a time. You are supposed to intersperse soup with bites of the main dishes. It is considered rude to clean up one or other bowl and then move on to the next.

...Nearly all their meals include clear soup, often drunk from lacquered wooden bowls, which you hold in both hands.

...The food is generally cool rather than hot. Custom has it that you eat what has been served warm first; these items are tastiest when warm.

...Their beer (excellent) is chilled.

...They do not go in for fancy desserts, except fruit (often oranges) at the end of the meal.

...The timing of a meal is important. The chef normally sends in dishes according to the pace of the diners, but the diners are supposed to keep a comfortable rhythm too. This means that when something is served, you should eat it, not let it languish while you are engrossed in conversation or in telling a long story!

...Whether you like it or not, be sure to eat what the host has ordered, and remark on how good it is. *Never ask the ingredients.* This is considered impolite.

...If you are served noodles, hold the bowl under your

chin and suck them up. Don't worry about the sound or the dribbles!

...If you have any food restrictions, be sure to tell your hosts about them in advance. Otherwise they will feel embarrassed if you cannot eat something they have ordered for you.

At the end of the meal, it is courteous to say *Gochisosama* to your host. If you say it to the waiter, he will go get your bill. It means: "That was an honorable meal."

Japanese greatly enjoy the sociability and the relaxation of a good meal, as well as the food. They will hope that you do, too. It is good to express this in two or three ways if you can—and to mention it again next time you see your host.

No-No's

It is absolutely repulsive to the Japanese to have anyone blow his nose in a restaurant or at the dining table. If you need to do it, excuse yourself and go to the rest room. Three other "no-no's":

1) Do not say that you are hungry;
2) Do not take large helpings;
3) Do not eat quickly.

Savor both the food and the company. It is distressing to the Japanese to have people rush through a meal.

Foods You May Encounter

As Japanese restaurants have spread through the major cities of the world—and even into the world's smaller towns as well—Japanese menus and names of foods are becoming more widely familiar.

However, it is still not always easy to know what you are being offered if you dine out with Japanese colleagues. A guide to some of the more common terms, types, and uses of food may, therefore, be helpful.

General Information

Fish is, of course, widely used in that island nation. Some of it is cooked, much of it is eaten raw. Many people do not like the idea of eating raw fish. However, those same people are often happy with eating raw oysters and clams, or beef "tartar" (*i.e.*, raw beef). Eating is much a matter of custom and habit.

In recent years, as the economy has improved,the Japanese have been eating less rice and more poultry and meat. Both chicken and pork are plentiful and relatively inexpensive. Beef, however, is VERY expensive there—$10 per pound and up—often way up, since it must all be imported. Because of the size of their country they cannot afford either the space or the feed necessary to support a cattle industry.

You will find that foods are often served in a single, communal dish from which everyone shares,especially in family groups.

Categories of Foods

Some kinds of food are frequently prepared at the table (as the Swiss do their fondues). Among these are:

Sukiyaki. This is a skillet dish of sliced meat and vegetables in a sweetened soy sauce. It is a kind of stew and is often served (using beef) for special occasions, including the visit of a guest.

Nabemono. This word means food boiled in deep dishes. Often fish, meat or poultry are boiled with Chinese cabbage, radishes, carrots, or other vegetables which have been sliced very thinly.

Yakitori. Meat (often chicken or chicken livers) are grilled on skewers, with a barbeque sauce.

Shabu-shabu. Beef, chicken, vegetables cooked in boiling water (often at the table).

Tempura. A combination of vegetables and fish, deep fried in a flour batter. (This is generally *not* done at the table.)

Individual Dishes:

Sashimi. Thinly sliced strips of raw fish, usually served with horseradish *(wasabi)* and shredded white radish *(daikon)*.

Sushi. Small blocks of rice cooked with rice vinegar, salt, sugar and *sake*. Topped with thinly sliced strips of raw or cooked fish. It is usually served with *wasabi w*hich is placed between the rice and fish, and pickled ginger *(gari)* which is served on the side.

The way to eat *sushi* is to pick it up with one's fingers or with chopsticks and turn it over to dip the fish side in the soy sauce. Don't try to dip the rice in the sauce. It will all fall apart! In the case of *sashimi*, chopsticks are always used.

It is common for the Japanese to eat sea urchins, kelp, squid, eels, prawns—also seaweed, dried and pressed into flat sheets.

Oden. Stewed vegetables and *tofu*.

Natto. Best advice is to stay away from it! It is sticky and has a bitter taste. It is made of fermented beans. When in a teasing mood, Japanese love to watch Westerners try it!

Katsudon. Pork cutlet with rice.

Ramen. Wheat flour noodles—popular in broth and with other vegetables.

Common Fruits

Mikan—mandarin oranges
Nashi—an apple/pear fruit
Kaki—persimmons

Foods from Other Countries

Tofu. This is a bean curd from China.
Curry and rice. From India.

"Fast" Foods. Young Japanese like pizza, hamburgers, spaghetti, fried chicken, and most other "fast" foods. They also like drive-in restaurants.

Because their diet has improved so much, the Japanese have been growing taller and heavier over the past decades. A study showed that in the twenty-five years between 1960 and 1986, for example, average twenty-year olds added three inches to their height. However, in the past decade, research shows a rise in colon cancer, a disease virtually unknown in Japan before the westernized diet. Perhaps "improvement" is premature.

Section 4:
Personnel Practices—In Japanese Terms

Graduated by Age

Fundamental changes are going on in the Japanese corporate world in terms of their management of personnel.

Until recently, company loyalty in the big firms had always been rewarded by a promotional system based almost entirely on seniority, rather than on individual merit. Those who worked for them had both personal and financial security from the cradle to the grave. Their whole life pattern was laid out for them, preordained, predictable, and certain—to be followed by retirement with a preordained pension. Children went to company schools from babyhood, housing was provided, recreation was provided— everything up to (and including) the needs of old age.

To some, this meant a welcome sense of security, to others, a sense of being trapped ... a pent-up frustration.

Chalmers Johnson put the matter well when he said: "The chief labor union goal in Japanese eyes in recent times has been 'living wages graduated by age', whereas the American labor union ideology has been 'equal pay for equal work'. These two different goals naturally have very different effects on management's incentive structure."[31]

Company loyalty and "lifetime employment" have been almost religious principles in Japan for decades. They have been given credit for much of the Japanese "economic miracle." Now the Japanese people are becoming ambivalent about it, however. The young look for more freedom, though, at the same time, they— and certainly their elders—are aware that greater personal freedom no longer provides the security, the harmony, the predictable relations that came with the older pattern of job and family security for life.

There is another major reason for the change as well: it is Japan's new affluence. The spread of wealth is creating a totally new set of priorities for Japanese workers. Now they demand money for goods such as televisions, cars, motorcycles, and washing machines, rather than cradle to grave security. They also want leisure time for themselves. Many now spurn six-day-week companies. The under-forty generation likes the chance to go fishing, or play with their children on their day off. The rising standard of living makes the security of company—dormitory life or compound life—less appealing. "When there is enough food, clothes, and places to live, peoples' interest is directed to other things, such as how to enjoy their life and spend their leisure time," explains Keimei Shimokawa of Gakusei Engo-kai.[32]

31 *Chalmers Johnson, "Japanese Style Management in America," California Management Review, Summer 1988.*
32 *Keiko Kambara, "Japs Try Out Job-Hopping," The Christian Science Monitor, 24 February 1989.*

Another factor has changed life for the younger Japanese. Japan's current labor shortage gives workers the happy feeling that if they leave one job, they will easily find another. Companies are growing and diversifying into new industries that require experienced workers. There is no longer the fear of having no job if one elects to move up the ladder at one's own pace by changing employers.

For The Old, too, The Tradition Changeth

In the past two or three decades, the shift from producing low-priced consumer goods to producing complex "high-tech" products and services has meant that many "old timers" have increasingly little to contribute to the modern market. More and more of them are being relegated to what are called the *Madogiwa-zoku*, meaning the "by-the-window" tribe. This phrase started about ten years ago. It refers to the increasing number of middle-aged (or older) employees who, though still ranked as senior managers, are no longer useful to their companies. They are what we might call "kicked upstairs," *i.e.*, given little to do except look out the window. They continue to be "respected" and paid but neither promoted nor given responsibility. Lifetime employment is now becoming exceedingly expensive at the very time when Japan is looking to reduce costs at home, in view of its global competition.

The Labor Ministry says that "one in three companies" now wants to get rid of its supervisors over age 50, in order to save on salaries built up by longevity, and to make room for young managers who are now eager to move up.[33]

As a result, Japan has increasing numbers of *heddo hantaas* (head hunters). There are more than 200 of them now, recruiting and moving managers from one company to another. Until recently, such an idea would have been

33 *Wall Street Journal, 14 March 1989.*

unthinkable in Japan. But now the greater number of young college graduates, together with the static seniority-based promotion system, means that there is a surplus number of middle level managers. They have little upward mobility. These are the people who feel the "squeeze" most acutely.

Another crucial factor changing the face of Japan's working world is the impact of high-tech, as opposed to previous labor-intensive manufacturing plants. Small, intensive companies look for creativity, and for informality in the work place. They absorb fewer workers. And where large scale manufacturing is still going on, the robot is replacing human hands to a growing degree.

What was once a landmark of Japanese business, namely stability in the work place, is therefore, rapidly changing on various fronts:

1. The idea that human value increased with the accumulation of years is now widely considered to be "fossilized, " and too expensive as well;

2. Many of Japan's industries are establishing themselves in other parts of the world—bringing new global ideas and new needs regarding personnel;

3. Young people now have the incentive, financial security and desire to "job-hop." The salary gap between major firms and the multitude of smaller "support" companies is narrowing. This makes it easier to "job-hop" without worrying about losing income.

In three short decades, the number of university graduates in Japan has catapulted from 3% of the population to 37%. As a result, many younger employees no longer see themselves as virtually "indentured servants" of the corporation that hired them. They see themselves as professionals, ready and able to sell their skills to the highest bidder, on an open market.

Clearly, safety and security in the company womb is no longer an acceptable goal for most of the new generation.

The Management and Coordination Agency in Japan reports that 2.36 million people changed their jobs during the year ending February 1988. This was a 34.9% jump from the previous year.[34]

Labor Shortage—Something New in Japan

For years Japan has had a worker glut. However, as the yen surged and as companies started transferring factories overseas in the mid-1980's, they became short-handed and are now looking around for new workers. They are importing more and more labor from South Korea and other parts of Asia. They are also hiring more high school graduates. Hitachi Ltd., for example, added 2,100 high school graduates in 1988—up from 250 the previous year. There is also a market increase in the use of part-time workers—nearly all women. Economists say that although 506,000 college graduates will enter the Japanese job market in 1989, companies will, in fact, need 948,000. One spokesman at a Tokyo job placement office said, "This is a complete seller's market."

Obviously this turn of events has changed the whole psychology of the marketplace. Not only are young and middle management people feeling more confident about finding new jobs, but also, as companies diversify into new industries and establish overseas plants worldwide, there is a growing need for experienced workers. No longer must the young wait patiently for much of their lives, hoping for one of the limited number of senior positions. Nor are they willing any longer to be at the company's beck and call from morning to night, especially as incredible rents in Tokyo force them to live farther and farther from the city, commuting longer and longer hours every day.

---

34 *Keiko Kambara, "Japs Try Out Job-Hopping," The Christian Science Monitor, 24 February 1989.*

Work Patterns are Changing

Offering flexible hours is one new trend. A number of Japanese companies are starting to experiment with these. Mitsubishi Electric, and Hitachi Ltd., for example, let workers choose their eight-hour day between 6 A.M. and 9:30 P.M., as do an increasing number of other firms.

Furthermore, there is a steady move towards shorter work weeks. The *Japanese Economic Journal* reports that in February 1989, the Federation of Bankers Association of Japan and the Post and Telecommunication Ministry both adopted a five-day work week! Currently, it reports, 1.1 million Japanese public sector workers have a 5-day week every other week! Little by little, Japanese workers are being brought closer to a goal that Western society has long accepted as its birthright.

The young of today's Japan are feeling a new sense of freedom. They have new confidence, wider opportunities, a higher standard of living, and more flexibility. It is a new Japan. They look at their contemporaries in other countries and realize that they, too, *can* lead lives of their own. Their personal lives and personal futures begin to take on a new kind of importance to them. The result is that many young Japanese are becoming less willing to work long overtime hours; they are demanding (and being given) longer vacations—and more of them. They travel more and play more in their leisure time. They are beginning to feel less keen about going out every evening with only their fellow workers. In short, many of them are becoming less "work-absorbed." The Japan Productivity Center reports that only 25% of white collar workers at major firms any longer think they should sacrifice their outside life for the good of the company; nearly 50% say they "have better things to do with their free time." Howell Hammond, Vice President and Director of Kodak-Japan Research and Development

Center writes: "There is an increasingly large segment of Japanese youth who find appeal in working for American companies in Japan itself. This is caused by the perceived freedom of having more control of your own destiny and being able to move up the ladder faster."[35]

A New Search for Affluence

Haruki Murakami, a 40-year old in Italy, is a best-selling author in Japan. He addresses himself primarily to his own generation: "There was an idealism in the 1960's," he says, "but it has disappeared. Now," he laments, "the rules of the game have changed, replaced by Japan's relentless search for affluence. In the 1960's my friends were all poor. But those people are now riding in BMWs and Mercedes—with telephones in the car." He is distressed by the "me" generation, where, as he says "Girls choose their boy friends by the car they drive. In the old days, everyone was poor, and loving somebody was a treasure, a way to kill time, everything. Things were simpler. It's getting more difficult to love somebody purely. You can get almost everything with money."

Murakami's books, such as *Norwegian Wood* and *Dance, Dance, Dance* have sold multi-million copies in Japan. Through his stories, Murakami says, he hopes foreigners will come to understand that there is another Japan from the one now apparent, and that it is struggling to establish its identity.

"My country has money, but it does not possess anything else," he writes. "I want Japan to become a country

35 *Howell Hammond quoted by Wil Lepkowski, "Americans Living In Japan Describe Life and Work There," as abstracted with permission from Chemical & Engineering News, 2 January 1989, 67 (1), p.11. © 1989 American Chemical Society.*

which others respect." He is resettling in Japan this fall (1989). "I have to settle down," he says. "I cannot escape for the rest of my life."[36]

How It Works at Home

Although changes are going on in Japan, personnel management still remains relatively easy for the Japanese in their own country, partly because of their great social and national homogeneity, and partly because of their uniform educational standards.

Japan has a nationwide curriculum set by the Ministry of Education. The Ministry controls the training of all teachers, and the selection of all textbooks. There is national school funding which provides remarkably equal distribution of education expenses per student—whether urban or rural—all across the nation. University exams are also set at the national level. The result is an extraordinarily predictable pool of recruits. The rigor, quality, and quantity of the Japanese educational system is far beyond that of most countries. Students work 5 days a week; their attendance is extremely high; their completion level and quality of work are also.

Japanese high school students compete favorably with U.S. *college seniors* in many areas. Year after year in international surveys that compare high school achievement levels in various countries, the Japanese rate at, or near, the top. High school graduates can be counted on to read and write well, and to be really competent in basic mathematics. Furthermore, they are also given a strong work ethic. They come out of school strictly disciplined, with the ability to follow instructions quickly and well. This, of

36 *Quoted from an interview by Keiko Kambara in Tokyo, reported in The Christian Science Monitor, 30 March 1989.*

course, means that they can be trained on the job with maximum ease. Furthermore, being part of that society, they think and work in terms of teams and groups. It is not difficult for them, therefore, to adapt quite easily and readily to the new "group" discipline of the work place. The system provides narrow, circumscribed standards, and judges by performance on the educational ladder.

In the West, there is more variety, more choice, more diversity, less pressure in schools. There is also, however, less discipline and far less predictability. The two systems point up the fundamental dilemmas between choice and concentration. It is hard to speculate on the future of the Japanese educational system as their national needs grow ever more global. In today's world, however, Western businessmen are dealing with products of a highly honed, carefully directed, demanding, and well-run educational system. Furthermore, Japanese schools are as yet scarcely troubled at all by drug or alcohol abuse. The firms, therefore, do not find this problem rampant in the young people whom they hire. In addition, the tradition of loyalty has always been strong. So one accepts and conforms. Personnel managers know reasonably well in Japan what they can count on in their workers. This makes their task relatively easy.

But Abroad

In other countries, however, there is a different picture. When Japanese start handling personnel problems in countries which have great national and ethnic diversity, they are often confounded by problems which arise.

Some of these stem from the lack of homogeneity to which the Japanese are accustomed. In diverse groups the workers no longer have the same work ethic, same heritage, same values and priorities as each other, nor are they necessarily the same values which are taken for granted in

Japan. Nor are Japanese managers accustomed to the rugged individualism and determined independence that they often find among workers in other countries.

Jeffrey S. Irish, a red-headed graduate of Yale, went to work for a Japanese company in Japan directly from college. He writes of his experience in a way that clearly shows the difference in attitudes and office procedures between the two countries. He tells how he once disagreed with a supervisor's decision on a business matter. He started to discuss it with him. The Japanese supervisor got very angry. "There is not a place for insubordinate actions or thoughts here," he said, "I am your senior, and you will do as I say. If you cannot accept this, you cannot work in a Japanese company."

Irish described the rigid daily pattern of the office. At 10 A.M.—and again at 3 P.M.—music was piped into the workroom for three minutes. Everyone leaned back, smoked a cigarette and (at least theoretically) thought about their work.

One had to sign in and out of the room on a chalkboard. In his company they were not supposed to talk to their colleagues. This indicated that they "were not concentrating"; it was considered also that they were "distracting to others."

Irish discussed the pervasive and constant feeling of competition with other companies. "It was our team against theirs all the time," he said, not only in his particular office but also reiterated in the company magazine and felt throughout the company. Their own progress and that of their competitors was constantly and steadily being compared and measured.

He is still working for the same Japanese company but is now in the United States. He writes: "In the USA Japanese companies compete just as they did in Japan. I am still the only *gaijin* (foreigner) on our 'team'; I am still part of the seamless fabric of Japanese work life. But now we

are competing in America; I am caught midway between two cultures, forever explaining the ways of each to the other, trying to come to terms with the person I have become. Sometimes it is as confusing as it is fascinating."[37]

Those who work under Japanese managers in other countries need to recognize some of the difficulties these managers themselves may be having in adjusting to—and understanding—the very different approaches of personnel in the new locality.

Ka Groups

The general work pattern in many Japanese plants on their own home ground, is to work through what are called *Ka* groups. These are basic work groups made up of about 15 workers—of various skills and ranks—plus a *kacho*, or chief. In Japan the groups are extremely closely knit. The men work and play together—they play ball; they go out together in the evenings after work; their bonds grow deep. Members often feel closer to their *Ka* colleagues than they do to their own families. They certainly see more of them. It is not surprising, therefore, being used to this group life, that when they are in other countries where family ties are strong so that most people rush home immediately after work, Japanese workers tend to be lonely. They often stick close together in order to fill the gaps they feel in their lives. This is frequently interpreted as being "offish" and "unsociable" by non-Japanese people who do not understand the reason for it. Often the fact is that these men are missing the sociability of their *Ka* companions and their after-work "togetherness."

37 *Jeffrey S. Irish, "A Yankee Learns to Bow," The New York Times Magazine, Business World Magazine Section, 8 June 1986.*

In a land where the individual blends in, rather than standing out, these *Ka* groups fill an extremely useful function. Praise and reward—or conversely blame—can be absorbed by the group rather than putting the responsibility—or the kudos—on a single individual. The Japanese have grown up with the system and are used to it. They miss that company "paternalism" and camaraderie. In a world of individuals, they miss their groups.

Section 5:
Negotiating: The Meeting of Business Minds

Most Westerners assume that business negotiations are focused entirely on "the bottom line"; that everyone is at all times constantly alert in watching out for his or her own interests. The Japanese are certainly focused on that as well. However, they also include a far greater concern than do most Westerners for *the quality of the relationship* during the process, and particularly at its conclusion.

As with everything in their lives, they aim to maintain smooth, harmonious relationships even as they pursue what may be a very tight negotiation. The human element is important enough to them that they will actually break off negotiations—however beneficial they might ultimately have been—if they consider that these interrelationships are not sufficiently solid.

Pressure

Aggression, "drive," and any sense of pressure are definitely counterproductive with most Japanese. Western-

ers—particularly Americans—tend to consider that "Time is Money." They are, therefore, preoccupied with efficiency. Concentration on speed, efficiency and productivity—as we Westerners see these—in fact often jeopardize our social and human relationships throughout the world, especially in Asia. Many Westerners plunge right into business without taking time to develop more than cursory personal relations. They really do not care much about these. They themselves are here today and somewhere else tomorrow. They want to "get down to brass tacks" quickly, get their business done, and be off. They hardly notice Mr. What's-His-Name, though they have his card "somewhere."

This bothers the Japanese. They want to explore the sincerity, depth, integrity, and goodwill of their opposite numbers before they start dealing with them.

As we have noted previously, the Japanese social system is a vertical one, meaning that class distinction and status are of great importance to them. Unless a Japanese knows the *status* of each negotiator, he feels ill at ease, uncertain how to act. Status distinctions are based on age, sex, and education, as well as a person's position in the firm. Therefore, time is needed not only for full introductory information, but also for the exploration of status relations. Age and seniority still mean a great deal. They are leery of representatives whom they consider to be "too young to have decision-making authority." Gray hair CAN be an asset! You may want to let the oldest-looking of your representatives make at least the opening remarks.

It is advisable, also, to start off being quite formally polite, not "Hail fellow...well met!" Play it cool, then, as the meetings go on; allow the Japanese to set the level of formality. They will be more comfortable if you do as they do, *i.e.*, show respect upwards and expect respect (rather than camaraderie) from those "below" you. This is not necessarily the Western way. Adaptations will take place as time goes on, but it is wise not to push informality too

hard at the start, especially with older Japanese. Certainly avoid using first names. Let the Japanese initiate these in their own time.

This awareness of "status" takes conscious effort on the part of Americans, Australians, Scandinavians, and many others who normally pay little or no attention to a man's "status" but take equality for granted around a bargaining table. In the interest of "getting on with it," Westerners often pass rather quickly over introductions and detailed qualifications. With the Japanese this attempt at speed can, in fact, *waste* time. Japanese absolutely must have adequate points of reference. They want to take whatever time is necessary to know quite a lot about each member of the negotiating team before they start.

What Westerners want to know is the other side's "group hierarchy." They are not so much interested in the background of each team member, but they do want to know:

Who is the key decision maker?

How much authority does he have?

Is there someone else invisibly in the background who is actually pulling the wires?

Is there really any "give" in the situation, or is there, in reality, a cut-and-dried, predetermined, one-position attitude resulting from an already completed *ringi* consensus decision?

Teams Negotiate—Not Individuals

There are such dissimilarities in our cultures that negotiations with Japanese people can often be difficult. Since overall consensus is their goal, their teams generally include members from various departments. Furthermore, their negotiating teams are often accustomed to working together, not brought together for just one given negotiat-

ing session, as is common in Western procedures. Often their teams have been trained over a period of time to work together, to depend on each other, to back each other up. They are often attuned to each other like an orchestra, extremely loyal to their fellow team members. They are also used to working closely with their seniors—whom they look on as their mentors. All this means that in negotiating with them, outsiders should take the time and effort to learn at the outset who is involved, what their lines of authority are, how to weigh each member, and how best to include them.

One or two lone Western negotiators meeting with a Japanese "team" can often feel overwhelmed by sheer numbers on the opposite side of the table. It is advisable that the Western side include not only several decision makers, but several well-qualified technical people as well. If your team cannot come up with detailed answers to precise questions, you are likely to lose position and respect. The Japanese have been described as "fanatical" about detail. They are quick to spot any fuzziness or "fudging." In addition to technical experts, it is often a good idea to have a marketing expert with you as well, and often a "disguised" lawyer. Bear in mind as you form your negotiating team that neither women nor young men are as effective as senior men in Japanese eyes. Westerners should try to have as many people on their team as the Japanese have. The more important the negotiation, the larger the group should be.

Japanese negotiating starts with a kind of "courting" process, usually at the middle management level. One who has frequently experienced the process writes: "The successful visiting executive never lets on what he is really thinking; he has unending patience, and is unfailingly polite. In short, he is very Japanese." [38] Understandably,

38 *"The Negotiating Waltz," Time, 1 August 1983.*

the tendency in one's own country is to negotiate on one's own terms and in one's own manner. However, those working with Japanese counterparts—wherever they may be—can ease their own path and in the end save themselves considerable time and trouble, if they make it their business to become familiar enough with Japanese "style" and "pace" that they can maintain the required relationships throughout the proceedings, whether in their own country or in Japan. This does not mean yielding one's ultimate position. It *does* mean adapting one's manner, and cutting one's cloth to fit the pattern. If you want to win a football game, you familiarize yourself in advance with your opposition; you plan your plays accordingly. There is nothing weak or yielding about that approach. It definitely pays off.

In their book, *Managing Cultural Differences*, Robert T. Moran and Philip R. Harris give a number of practical tips for interacting with Japanese businessmen. They stress the importance of third party introductions, *i.e.*, a go-between, or arbitrator, who may be involved throughout the whole negotiation. They suggest that your initial approach to an organization should be at the highest possible level, because the first person contacted is likely to be involved throughout the negotiation.

They suggest that you avoid communicating directly about money, saying this is better done by the go-between or by staff at lower levels. They stress the element of patience, saying "Wait patiently for meetings to move beyond preliminary tea and inconsequential talk."

They reiterate the vital importance of saving face and maintaining the harmonies, urging that one should never put any Japanese person in a position where he must admit failure or the inability to produce some necessary element. They stress the imperative need for an emotional "coming together" by both sides rather than operating with a purely intellectual approach. They explain this as meaning that

the atmosphere must be one of "dealing with a known business associate, rather than a stranger."

One more point that might be unfamiliar to many Westerners is their advice to "avoid praise of your own product or services; let your literature or the go-between do that."[39]

Never underestimate Japan's "middle managers." They are important. Their recommendations are given considerable weight by men of higher rank—who often only start easing into the discussions after the preliminaries are well underway. Don't be surprised if new faces drift into the sessions from time to time, while others disappear.

Precision—Or Lack of It

What Westerners perceive as "ambiguities" in the Japanese are often a major stumbling block in relationships. **(See pg. 94 Part III, Section 2: Can Anyone "Read" A Japanese? on "Ambiguous Replies.")** Germans, Americans, British, and others tend to state facts as clearly and precisely as they can. When the two sides do not agree, they argue with each other trying to persuade the other of each viewpoint. Japanese, however, do not like to argue and will rarely do so. If they feel they are right they see no point in discussing the matter. Anyway, it would upset the harmonies and show lack of respect. So, at key points they often go silent or speak "obliquely." Westerners must understand and recognize this situation. Watch for skillful side-stepping and read it as a clue indicating that you may be touching on important fixed points.

Another area in which Westerners must be alert relates to the Japanese two-level system of *tatemae, i.e.,* official

39 *Robert T. Moran and Philip R. Harris, Managing Cultural Differences, (Gulf Publishing Co., 1987; 2nd edition, 1989) p. 391.*

principle or policy, and *honne*, their true thoughts or real intentions.

They shift back and forth between these two levels in response to their perception of the relationships in the group. If they see that negative or controversial feelings are rising, or if a confrontation appears to be brewing over some point, they will, in all probability, back off from the more open *honne* and fall back on the "official" stance. They may play for time. The *gaijin* often becomes confused. He often perceives this shift of gears as being evasive—even dishonest—certainly perplexing. Actually, the Japanese are not doing this to be evasive. They are more often trying to keep relationships at a harmonious enough level that agreements *can* be reached. It is a little like easing your foot off the accelerator as you approach a dangerous corner. You are still going forward, but you adapt your speed to the circumstances. They, too, "adapt" as they come to what they see as a crucial corner or a change of mood in the negotiations. It is a mistake to judge harshly and get irritated. We, too, "play for time" when we want to ease off a point or want to come at it in some other way— or at some other time. We just do it differently.

Differences in techniques between both sides are more often matters of perception as to priorities and approach than they are basic matters of honesty and ethics. It is very important to keep remembering that, and to give leeway for it.

Bargaining Chips

It may surprise some Westerners to learn that the Japanese frequently perceive us as being "evasive" and perplexing in negotiating situations, just as we do them.

Westerners generally come to a meeting with a number of demands and proposals which they are quite prepared to give away. These are recognized (by us) as our "bargaining

chips." As we start to yield on one point after another, however, the Japanese become confused.

"We might be able to shave the price a bit perhaps," we say on the third day—after having been adamant on the first and second day that the price was "firm." Or we say, "Would it help if we adjusted the conclusions to read..." or, "Well, we did say it was final, but perhaps we could..."

The Japanese start to wonder what the position really is. How much more is open to change? What is making the other side shift? Who is calling the tune?

They understand a firm position (with clearly identified upper and lower ranges, if necessary), but they do not understand "waffling." They interpret this as weakness-unreliability. Respect and trust are lost more often—on either side—through misunderstandings such as these, than they are through fundamental disagreements with the basic proposal.

Consensus

It is important to remember that consensus is *always* their goal. It is not a Japanese concept to "stand up and be counted" on a one-by-one, individual basis—each person defending his particular point of view. "Joe, what do you think of Pete's proposal?" puts both men on the spot.

Edward C. Stewart writes: "The Confucian ethic, which still governs Japan, demands unanimity. In order to respect the rights of the minority, the majority will compromise on almost every issue until a consensus of some kind is reached...no one must ever be completely defeated, because if he is, he 'cannot hold up his face'. In other words, 'leave everyone with something.' Decisions will often be postponed or the entire proposal cancelled if a consensus cannot be reached." [40]

40 *Edward C. Stewart, American Cultural Patterns: A Cross Cultural Perspective, quoted by Robert T. Moran and Philip R. Harris, Managing Cultural Differences, p. 14.*

Decisions by consensus are, by their very nature, extremely slow. But the Western "Let's get this show on the road" approach, tends to stiffen Japanese backs. One needs always to remember that the basic goals are, in fact, different: Westerners are trying to negotiate a final written contract; the Japanese are trying to negotiate a *relationship*. These are two very different things. So you talk and work together. They are trying to "get to know you." You are trying to "finalize points." Westerners are eager to culminate a deal, sign a contract, and be off to the next appointment.

Directness

The Japanese approach in any negotiation is to go deliberately, step by step, asking massive numbers of detailed questions which may seem to Westerners to be off the point, superfluous, time-consuming, and unnecessary. To them they *are* necessary, however, so one needs to take the time to answer them. Time is what they have and what we usually do not... or think we do not have.

Western directness and Japanese indirection often come face to face quite early in negotiations, as Westerners try their best to be sure that every point is lucidly clear in a series of agreements. Every word is weighed to make sure it carries the intended sense. Issues are stated directly and qualified carefully—often in writing.

However, the more the West pushes to get similar clarity and directness from the other side, the less progress is likely to be made. Western voices then begin to rise; Western negotiators, with their approach of logic and analysis, begin to separate out individual issues, searching to see if the log jam can be resolved piecemeal; trying to find out exactly where any problems lie and what is causing them. Western representatives often become increasingly strident, partly from frustration, and partly because they

are always pressured by the sense that precious time is passing. They want to "get this thing settled." Irritation mounts. An air of confrontation grows. The all-important consideration of "face," and any feelings of "group harmony," are lost and forgotten.

Japanese counterparts grow more and more silent. They watch each other's signals. Forward progress ceases. They do not make decisions on any of the now "separated-out" issues. Indecision and confusion of this kind can quite readily turn into a firm negative response. Why?

In the Japanese scheme of things, nothing is ever settled piecemeal. Nothing is settled at all, in fact, until the last stage of the negotiation. Things, to them, are not black/white, right/wrong, possible/impossible. As we have said elsewhere, they think in terms of continuums—shades of gray, points merging and converging—rather than in terms of clear-cut segments.

The Meeting Itself

Generally speaking, the Japanese will make two offers, neither of them very far apart. They will normally come into the negotiations having had long internal discussions, and therefore, having already arrived at a carefully considered "consensus" viewpoint of their own.

After negotiations have been going on for some time, it is not unusual for them to fall into a long silence. This is perplexing and disturbing to non-Japanese. These silences are easier to handle if you have some clue as to what may be going on. They may occur for a variety of reasons:

1. The negotiators may, in fact, be taking time to consider the question.

2. Perhaps they do not want to answer—so they go silent. As we have said, they rarely argue.

3. Something you said may have startled them—changed their way of thinking or upset their understanding of your

proposal. In that case, they will be waiting to regroup, so they can discuss the new element in private.

4. They may simply feel that it shows greater respect to the questioner not to answer too quickly and easily. It feels to them more "sincere" when people take a reasonable time before answering a question, even if, in fact, they know the answer quite well and could give it quickly. They themselves mistrust too "glib" and quick an answer, so they may be giving the appearance of deliberating for some time before answering, just to be polite.

5. They work on long-term time frames. They may, therefore, be operating slowly and deliberately in order to get to know you a little more. They want to be sure there is real mutual understanding and goodwill on your part. If this is the reason for their silence, they will be watching to see what you do, listening to hear what you say, assessing you carefully.

When there seems to be an impasse—any unexplained halt in the procedures—it may be wise to call for a recess. This allows the Japanese an interval in which to reassess their own group consensus and touch base with their colleagues. It gives both sides the chance to confer informally, to feel out attitudes and reactions, even if briefly. If the "harmonies" have indeed begun to fray, a break in the proceedings may be vital in order to allow time to reestablish the atmosphere.

Preparing in Advance

When preparing for a negotiating session, it helps to:

1. *Select* as your representatives those who are known for their patience and their courtesy, as well as for their competence and knowledge of the subject involved. Patience, with no sense of time pressure, is a *vital* component in a successful session. The hard-pressing "Type A" Westerner is less likely to succeed than one who appears more

conciliatory, less in a hurry, more willing to listen, quieter.

2. *Ease the process* by supplying as much relevant material as possible in writing and in advance. This shows "sincerity" in Japanese eyes. Furthermore, it provides a common base of summarized, accurate, identifiable information. In addition, it is almost always easier, in any unfamiliar language, for people to handle written material than to understand the spoken word. It makes sense, therefore, to provide as much advance, written back-up information as possible. One should also supplement that at the meeting with as much relevant audio-visual material as possible—in Japanese if you can.

3. *If you want to tape the negotiations*, be sure to discuss this with the Japanese in advance. Everyone should agree to it before you do it.

4. *Provide an interpreter*. Unless spoken language is fluent on both sides, it is wise to have an interpreter at any really important meeting. Everybody gets tired as the hours go on; if people have to operate in an unfamiliar tongue a lot of points get missed. An interpreter is valuable not only to translate accurately what is said, but also (and this is very important) to overhear what the Japanese are saying in asides among themselves. Which topics seem most important for them? What do their hang-ups seem to be? Furthermore, at break times, an interpreter can give you considerable insight into what has been going on in the area of nonverbal language as well, among the negotiators. This, too, can be very helpful. (**See also "Using Interpreters," Business Environment Part V: Person To Person p. 208**)

5. *Hold pre-discussion meetings for your own team.* Make these intensive and *thorough*. Be sure that everyone has done his homework carefully. Your team must speak with one voice without dissension, arguments, internal discussions, or visible uncertainty among your members. "Wobbling" or uncertainty among your members can be

extremely destructive not only to the "harmonies" but particularly to the Japanese trust in you, and therefore, to the success of the whole negotiation.

Disagreeing/Criticizing

A subtle but important way to show respect is by avoiding direct negatives or critical responses. This is often hard for us Westerners. We are accustomed to say what we think as we think it. It makes a great deal of difference to their success, however, if Westerners try to soften their negatives and criticisms rather than coming right out with them bluntly. Instead of saying "Oh, no. That would not work at all," or "We are not interested in doing that," one can say, "Perhaps we can think about that later," or "We will see if that is possible," or "We could ask the engineers what they think..." Polite "stalling" is very familiar to them. They will get your meaning perfectly clearly, but it will avoid any sense of confrontation or superiority. (**See Patterns of Communication p.131**)

In reverse: Westerners also need to be alert and sensitive to the fact that Japanese negatives are likely to be couched in roundabout terms. It is important to train your ear to catch them, for pressure on a man who has already said "no"—however gracefully and obliquely—is not appreciated, and is not effective. One needs to yield gracefully at the moment—then come back to the point at another time, in another way, if necessary. Don't batter or argue. It will not advance your cause. Sometimes, as the French saying goes: "One must step back in order to jump forward better." "Coming right out with it" is nearly always counterproductive in Japan. The reason is that in their eyes a person is not separate from his words. In Western cultures he is. You can have rapport with a person even if you have basic disagreements with his ideas. The Japanese feel that if you question or negate what someone

says you are questioning or negating the man himself. This brings us back to the matter of "face." It is why they use so much "indirection."

If you want to work smoothly with them, especially in critical business conversations, you, too, must learn to raise your questions or your doubts obliquely, rather than making a head-on, cut-and-dried denial or defense of an idea. You can soften the edges by saying such things as: "I thought I understood from somewhere ..."; "I had not realized that was true ..."; "That's a new approach to me. I must think about it..."; "Would you think that is always the case?...", *etc*. If you make a few such oblique comments, they will clearly and quickly understand your position is one of doubt, but they will not have lost face by an outright challenge, nor feel insulted. It may seem tedious and laborious to you—and time-consuming—but the more you learn to talk around a point rather than arguing or denying it, the better it will pay off for you.

For the same reason—that a man is not separate from his words—the Japanese seldom interrupt anyone who is their superior, be it in rank, position, or age. They consider it to be *extremely* rude when we interrupt, especially a senior, a superior, or a guest. They will rarely, if ever, comment on this, but they will notice, inwardly react, and generally remember.

A Different View of Contracts

Quick decisions are quite common in the West. Once the facts are known, the costs agreed upon, and the benefits discussed; once each person has presented his position—giving a bit here and a bit there on both sides to make acceptable concessions—then the agreement can be finalized. On to the next problem...

This procedure can often be quick, efficient, and very clear— at least to Western eyes. When a contract has been

signed, everyone knows where everyone else stands... nothing is left vague or open-ended. If a legal document has been signed, everyone will honor it. Mission accomplished. Yes?

Not necessarily so. In Japanese eyes, drastic changes can be suggested after the signing if circumstances change. Why not? What is so magic about a piece of paper? Financial conditions, world prices, availability of raw materials, labor unrest, changes in world markets, or other vital variables may not stay the same as when the contract was signed. "Why can there not be 'reinterpretations' in view of new facts?" they ask.

These are two profoundly different points of view as to the meaning and purpose of a contract. It may be advisable, in order to increase mutual trust and understanding on both sides, to discuss the final form of the contract and the points to be covered before the contract is actually drafted. Some people suggest further that in the interest of the often-needed "leeway," that there be an agreement to meet once again, at a specified time after the signing, to reassess the validity of the contract. All patents and copyrights should, of course, be included in the contract. Westerners should show the final copy to Japanese lawyers as well as to their own. Every effort should be made to be sure that both sides are in real agreement and full understanding.

Despite their more "flexible" view of contracts, one needs to be prepared for considerable ceremony when the final papers are to be signed. Senior executives and both negotiating parties normally attend and give speeches. Gifts are often exchanged; photos are often taken. Afterwards the chief executive officers of each company exchange letters of congratulations. The Western handshake, quick gathering up of papers, and relatively hurried departure are frequently counter-productive. It is worth taking a small amount of extra time to cement relationships in a formal "harmonious" way.

The Law

The use of a codified legal system was a post World War
II Western import into Japan. Their legal system today is
based almost entirely on U.S. and European models. It
does not feel comfortable to them. They greatly prefer
mediation. There is little in common between their traditional, flexible concepts and the rigid legal codes familiar
to most Westerners. Both sides start from basically different premises.

British Common Law (the basis not only for British law
but also for USA, Canada, and most of the Commonwealth
countries around the world) is based on precedent. Negotiators who have been trained under these laws emphasize
contract terms. By these terms the rights and obligations of
both parties are set out in written form, agreed to, then
adhered to, strictly for the specified length of the contract.
Japanese relationships, however, are based not on contrac-
tual obligations, but on mutual trust. As a result, they rarely
start civil proceedings among themselves. Their emphasis
is on moral commitment rather than on legal verbiage. One
needs to understand the full implication of this in terms of
working with them. It means that one needs to be extremely
careful not to promise anything casually; never say something that you do not really intend to back up. For the
Japanese a verbal agreement is just as binding as is a
written one.

This emphasis on moral commitment (rather than legal-
ity) can affect their reaction to Western insistence on written details as well. One needs to be careful, and fully aware
of their sensitivities, lest they consider insistence on writing everything down as showing a lack of faith in their
moral integrity. That is, of course, insulting to anyone.
Make sure they feel that you trust them—even if you need
to have everything on paper "for the home office," or for
the record.

Until recently Japanese rarely used lawyers or courts. To them the whole concept was "confrontational." "Law to them," someone has said, "is like a ceremonial sword—meant to be brandished but not used to kill."

Nowadays, however, with their widespread global operations, they are, of course, using lawyers to a steadily increasing extent. The complexities of international law and international finance have changed the picture. A large company, like Mitsui Trading Company, for example, has between 50-100 lawyers in its legal department. Smaller companies usually retain law firms. Many young Japanese study at prestigious law schools throughout the West. Increasing numbers of them are now positioned on boards of directors to help their companies avoid legal action.[41]

Basically, since Japanese greatly prefer mediation, they look for intermediaries if they have disagreements among themselves. **(See Part III, Section 1 for "Go Betweens," p. 74)** Laws based on "individual rights" are quite contrary to their "group" feelings, so mean little to them. "Scholarly opinion," aged and respected views, are what they greatly prefer in place of legal confrontation. Conciliation—out of court—suits Japan's paternalistic system far better than any adversary relationship. If they must go to court, they look for judge-oriented—rather than lawyer-oriented-justice. In their view, judges are more likely to be interested in the truth than are competing lawyers. Even today, lawyers in Japan are primarily involved in matters concerning foreign firms, international disputes, and problems with local foreigners.

Among themselves they still prefer more conciliatory approaches to conflicts.[42]

41 *Robert T. Moran, Getting Your Yen's Worth: How to Negotiate with Japan, Inc. (Houston, TX: Gulf Publishing Co. , 1985) p. 22.*

42 *Ibid. p 21.*

When in the West, the Japanese carefully abide by each country's rules and regulations. When they do find themselves enmeshed in a lawsuit, they rarely fight the case. They are far more likely just to pay quietly.

As can be imagined from the above, willingness to compromise is seen as a strength in Japan. In many other countries, compromise can be seen as capitulation. For the Japanese, however, it is more often a sign of strength. For them, the overall harmony and stability of a group (or company) takes precedence over almost any disagreement. Inability (or unwillingness) to compromise creates an embarrassing loss of face on one side or the other, as they see it. With compromise, both sides can hold up their heads. That is strength.

Persuasion—Or Lack of It

Westerners frequently use negotiating sessions as opportunities to "persuade." They expect there to be lively discussions—often some confrontation, arguments, and debates—but out of it all, they expect there to emerge a greater understanding of the situation on the part of everyone, leading to new agreements—at least to some degree—and with no hard feelings.

In Japan's vertical society, this would never do. The people of the highest status would always win! Furthermore, all losers would lose face. The situation would be fraught with the very confrontations which they struggle so hard to avoid at all costs. In their eyes a negotiation is, as Robert T. Moran describes it, "almost the ritualistic enactment of a predetermined agreement."[43]

He quotes Howard van Zandt as saying that the Japanese are more likely to be persuaded by a written than oral presentation. "The reason is," Dr. Van Zandt says, "the

43 *Ibid. p. 76.*

Japanese feel that if a man is willing to put his case in print, where all may challenge what he has said, it is likely that he will be accurate, so as not to lose face."[44]

Agreement and Disagreement

For some reason, many of us Westerners have a tendency to focus on points of *disagreement* when we have a conference. Since these are potential pitfalls, we latch onto them; we try to explain them away; we point out why they should not be perceived as they are, or how they could be modified. We appear to dwell on them.

In dealing with people or other cultures—especially in the East—it is far better to concentrate on *agreement*. Seek out all the pluses and build on them; develop all possible affirmative angles, working with your opposite numbers, getting their input as much as possible, focusing on the benefits you see accruing for both sides. The vital harmonies will best be maintained if you work together on the joint process of building an *affirmative* approach, aimed at *mutual* advantage.

In doing so, it is important to keep the picture whole, insofar as possible. Our Western approach of dividing problems into parts, or steps, or sections, often makes the Japanese feel uncertain and uncomfortable. They tend to become apprehensive when faced with too many details, or too many "parts." Remember: we who stem from the ancient Greek and Roman heritages have an inborn tendency to take everything apart and analyze it. People of the East are more in tune with the continuum—an overall whole—a "merging" world without sharp edges.

In making a presentation, therefore, it is vital to keep the totality of the whole proposal clearly in focus. The "big

44 *"How to Negotiate in Japan," Harvard Business Review, Nov.-Dec. 1970, pp. 44-46.*

picture" should frequently be referred to; summaries throughout the discourse are helpful, as are charts and diagrams. One needs to do whatever one can to keep the overall "whole" from getting lost in the details. Conscious care taken in this regard helps to build their trust and confidence. If you operate from that base, and at their pace, giving them leeway for the translation of ideas—as well as words—the strength of your relationship is likely to grow as you proceed.

Words

One has to remember at all times that however fluent they may seem, most Japanese are working in a foreign—and difficult—tongue when they speak anything other than their own language. Understandably, therefore, words sometimes convey quite different meanings from those that were intended. For example, if you say (as President Nixon did during a speech in Japan): "Our nations have parallel interests and goals," English-speaking people will take it to mean "our goals are similar; we are going in the same direction; we can work together." The Japanese, however, understand that parallel lines never meet. So to them the former President's comments implied opposition, a splitting apart, rather than a similarity or linkage.

This kind of "slippage" of meaning is understandably very common between people of different tongues.

One needs to stay alert to the possibility that you and your Japanese colleague may find yourselves on different wave lengths from time to time, without realizing why. It may be merely through the difficulties of language. If you feel that you are "off track" and not "getting to" each other, it may help to look back to see whether "slippage" of meaning and understanding has occurred on one side or the other.

In Sum

The Japanese look for flexibility. Getting things "down on paper" holds no great allure and no great importance to them. Getting things to "feel right " is their fundamental focus. If we both understand our differences in that regard, in all their ramifications, we can both work more easily together. One needs to understand first. Only then can one adjust, compromise, or give each other that crucial "leeway."

The Japanese are not looking for short term "wins." Efforts focused on "cutting the best deal" are likely to fail with them. Their interests are far more concentrated on the long term. They look for agreements to be based on true, long-lasting compatibility. If they do not "feel" that will be the case with their negotiating opposites, they will not hesitate to call the whole thing off. The unspoken "feel" of negotiation is *that* important to them.

PART VI

FINALE:
UNCHARTED SEAS

Gujo-hachiman Castle, Gifu-ken

(photo by Kenji Arai)

When the European Community achieves economic integration-planned for 1992 and thereafter—it will become the third great power on the Eurasian mainland, along with the Soviet Union and China.

In the Western Hemisphere, the United States is also working to achieve a major "mass" market. It has already signed a free trade pact with Canada, which started operating to some degree in 1989. Plans towards forming a full Western Hemisphere unit (northern) by developing an agreement with Mexico are in process as well. New continental economic blocs are thus being formed in both Europe and North America; the Asian countries are talking together about regional economic cooperation as well. **(See Part II, Japan's Fast-Changing World Role, Section 2 "Japan and Southeast Asia")**

What of Japan?

"The State", as symbolized by the Emperor, used to be the supreme authority. Under that system Japan's national integrity was to be defended at all costs. Nothing foreign was welcome. The Japanese monarch's significance was chiefly that of holding the nation together—in isolation. He did this by what was virtually Emperor worship.

Nowadays there is a new philosophy: that of working together with other nations, developing mutual dependencies across the world and breaking down—at least economically—the barriers of national boundaries.

Japan is not now in a position to spearhead an Asian version of the European Community among the Pacific Rim nations, nor with the Asian mainland. However it is in a position to ease current frictions with both developed and developing nations in many parts of the world by promoting mutual prosperity. It is perhaps starting to respond to that challenge.

In an article in *Chemtech* (6/89), Peter F. Drucker points

out that the Japanese are competing increasingly for western markets in terms of quality, rather than price. They are making better—not merely cheaper—cars—electronic equipment— robots—

"In addition," Mr. Drucker says, "they are automating their workplace far more rapidly and effectively than either the USA or Europe. Thereby," he says, "they are defending their cost structure against newcomers such as South Korea."[1]

As we have seen throughout this book, the Japanese have also "gone international" with tremendous vigor during the past two decades. They are rapidly increasing the pace of this internal revolution. Much of their manufacturing is being moved out of Japan, being reestablished primarily in countries where labor is low-wage, or in countries which give Japan easy access to major world markets ... or both.

As Japan grows more and more global, the need intensifies for it to develop into a more multinational and multiracial society at home—a far cry from the island isolation of previous times. Whether this will, in fact, happen increasingly or not, lies in the hands of the new, younger generation of Japanese.

Coexistence with "foreigners" becomes increasing crucial for the Japanese in today's world. Their islands are small. How will they adjust to the new and ever-greater demands that will be made upon their nation?

...To what extent can they integrate foreign workers into Japanese companies at home? How many?

...Will Japanese and foreigners be able to work together in "harmony" in other parts of the world? Where? Where not?

...As Japanese people get more and more dispersed

1 *Peter F. Drucker, "Japan's Choices—Somebody is Gaining on Japan", Chemtech, June 1989.*

across the globe, what will happen to the "Japaneseness" of the Japanese culture?

Many in Japan still believe deeply in the unique "separateness" of their nation. They feel it is uniquely superior. In addition, they worry that if they become too dependent on outsiders, they could find themselves defenseless in case of an emergency. [The irony is that if they carried that thought to its logical conclusion, they would find themselves returning to Japan's age-old concept of isolation!]

Mr. Shozaburo Kimura, professor of Western History at the University of Tokyo, writes: "I can find an analogy in the world of sport for Japan's present position."

"Golf," he says, "is a sport in which the players can relax between shots and talk to one another while walking along the fairways."

"Yachting, on the other hand, is a sport that requires constant vigilance. Wind direction and many other factors must be calculated so that the boat can be sailed safely and kept on course. It is the ability to handle a large number of variables in a fast-changing situation that the Japanese must cultivate. The Showa era drew to a close in 1989 with the death of Emperor Hirohito. Japan is undergoing momentous changes. The leaders that the country needs must now display the qualities of yachtsmen—not golfers."[2]

To continue the analogy of the sailor a little further: We are all competing in the same race. We are tacking and yawing in the same uncharted waters; we are adjusting our sails to the new and powerful winds of globalization. We have no choice but to reset out sights, for we navigate now by new and different stars and must be alert for new and different reefs. The ocean is wide. There is room for us all, but we need to be out on deck, alert to the unexpected elements of the world's new course.

2 *Shozaburo Kimura, "Culture and Society. The Showa Period", Look Japan, February 1989, pp. 6-7.*

APPENDICES

APPENDIX I

All Nations Stem from Their Historic Roots: So, too, the Japanese.

Since nearly all people are proud of their own national heritage, it is a sign of respect—as well as an easy source of conversational material—to know at least a little about Japan's long history.

Origin

According to Japanese legend, the Empire was founded as early as 660 B.C. by Emperor Jimmu. The earliest records—as distinct from legend—started roughly 1,000 years later.

Chinese influence was strong in the formation of Japan's civilization, with Buddhism, Confucianism and some technologies being introduced into the country before the 6th Century. All three revolutionized this society.

Feudal Power

Powerful, feuding, noble families, with their retinues of warriors, dominated the country from as early as 1192 until the eighteen hundreds. They ruled as *shoguns*, or generals, in the name of the Emperor. One can think of this long period as one of unrelenting military dictatorship, cruel and demanding.

Isolation

Some European missionaries came to Japan in the early and middle parts of the 16th Century, chiefly into the southern areas. Fearing that potential interference would take place through this foreign contact, the Japanese of the *Tokugawa Shogunate* forbade Christianity and, during the 1630's, closed Japan's door to ALL foreigners, except for a few Dutch and Chinese traders who were confined to one small island. For two and a half centuries this was Japan's only window to the outside world. The effects of this long period of extreme repression and isolation have not yet disappeared from the national character.

Modern Period

By the end of the 18th Century, the *Tokugawa Shogunate* was starting to show internal decay of power, and Japan came under increasing pressure to open its ports to trade. Throughout the 16th and 17th centuries, Portuguese and Dutch ships had been coming and going in minor trading.

In 1853, Commodore Perry came from the United States, making a show of force with his fleet, to "establish relations" with Japan. The next year a Treaty of Amity and Friendship was signed. This was soon extended to other countries as well, and was the first step in Japan's participation in the world. It is hard today to realize that this was less than 140 years ago!

Meiji Period

As a result of these developments, an Emperor was restored in 1868, in what is known as the *Meiji Restoration*. The capital was established in Tokyo at that time, and the country entered a period of transformation. Western science, technology, and civilization surged in, brought by ships and men of many nations. The country modernized

rapidly in terms of industries, political institutions, and social patterns. Japanese and Western cultures explored each other and were, to a degree, "harmonized." Japan adopted many western technologies and put energetic emphasis on restructuring both its industries and its education. It took Japan remarkably few decades to adopt and absorb so much that it was soon ranked with major western development in many areas—such as medicine, for example.

Wars

In the late 19th century, Japan embarked on military expansion. From then until 1945, much of Japan's history involved war with other countries:

…In 1884-85, Japan fought China in what was called the **Sino-Japanese War**. At this time, Japan took over rule of what is now Taiwan.

…Hardly had this war terminated when the **Russo-Japanese War** broke out (1904-5).

…In 1910, Japanese rulers annexed Korea.

…Japan entered **World War I** as a British ally. They took over various German Pacific Islands and other territories. By the end of the war they were recognized as a growing world power.

…In 1931 Japan took Manchuria by force, and in 1937 invaded China. This started a long-running war with China which merged into **World War II.**

…Westerners, especially Americans, will never forget the Pearl Harbor attack on December 7, 1941. This launched all-out war with the U.S. and its allies.

Post World War II

World War II did not end until August 14, 1945, at which time Japan was occupied by foreign forces for the first time in its history. Occupation troops were under the control of

General Douglas McArthur of the USA. The occupation lasted until 1947.

Under its new Constitution, adopted May 3, 1947, Japan renounced the right to wage war; the Emperor gave up claims to divinity; political power was shifted from the Emperor to the people, and the Diet was made the sole law-making authority of the country. Although the Japanese military was "abolished" by the new Constitution, Japan was allowed to maintain several branches of a "self-defense" force, in order to maintain its own security.

Economic Growth

A scant ten years after the end of the war (*i.e.*, 1955), the Japanese economy had recovered to pre-war levels of national production and consumption, even though, in their words, they had been "completely ravaged" at the war's end.

As early as the 1970's, the Japanese were enjoying higher growth rates than any of the developed countries. By 1983 it had the second largest GNP in the world, partly as a result of changes in industrial structure; partly because of their innovative technology; partly from concentrating their industries and population in metropolitan areas; and partly because of their extraordinarily high rate of savings (and low standard of living). During this period they moved from being an agricultural society to becoming an urban, industrialized one. Manufacturing has been the basis of their growth; now they are also consummate handlers of money.

Living standards have risen somewhat as the years have passed, but not in comparison with their national wealth [although this is undergoing rapid change in the 1980's].

Trade barriers and the competitiveness of Japanese products overseas have contributed to trade deficits among Western nations.

International Relations

In 1972 China and Japan resumed diplomatic relations. As yet Japan and the USSR have not done so, due to their failure, to date, to resolve disputed claims of sovereignty over four of the Kurile Islands which the Soviets occupy, but which the Japanese claim as theirs.

Current Problems

During the 1970's and 80's, the environment has become an increasing matter of concern for Japan, as it has for much of the world. The oil crisis in 1973 showed Japanese leaders the need for adjustments in both economic structure and in society, in terms of stable economic growth.

Aging of the population (which is occurring faster in Japan than in most other industrialized nations) is a matter of serious concern for Japan's future as well. So is the matter of fishing rights. Numerous disputes are heating up with various countries which are vehemently protesting what they call Japan's "extinction" fishing. This means the use of enormously long drift nets— some as long as thirty MILES, to net and kill tens of thousands of marine animals and fish indiscriminately, day after day.

Currently (1989) Japan is also undergoing political disturbances and internal changes of power.

APPENDIX II

Background Information

Japanese Government

Japan is a democratic country. People elect representatives to the National Diet (*i.e.*, the country's law making body); as well as to prefectual (state) and local assemblies.

The Diet

Like Congress it has upper and lower houses; the Diet has various powers over government budgets, taxation, social programs, *etc.*

Emperor

The Emperor is symbolic of the country and of the "unity of the People." He has no power of government. He presides at official ceremonies, receives foreign dignitaries, and the like.

Prime Minister

Equivalent to a President. As in the British system, he is not elected by the people, but is selected from the Diet by its members. The Diet can remove the Prime Minister from office when it so desires. The Prime Minister can dissolve the Diet and ask for new elections.

Cabinet

Members of the cabinet, who head up various government ministries, must be approved by the Diet.

Parties

They have a multi-party system with six major parties.

Courts

Courts are independent of both the legislative and executive branches of government.

Vote

The voting age is 20 or over; 70% of qualified voters took part in the 1986 national election (compared to under 50% in the last U.S. Election).

Troops

The U.S. has 46,600 troops in Japan (1988) as a result of the security alliance; Japan provides $1.4 billion a year in host country support to help defray costs.

World Aid

Japan is now one of the world's largest donor nations. It is playing an increasingly constructive role in both aid and technical assistance in many parts of the world.

APPENDIX III

Social Conditions

Health standards are among the world's highest: 2nd highest in life expectancy (after Iceland).

Infant mortality is about half that of the USA; malnutrition and starvation are virtually nil.

There are several national health plans that provide low-cost medical care; like the U.S., the big killers are cancer, stroke, heart disease—illnesses thought to be connected with the tensions and pressures of life in modern industrial societies.

The Japanese are big physical fitness buffs—joggers, cyclists, aerobics, *etc.*

Class

Studies show that 80% of all Japanese consider themselves to be members of the middle class.

APPENDIX IV

Business Figures*

Japan is 2nd (after USA) in the free world in economic production (GNP). USA is Japan's most important trading customer; Japan is the second most important trading partner for the USA (after Canada); the two-way trade between them was $110 billion (3/88). 35% of Japanese exports go to the USA (mostly consumer industrial). 20% of Japanese imports come from the USA (agriculture, coal, lumber, heavy machinery, chemicals, aircraft, consumer goods).

* *(all of the above figures are from the Japan Information Center—1989 unless otherwise noted.)*

Wages

Higher than France or Italy; comparable to U.S. Average per capita income about the same as in USA.

Salaries between different occupations vary less than in most countries. Teachers, factory workers, farmers, *etc.*, earn roughly the same income. The difference between management and labor is less extreme than in most other countries.

Japan can be considered a modern, affluent society:

98% of homes have washing machines, refrigerators, color TVs

67% have cars

50% have air conditioners

33% have VCRs

APPENDIX V

Business Names to Recognize

As of 1989:
Leading Trading Companies:
1) Mitsubishi
2) Mitsui and Company
3) C. Itoh and Company
4) Sumitomo
5) Marubeni
6) Nissho Iwai
7) Toyo Menka
8) Nichimen
9) Kanematsu-Gosho

The above companies handle 60-65% of the export/import business of Japan.

(Figures and information from JETRO, New York, April, 1989.)

Major Japanese Banks 1989
(As measured by size of deposits)
1) Dai Ichi Kangyo Bank
2) Sumitomo Bank (highest earnings; 2nd in fund volume)
3) Fuji Bank
4) Mitsubishi Bank
5) Sanwa Bank (Osaka)
6) Tokai Bank (Chubu)
7) Mitsui Bank
8) Taiyo Kobe Bank
9) Daiwa Bank
10) Bank of Tokyo (largest in lending to debtor nations)
(Information from JETRO, April 1989.)

APPENDIX VI

Sources of Information

(Some or all of the following organizations have branch offices in many major cities of the world. It may be worth looking in local phone books to check for your area. They can be valuable sources of business, trade, and cultural information. They may have somewhat different names in countries other than the USA.)

Consulate General of Japan
Japan-American Societies (See Appendix VII)
Japan External Trade Organization (JETRO)
Japan Information Center
Japan National Tourist Office
Tokyo Trade Center

APPENDIX VII

Japan-American Societies in the USA

The following organizations across the United States may be helpful to our readers. [Those in some other countries may find similar groups in their lands too.]

The Japan Society of Boston, Inc.
22 Batterymarch Street
Boston, MA 02109
617/451-0726 FAX 617/451-1191

Japan-America Society of Kentucky
P.O. Box 333
Lexington, KY 40584
606/231-7533

Japan-American Society of Central Florida, Inc.
P.O. Box 23744
Tampa, FL 33623
813/223-2550

Japan-America Society of Maine
One Union Street, Suite 303
P.O. Box 288 DTS
Portland, ME 04112-0288
207/774-4014

Japan-America Society of Chicago, Inc.
40 North Dearborn, Suite 910
Chicago, IL 60602
312/263-3049 FAX312/263-6120

Japan-America Society of Minnesota, Inc.
c/o Asian International Travel Services
7320 Ohms Lane
Minneapolis, MN 55435
612/897-3590

Japan-America Society of Dallas
c/o The Staubach Company
6750 LBJ Freeway # 1100
Dallas, TX 75240
214/385-0500 FAX 214/386-0026

Japan Society, Inc.
333 East 47th Street
New York, NY 10017
212/832-1155 FAX 212/755-6752

The Japan-American Society of Georgia
225 Peachtree Street N.E.
Suite 801, South Tower
Atlanta, GA 30303
404/524-7399 FAX 404/524-8447

The Japan Society of Northern California
350 Sansome Street, Suite 630
San Francisco, CA 94104
415/986-4383 FAX 415/986-5772

The Japan-America Society of Honolulu
P.O. Box 1412
Honolulu, HI 96806
808/524-4450

The Japan-America Society of Oregon
c/o Portland Chamber of Commerce
221 N.W. Second Avenue
Portland, OR 97209
503/228-9411 FAX 503/228-5126

The Japan-America Society of Houston, Inc.
17 S. Briar Hollow Lane #301
Houston, TX 77027
713/963-8376

The Japan-America Society of Pennsylvania
600 Grant Street, Suite #4444

Pittsburgh, PA 15219
412/281-4741 FAX 412/281-8143

Japan-America Society of Phoenix
P.O. Box 654
Phoenix, AZ 85001
602/966-4347

The Japan-American Society of St. Louis, Inc.
111 S. Bemiston, Suite 221
St. Louis, MO 63105
314/726-6822

The Japan-America Society of Rhode Island
222 Richmond Street, Suite 107
Providence, RI 02903
401/272-7790

The Japan-America Society of the State of
Washington
One Union Square Suite 1925
Seattle, WA 98101
206/623-7900 FAX 206/343-7930

The Japan America Society of Southern California
ARCO Plaza
505 South Flower Street
Los Angeles, CA 90071
213/627-6217 FAX 213/627-1353

The Japan Society of Vermont
135 Church Street
Burlington, VT 05401
802/658-4972 FAX 802/863-1240

The Japan-America Society of South Florida, Inc.
1500 Bay Road, # 683
Miami Beach, FL 33139
305/532-1855

The Japan-America Society of Washington, Inc. (D.C.)
Bacon House Mews
606, 18th Street, N.W.
Washington, D.C. 20006
202/289-8290

RECOMMENDED   READING

Cultural and Social Books
Business Related Books
Articles and Books (in English) by Japanese Authors
Articles 1988
Articles 1989

There are a great number of excellent books about Japan and about working with the Japanese people.

In this brief listing, I have pinpointed some books which seem to me to be particularly helpful, together with a number of articles which I found informative and useful as well. Most of these are in addition to those mentioned in the footnotes.

Because Japan is changing so much and so quickly, I have tried to keep my recommendations as current as possible, but have included some solid, informative, older books as well, that can be considered almost "classics."

I hope that this listing will provide a good starting point for those who are coming in contact with increasing numbers of Japanese people, and would like to learn more about them.

I. CULTURAL AND SOCIAL BOOKS

Chambers, Kevin. *The Traveller's Guide to Asian Customs and Manners*. Deephaven, MN: Meadowbrook, Inc., 1988.

Christopher, R.C. *The Japanese Mind: The Goliath Explained*. New York: Fawcett Columbine, 1984 (paperback).

Readable interpretation of Japanese culture and society— many illustrative anecdotes about how Japanese feel, think, work and react.

Condon, John C. *Interact: Japanese and Americans*. Chicago: Intercultural Press, 1983.

Condon, John C. *With Respect to the Japanese: A Guide for Americans*. Yarmouth, ME: Intercultural Press, Inc., 1984.

Condon, John C. and Kurata, Keisuke (photos by Yasuo Kubo). *What's Japanese about Japan*. Tokyo, Japan: Shufunotomo Co. Ltd., 1987; 6th printing.

A beautifully melded book of photographs and text which is a remarkably clear introduction to the life-style and ways of thinking of the Japanese.

Condon, John C., ed. and Saito, M., ed. *Intercultural Encounters with Japan : Communication, Contact and Conflict*. Tokyo: The Simul Press, 1974.

Copeland, Lennie and Griggs, Lewis. *Going International: How To Make Friends and Deal Effectively in the Global Marketplace*. New York: Random House, 1985.

Fallow, James. *More Like Us: Making America Great Again*. Houghton Mifflin, 1989.

Fields, George. *From Bonsai to Levis*. McMillan, 1983.

Gudykunst, W. and Yong, Y. *Communicating with Strangers: An Approach to Intercultural Communications*. Reading, MA: Addison Welsley, 1984.

Halberstam, David. *The Reckoning: Made in America or Japan?* New York, NY: William Morrow, 1986.

Hall, Edward T. *Beyond Culture*. Garden City, NY: Anchor Press/Doubleday, 1987.

Not specific to Japan but solid basic material about the interrelations of cultures.

Hall, Edward T. *Silent Language*. Garden City, NY: Doubleday, 1959; Anchor Press/Doubleday, 1973 (paperback).

Hall, Edward T. and Hall, Mildred Reed. *Hidden Differences: Doing Business with the Japanese*. Garden City, NY: Anchor Press/Doubleday, 1987.

Very valuable book, full of wisdom and insight about the Japanese.

Morton, W. Scott. *Japan: Its History and Culture*. McGraw Hill, 1984 (paperback).

One-volume introduction to Japanese civilization from early times to the present. Recently updated (in 1984). Provides panoramic overview of old and new Japan.

Mossback, Helmut. *Etiquette in Japan*. Paul Norbury Publishers, 1984.

Pegel, C.C. *Japan vs. the West*. Hingham, MA: Kluwer Academic Press, 1984.

Reischauer, Edwin O. *The Japanese*. Belknap Press of Harvard University Press, 1977 and 1981.

A monumental work by the Harvard historian and former Ambassador to Japan. Analyzes Japan and its people in their historical and geographical setting; analyzes the Japanese personality, identifying ways in which the Japanese differ from Westerners. A classic in the field.

Van Wolferen, Karel. *The Enigma of Japanese Power*. Knopf, 1989.

An excellent critical analysis of the vital issues of trade and international relations. A valuable contribution to the general thinking on a question of world importance.

Varley, H. Paul. *Japanese Culture*. Honolulu, HI: University of Hawaii Press, 1984 (paperback).

Traces the evolution of Japanese arts and literature from prehistoric times to the present, relating them to Japan's social and political history. Good illustrations. Also published under the name:

Varley, H. Paul. *Japanese Culture: A Short History*. Rutland, VT: Charles E. Tuttle Co., 1985 (paperback).

Vogel, Ezra. *Japan as No.1: Lessons for America*. Cambridge and London, England: Harper and Row, 1980. What Americans can *learn* from the Japanese.

White, Merry I. *The Japanese Overseas: Can They Go Home Again?* New York: Free Press, 1988.

Discusses resettlement problems of Japanese families who have had long assignments overseas (U.S. and Europe). Focuses on three professional families.

Wilkinson, E. A. *History of Misunderstanding: Europe vs. Japan*. Tokyo, Japan: Chuokoron-sha, Inc., 1981 (English language edition); Penguin, 1983.

II. BUSINESS-RELATED BOOKS

Graham, J. L. and Yoshihino, S.*Smart Bargaining: Doing Business with the Japanese*. Cambridge, MA: Ballinger, 1984.

The Economist Business Traveller's Guide: Japan. Prentice Hall Press, 1987.

Moran, Robert T. *Getting Your Yen's Worth: How to Negotiate With Japan, Inc*. Houston, TX: Gulf Publishing Co., 1985.

Moran, Robert T. and Harris, Philip R. *Managing Cultural Differences*. Houston, TX: Gulf Publishing Co., 1987; 2nd edition, 1989.

Morishima, M. *Why Has Japan Succeeded? Western Technology and the Japanese Ethos*. New York: Cambridge University Press, 1982.

Pascale, A.T. and Athos, A. G. *The Art of Japanese Management: Applications for American Executives*. New York: Simon and Schuster, 1981.

Tasuno, S. *The Technological Strategy: High-Technology and the Control of the Twenty-first Century*. Englewood Cliffs, NJ: Prentice Hall, 1986.

Thurow, Lester C., ed. *The Management Challenge: Japanese Views*. Cambridge, MA: MIT Press, 1985.

Trevor, Malcolm. *Japan's Reluctant Multinationals: Japanese Management at Home and Abroad*. New York: St. Martin's Press, 1983.

Tung, Rosalie L. *Business Negotiating With the Japanese*. Lexington, MA: D.C. Heath, 1984.

Zimmerman, Mark. *How To Do Business With the Japanese: A Strategy for Success*. New York: Random House, 1985.

III. ARTICLES AND BOOKS (IN ENGLISH) BY JAPANESE AUTHORS

Imai, Masaaki, *Never Take "Yes" for an Answer*. Tokyo: The Simul Press, 1973.

————. *16 Ways to Avoid Saying "No"*. Tokyo: Nihon Keizai Shimbun, 1981.

Nakane, Chie. *Japanese Society*. Berkely, CA: University of California Press, 1972 (paperback).

Odaka, K., Crondine, R., Mizushima, S. *Corporate Strategies in Japan*. Longman, 1985.

Ohmae, Kenichi. *Triad Power: The Coming Shape of Global Competition*. New York: Free Press, 1985.

Sogo, Shinsaku. *Gaining Respect: The ABC's of How to Get Along With Your Japanese Staff*. Tokyo: Keizai Koho Center, 1981.

Takie, Sugiyama Lebra. *Japanese Pattern of Behavior*. Honolulu, HI: University of Hawaii, 1986 (paperback).

Describes and explains various aspects of Japanese social behavior. How the Japanese place great importance on social interactions and relationships, and less emphasis on individuality.

Tatsuo, Hatta. *It's Not What You Learn But Where You Learn It*. San Francisco: The Asia Foundation, article from the Japanese Press, TSC 886, 1987. (Author is a professor of economics at Osaka University.)

Yoshiyuki, Noda. *Introduction to the Japanese*. Tokyo: Tokyo University Press, 1976.

IV. ARTICLES 1988

"Canada—The Risk of Kissing Japan Off." *MacLean's*, **101** (11 April 1988): 36.

"Great Britain/Japan Relations." *The Economist*, **306** (16 January 1988): 50.

"Polite Resentment (Japanese/U.S.)." *The Economist*, **306** (16 January 1988): 26.

"Fitting Into Global Economy." *U.S. News and World Report*, 26 December 1988, p. 80.

"Japan Compared—Pity Them." *The Economist*, **309** (24 December 1988): 48.

"The Japanese Menace." *Today*, February 1988, p. 28.

"How To Survive a High Yen."*The Economist*, **306** (9 January 1988): 6.

"Selling To Japan." *Inc.*, November 1988, p. 15.

"Tapping Japan's Lucrative Market." *Nation's Business*, November 1988, p. 85.

"Deals In Japan. U.S. May Find Footing." *Industry Week*, 2 May 1988, p. 32.

"How Competitive Are We?" *World Press Review*, August 1988, p. 64.

"The World Is Buying Japanese." *Business Week*, 30 May 1988.

"How To Tackle Japan, Inc." *Time*, 9 May 1988.

"Japan and The Four Tigers,"*Management Today*, May 1988, p. 27.

"The Opening of Japan." *The Economist*, **309** (17 December 1988).

"Japan's Investment in U.S. Is It a Challenge?" *Challenge*, November/ December 1988.

"Head of Sony on Japanese Success." *World Press Review*, October 1988, p. 31.

"Japan: Country in Transition."*Fortune Magazine*, 1 August 1988.

"American Power; The View from Japan." *New Perspectives Quarterly*, 5 (Summer 1988): 20.

O'Reilly, Brian. "Japan's Uneasy U.S. Managers." *Fortune Magazine*, 25 April 1988.

V. ARTICLES 1989

"To Have and To Have Not in Japan: Not the Good Life." *U.S. News and World Report*, 13 February 1989, p. 41.

"How to Ride Japan Inc.'s Raging Bull." *Business Week*, 6 February 1989, p. 26.

"To Sell in Japan: Meet the People." *Nation's Business*, February 1989, p. 10.

"How Do U.S. and Japan Compare in Labor Market Changes?" *Monthly Labor Review*, February 1989, p. 31.

"Export Machine Revs Up." *The Economist*, **310** (7 January 1989): 58.

"The Asian Challenge: Why U.S. Has Trouble Cracking the Market." *Newsweek*, 13 February 1989, p. 48.

"The Hard Life: Japanese Stoicism." *Atlantic*, March 1989, pp. 16-18.

"U.S. Exports/ Imports Going Up." *Business America*, 10 April 1989, p. 29.

Review of "Should We Be More Alike?" *Newsweek*, 3 April 1989, p. 45.

"Power Without Purpose: Japan's Global Crisis." *Harvard Business Review*, **67** (March/April 1989): 71.

"Where the Jobs Are."*Newsweek*, 2 February 1989.

Epstein, Edward Jay. "The Japanese Are Different." *Lear's Magazine*, July/August 1989.

"The Cop and the Benefactor (U.S. and Japanese Foreign Aid)." *Newsweek*, 6 February 1989.

Burstein, Daniel. "A Yen for New York: What the Japanese Own—What They Are After." *New York Magazine*, 16 January 1989.

THE RISING SUN ON MAIN STREET

—Working with the Japanese—

A YOHAN LOTUS BOOK/Published 1991

Cover design by Takashi Suzuki

Printed and distributed in Japan by arrangement with
International Information Associates.

YOHAN PUBLICATIONS, INC.

14-9 Okubo 3-chome, Shinjuku-ku, Tokyo, Japan

Printed in Japan

THE RISING SUN
ON
MAIN STREET

WORKING WITH THE JAPANESE

ALISON R. LANIER

The Chinese word Nihon, from which comes our word
"Japan", was written with two characters. One stood
for "sun"; the other for "origin". Since Japan lies east
of China, it was known to the ancient Chinese as "The
Land of the Rising Sun". It has kept that name, worldwide, ever since.

YOHAN PUBLICATIONS, INC.